**British Writing
on Disarmament
from 1914 to 1978**

British Writing on Disarmament from 1914 to 1978

a bibliography

**Lorna Lloyd
and Nicholas A. Sims**

© Lorna Lloyd and Nicholas A. Sims

First Published in Great Britain in 1979 by
Frances Pinter (Publishers) Limited
5 Dryden Street, London WC2E 9NW

Published in the U.S.A. in 1979 by
Nichols Publishing Company
Post Office Box 96
New York, N.Y. 10024

ISBN 0 903804 40 9

Printed in Great Britain by Billing and Sons Ltd, Guildford & Worcester

Library of Congress Cataloguing in Publication Data

Lloyd, Lorna.
    British Writing on disarmament, 1914-1978.

    1. Great Britain – Foreign relations – 20th century –
Bibliography. 2. Disarmament – Bibliography.
3. Peace – Bibliography. I. Sims, Nicholas Roger Alan,
joint author. II. Title.
Z6465.G7L56   1979   [DA566.7]   016.327'174   78-26854
ISBN 0-89397-052-2

Frances Pinter Ltd., London
Nichols Publishing Co., New York

CONTENTS

PREFACE

In compiling this bibliography between 1974 and 1978 we came across some of the entries in our day-to-day reading, but the vast majority, particularly of the earlier publications, were found in bibliographies and library catalogues. Of these the most important were

The British National Bibliography
The British Humanities Index and its predecessor, the Selected Index of
    Periodicals
The British Library of Political and Economic Science Catalogue
The British Museum Subject Index of Books
The Hoover Institution Catalogue (Stanford University)
The International Index to Periodicals
The League of Nations: Annotated Bibliography on Disarmament and
    Military Questions (Geneva, 1931)

Specialised bibliographies in this field are few. We consulted the *Disarmament* bibliographies for 1962-1966 and 1967-1971 respectively published by the United Nations (Dag Hammarskjöld Memorial Library); in neither, however, is British writing adequately represented. This is even more true of Richard Dean Burns' *Arms Control and Disarmament: A Bibliography*, published by ABC-Clio for the Center for the Study of Armament and Disarmament in 1977, which became available in British libraries after our own compilation was complete and, although massive in scope, is overwhelmingly preoccupied with American contributions to the literature.

Whenever it was needed, we found ready assistance and guidance in the following libraries which we used in compiling the bibliography. Our first thanks are due to the Librarians and staff of the British Library of Political and Economic Science, the British Museum, North Staffordshire Polytechnic Library, Friends House Library and the Buckinghamshire County Library at Elgiva Lane, Chesham. We also enjoyed access to the literature files of the Campaign for Nuclear Disarmament and the library of the Conflict Research Society.

Thanks are due also to the Rt. Hon. the Lord Noel-Baker who has always been willing to share his unrivalled knowledge of disarmament and who stimulated us to think more deeply about the subject; to Professor Alan James and the Joseph Rowntree Charitable Trust for their encouragement and support; and to all those friends, in particular Melanie Barber and Cecil Evans, who have helped us carry this project through to completion. Any errors whether of fact or judgement are, however, ours alone.

We acknowledge the kind permission of Professor A.K.S. Lambton to quote extracts, in our introduction, from the Cecil Papers for which she holds the copyright and to the Earl of Balfour for permission to quote a letter from the First Cecil of Balfour to Viscount Cecil. We crave the indulgence of any copyright holders whose rights we may, despite exhaustive searches, unwittingly have infringed.

ABBREVIATIONS

The following are abbreviations which occur in the titles of books and articles, or in the names of periodicals or publishers, included in the bibliography.

CBW   Chemical and biological warfare/weapons
CND   Campaign for Nuclear Disarmament
LNU   League of Nations Union
NATO   North Atlantic Treaty Organisation
RUSI   Royal United Services Institution; *subsequently*, Royal United
       Services Institute for Defence Studies
SIPRI Stockholm International Peace Research Institute
UNA   United Nations Association

EDITORIAL NOTE

The entries comprise name of author; title (and subtitle, if any) of book, pamphlet or article; journal or periodical with volume or number of issue if not in volumes, and page numbers and/or date of issue; publisher and date and place of publication, in the case of books and pamphlets; series if any (e.g. *Adelphi Papers, Fabian Tracts, Peace Aims Pamphlets*) and number in the series; number of pages; format (hardback, paperback, pamphlet); so far as we have been able to trace all these details. Place of publication is given for journals or periodicals only when not London and not clear from the title. We have also included certain entries which relate to chapters on disarmament in books on more general or different subjects by a single author, or in collections of essays. Cross-references are limited to *directly* related entries, e.g. critiques of a report.

Some entries which are under the name of a single author might equally well be written under the name of an organisation, and vice versa. In general, we have followed title-pages and made cross-references (in the index) to rapporteurs, chairmen, etc., where they are not included as authors; occasionally we have 'upgraded' them to authorship.

With rare exceptions, we have entered items once only, in the section considered most appropriate. In the list of sections, and at the beginning of a section, we have indicated related sections which it may be useful to consult for material which may span more than one category.

The following paragraphs explain how we understand the criteria for inclusion, taking the different elements in the title of our bibliography in turn.

British
We have included British authors and organisations, and certain authors from other countries who, while living and working in Britain, have made a significant contribution to thought on the subject. (Examples under the letter B alone are Beaton and Buchan from Canada, Bull from Australia, Bertram from West Germany.) Occasionally we have been unsure and have had to assume an author to be British.

Writing
Apart from unpublished doctoral theses we have excluded all non-printed material, such as duplicated pamphlets. Among printed articles, we have excluded those printed in newspapers and magazines and running to less than two pages.

Disarmament
This is naturally much the most difficult element in our title for which to adopt and apply criteria. What one person regards as 'writing on disarmament' may well appear to another as nothing of the kind. In deciding to play it largely by ear, we have exercised our discretion as compilers to stretch the boundaries of the subject of disarmament to embrace, for example, topics for which there is no ready alternative bibliography or topics which, at a particular time during the century, were closely associated with disarmament. Similarly, we have allowed greater flexibility in the subject-matter admitted to our bibliography as having a bearing on disarmament when the author is a major figure in the history of British thinking about disarmament: thus such authors' contributions can be seen more readily 'in the round' than if a more stringent criterion of 'writing about disarmament' were rigidly applied in every instance.

1914–1978
While this bibliography comprises publications from 1914 to the present day, we have included a pre-1914 section which, while incomplete, includes books and pamphlets either indicative of pre-war thinking on the subject or which, like Norman Angell's *Great Illusion*, affected the way people approached disarmament.

Addenda

No doubt sharp-eyed readers will discover omissions. We shall be glad to receive notice of items which readers consider deserving of inclusion in any future edition, and of any inadvertent errors in the entries contained in this one.

LORNA LLOYD
Department of International
  Relations
University of Keele
Keele
Staffordshire
ST5 5BG

NICHOLAS A. SIMS
Department of International
  Relations
London School of Economics
  and Political Science
Houghton Street
London WC2A 2AE

INTRODUCTION

Part One

1900-1919

By the end of the 19th century the activities of peace societies, as seen in their intense disarmament campaign in the mid-1890s, had succeeded in gaining widespread sympathy for disarmament. The century, itself, had closed with the First Hague Conference, called by Czar Nicholas to seek:

> the maintenance of universal peace and a possible reduction in the excessive armaments which weigh upon all nations.

The Conference did succeed in furthering another aim of the peace societies — arbitration — with the establishment of the Permanent Court of Arbitration, but that it did nothing for disarmament was underlined when the Czar deliberately omitted it in his invitation to the Second Hague Conference of 1907.

Especially active within the peace societies were the nonconformist churches, whence the Liberal party derived important electoral support. Hence the Liberal party came to espouse the cause of disarmament. In an Albert Hall address in 1905, Campbell Bannerman said:

> I hold that the growth of armaments is a great danger to the peace of the world. The policy of huge armaments keeps alive and stimulates and feeds the belief that force is the best, if not the only, solution of international difficulties.

At the same time Socialists advocated disarmament holding that, 'the fight against militarism and war must be an integral part of our struggle to overthrow capitalism'. Within the capitalist economy, they argued,

1

private armaments firms unduly influenced government arms policies, a theme which found expression in their literature and seemed exemplified in the Mulliner scare of 1909.

Disarmament, however, shifted to the background of liberal consciousness as Europe moved closer to war and turned its attention to preparing for that war. The outbreak of war demonstrated the weakness of international socialism but it also demonstrated a certain weakness in the peace societies. Although a large number of people did continue to hold to pacifism, members of many peace bodies, which were theoretically anti-war, in practice supported the war. For example, Joseph Pease, Asquith's Education Minister, Quaker and President of the London Peace Society (founded in 1815 under Quaker auspices and the only peace society with unqualified pacifism written into its statutes) approved the declaration of war in August 1914 and did not resign the presidency of that society until May 1915.

The main burden of writing and action during the war continued to come from Churches and Socialists while new bodies were founded to further these aims. The League of Nations Society and its temporary offshoot, the League of Free Nations Association, directed their attention towards a post-war League of States. Although pacifism received its major stimulus from the introduction of conscription in 1916, the Fellowship of Reconciliation, formed as early as December 1914 by Christian pacifists, was a small group concentrating on uniting people of like belief, rather than acting politically. In sharp contrast, the No-Conscription Fellowship (NCF) took direct political action and accordingly suffered mounting harassment from the authorities so that by 1918 almost all its leaders had been jailed as conscientious objectors. The NCF had originated in November 1914 in an appeal by the editor of the *New Leader* (the organ of the Independent Labour Party), Fenner Brockway, for potential conscientious objectors should conscription be introduced. Under the chairmanship of Clifford Allen (later Baron Allen of Hurtwood) it attracted a varied membership of 10,000 (of whom about 6,000 were ILPers, the next largest group being Quakers); it was extremely efficiently organised and, besides its weekly journal *The Tribunal*, it produced over a million pamphlets and leaflets.

Within the House of Commons, the 'peace' party was an amorphous group of roughly 40 M.P.s and contained a number of future Labour Ministers. There were 5 ILPers including MacDonald and Snowden, other Labour members and some 25 independent Liberals, including the vociferous Union of Democratic Control with such men as E. D.

2

Morel, Arthur Ponsonby and Charles Trevelyan. All who opposed the war paid a price: Clifford Allen nearly died from treatment he received as a conscientious objector, Ramsay MacDonald was branded a traitor, hounded during the war, lost his seat in Leicester in the coupon election and continued to face taunts when he stood for Woolwich in 1921.[1]

1919-1934

The wealth of literature for this period reflects the fact that at this time disarmament gained its greatest popular support and that it was a major political issue. This can be attributed to the experience of the First World War, the popularity and ceaseless activity of peace societies, and, with the establishment of the League of Nations, the attempt to transfer liberal-democratic principles to international relations.

For twelve years, from 1922 to 1933 disarmament was at the forefront of activities of the League of Nations. The League of Nations Union (LNU), as often as not at odds with the Government of the day, was the most important of the pressure groups. By 1933 it had 3,000 branches and nearly a million members, but as early as 1923 Arthur Balfour was writing to his cousin, Robert Cecil:

> The point about the League of Nations Union is this. It is a very widespread organization — probably at certain moments, wielding considerable electoral power and regarded by an ignorant British public as the British representative — so to speak — of the League of Nations.[2]

The LNU published numerous leaflets and pamphlets as well as its journal *Headway*, arranged meetings and petitions (such as the mammoth anti-war petition organised in the summer of 1925 in conjunction with the No More War Movement) and, under the Presidency of Grey of Fallodon, attracted most of the leading figures of the day including Arthur Henderson, Gilbert Murray and its most indefatigable supporter in the public eye, Robert Cecil.

[1] For a fuller account of this period see Gerda Richards Crosby, *Disarmament and Peace in British Politics, 1914-1919* (Cambridge, Mass.: Harvard U.P., 1957).

[2] Lord Balfour to Lord Cecil, dated 4 June 1923. Cecil Papers. British Museum Add. Ms. 51071.

On the other hand, the older peace movement and sections of the Labour movement were critical of the League as a League of victor states. They eyed askance the sanctions provisions of the Covenant. They wanted the League universalised and democratised to form a world 'parliament'. Socialists associated the advent of peace with the achievement of socialism while maintaining, however, strong support for present attempts to achieve disarmament. In *National Defence*, written in 1917, Ramsay MacDonald had compared a belief in the possibility of permanent peace without disarmament to 'expecting a warm, gentle, nourishing rain when the temperature is below zero'.[3] A pamphlet, received in the TUC Library in 1931, written by 'an old war horse' and entitled *The futility and suicidal policy of war*, is dedicated:

> to the *Churches* and all *Cabinet Ministers* under Warmongering Governments who prattle, squirm and prate about disarmament with reservations but who have not the *Abolition of War* at heart.

The No More War Movement (NMWM), established in 1921 to replace the NCF (dissolved in 1919) drew its leadership from former NCF members such as Arthur Ponsonby. Of all European countries, Britain was perhaps the most receptive to peace movements and the NMWM, like the LNU, expanded rapidly in the 1920s while particularly appealing to Labour pacifists since socialism as well as pacifism was written into its programme. Similarly Britain provided a large and active membership for international bodies such as War Resisters International and Pierre Cérésole's Service Civil International.

The Churches provided members for these groups while maintaining their distinctive contribution. The Bishop of Chichester's Council of Christ and Peace Campaign, launched in 1929, was endorsed by seven of the free churches.

With the Disarmament Conference the disarmament literature reaches its peak. In fact so much was written at this time that manageability alone necessitated dividing the period 1931-1935 into two sections as well as having a separate section on the Conference. The volume of writing on naval disarmament reflects not only the number of conferences and attention given to this in disarmament negotiations but also particular British preoccupations: the traditional importance of the navy, the role it had played during the war and its role generally in imperial defence. Far less was written on land and air disarmament although anxiety was expressed about the role of the bomber.

[3] Cited in David Marquand, *Ramsay MacDonald* (London: Jonathan Cape, 1977), p. 205.

4

After the failure of the Disarmament Conference writing on disarmament drops off sharply. As tension increased in the world and Britain rearmed so writers turned their concern to rearmament and it has been felt worth while to include two sections on this subject for those interested in examining its relationship with disarmament. Excellent studies on disarmament did, however, continue to appear, as with Philip Noel-Baker's *The Private Manufacture of Armaments*.

The falling away of the literature does not indicate that the peace movement had worn itself out; on the contrary, it remained strong. The Peace Ballot of 1935 represented the views of half as many people as normally voted in elections, and the Peace Pledge Union (PPU), which Canon 'Dick' Sheppard formed in 1936, attracted roughly a hundred thousand members and a formidable array of sponsors. The following year, 1937, the PPU merged with the NMWM and shortly before the outbreak of war in 1939 had a membership of around 125,000. However, the significance of the Peace Ballot and the PPU lies in the realm of aspiration and in demonstrating the success of the peace movement in spreading its ideas: the Peace Ballot demonstrated the enormous popular support for disarmament but provided no solution to inherent political problems, the PPU offered an apparently easy way to avoid the coming war but, once the war had actually broken out, large numbers abandoned pacifism and devoted themselves to the war effort.

Events in the Far East and Europe had brought an earlier parting of ways between those who remained staunch pacifists and those former pacifists who became converted to collective security. This division was sharply illustrated at the 1935 Labour Party Annual Conference in the clash between Bevin and Lansbury who had taken over the party leadership when MacDonald formed the National Government. Later Lansbury did admit to having had increasing 'difficulty in squaring my pacifist principles with the policy of my party'.[4] At the same time those who became convinced of the necessity of the 1939-1945 war by no means abandoned their faith in disarmament. When Cecil's *Great Experiment* came out in 1941 in the middle of the war, he wrote on the flyleaf of the copy he gave to Noel-Baker, 'Le jour viendra'.

The inter-war years saw the failure of an attempt to create a new, disarmed world, but the attempt was not futile. Noel-Baker argues that by 1932 every technical problem of land disarmament had been

[4] Cited in Peter Brock, *Twentieth Century Pacifism* (Van Nostrand, Reinhold, 1970), p. 134.

solved,[5] but the political difficulties were not solved. The writers did, however, examine every aspect known at the time. Certain works, like Madariaga's *Disarmament* (1929), remain important today. The British peace and disarmament movement was the strongest in Europe, attracting many of the ablest people of their generation. It is not insignificant that the bibliography has ample representation of the writing of four Nobel Peace Prize winners (Angell 1933, Henderson 1934, Cecil 1937, Noel-Baker 1959). For modern cynics who belittle the cause of disarmament and the efforts of this century, Lord Grey's answer remains valid today:

> If you tell me it is utopian I reply that I prefer the chance of utopia to the certainty of destruction.[6]

Lorna Lloyd

Part Two

1941-1955

As the 1940s unroll into the early 1950s several features of the disarmament literature of the time emerge more clearly. The two outstanding features are the concern with nuclear (or, as they were generally known up to the mid-fifties, *atomic*) weapons — almost, it now seems, to the exclusion of all others — and the prominence of working scientists among our authors. Kathleen Lonsdale, the eminent Quaker crystallographer, is perhaps the most prolific but other chemists and physicists are there in plenty. This trend reflects popular anxieties and the novelty of atomic *energy* (let alone atomic weapons), which the scientist was expected to explain as well as to civilise — into peaceful applications, which were long regarded as being almost wholly advantageous.

In this period, too, Christian concern took a form which was to shape the debates of the moral theologians and the church leaders of succeeding decades. In brief, it was the (uneasy) marrying of two barely compatible partners: modern strategies deploying the supposed

[5] Philip Noel-Baker, *The Arms Race* (London: Atlantic Book Publishing Co. Ltd., 1958), p. 8.

[6] Robert Cecil Papers, British Museum, Add. Ms. 51204.

deterrent effect of atomic weapons, and traditional concepts of the Just War and proportionality in the means adopted by belligerent states. The pacifist challenge to non-pacifist orthodoxy acquired a fresh relevance, although this was more often than not obscured by the prevailing uncertainty over the *kind* of statement the Churches ought to be making in a world of atomic weapons and deterrent strategies. The great figures of the ecumenical movement — George Bell, Bishop of Chichester, and Dr. J. H. Oldham — played their part in launching this unfinished debate between two streams of British Christian witness and thought.

Non-governmental organisations are not, perhaps, as strongly represented in the literature of the time as they had been earlier and were to be later. With notable exceptions, such as the massive National Peace Council report *World Disarmament* (1953) which brought such different Members of Parliament as Ian Mikardo, Philip Noel-Baker and Harold Wilson together in a common exercise over three years, the non-governmental banner is kept aloft principally by the unfailingly productive Friends Peace Committee. Its Secretary, Karlin Capper-Johnson, was particularly prolific in writings which related disarmament to wider themes of world order in the context of the United Nations' creation between 1944 and 1947. ('Federation: Disarmament; the two things go hand in hand. The Christian pacifist is called to achieve them.')[7] In passing, it may be remarked that the Director of the National Peace Council was still, up to 1948, that very energetic Quaker, Gerald Bailey, who was to be no less active in the Friends East-West Relations Committee of 1951-1965 and its successor, until his death in 1972. In the same way, leaders of the United Nations Association and the pacifist organisations through to the 1970s tended to be those who had been active in the inter-war period.

The 'borderline' problems of classification which are most apparent in the sections of the bibliography relating to this period have to do with the fact that disarmament is largely subsumed under, first, the subject of postwar reconstruction or world order-building, and second, the grand themes of the Cold War (reducible much of the time to the question, 'How shall we deal with Stalin/the Russians?'). The first theme gives way to the second around 1946-1947. In both cases the subsuming of disarmament means that it is seen as an aspect of politics

---

[7] Karlin Capper-Johnson, *Enter the World State: A Christian Pacifist Comment* (London: Friends Peace Committee, 1946), p. 8.

among the powers rather than as a distinct process of international relations with its own diplomatic and technical problems. There is rather little *contemporary* analysis of the disarmament negotiations which were taking place under the auspices of the United Nations, with rival proposals being tabled in vain by each of the big Four: the admirable accounts we have today, from the pens of Goodwin (1957), Nutting (1959), Luard (1965) and others, were all written some years afterwards.

1956-1965

The literature of disarmament 'peaked' in 1956-1965 as it had done no less dramatically some thirty years before. This time not a little of the increase was occasioned by the rise of the movement for unilateral nuclear disarmament by Britain. The Campaign for Nuclear Disarmament (CND) was founded in 1958. CND, itself, the smaller unilateralist groups and the equally vociferous opponents of the unilateralist cause produced a mountain of literature, most of it polemical, much of it ephemeral, some of it, however, possessing a more lasting value. CND, in particular, was remarkably fortunate in the literary and scientific talent on which it could call. The novelist Mervyn Jones, Chairman of the CND Literature Committee in the early 1960s, was only one of its brilliant pamphleteers.

The unilateralist movement and its critics were not, however, anything like the whole story.[8] This period also saw the establishment of the Institute for Strategic Studies (1958), international from the outset in fact though not for many years in name, the Conference (now Council) on Christian Approaches to Defence and Disarmament (1963) and, through a reorganisation of Quaker committee structure, the Friends Peace and International Relations Committee (1965). It saw a resurgence of interest in disarmament among such established and influential pressure groups and pamphleteers as the Fabian Society and the United Nations Association, and a burgeoning of ecclesiastical concern which affected each of the main confessional groups — Church of England, Church of Scotland, Catholic and Methodist — as well as the British Council of Churches. These non-governmental developments

[8] For an interesting account of *British Thinking About Nuclear Weapons* during this period, see A. J. R. Groom's book of that title (London: Frances Pinter, 1974).

had their parallel within the Foreign Office, with the creation of an Atomic Energy and Disarmament Department (1958), followed by an Arms Control and Disarmament Advisory Panel (1964) and Research Unit (1965). Disarmament, once again, had seized the attention of Britain and, in some degree, the world.

One of the more curious features of the literature of this time is the appearance of isolated contributions to British writing on disarmament by well-known public figures who had written nothing on the subject before and would write nothing thereafter. Yet they found, it seems, little difficulty in obtaining an airing for their generally unremarkable views. It is almost as if some kind of cultural or intellectual compulsion was abroad, adding, to the ranks of those who knew what they were writing about, many whose names exceeded in renown the depth of their knowledge or originality of their thought on the particular subject of disarmament. Professor J. H. Fremlin's splendidly deflating phrase – 'a large number of people, some of them very eminent in fields other than that which they were discussing' – might have been coined to describe this sudden influx of literary and political personalities.

As everyone knows, the unilateralist movement spilled over into many aspects of British society in the 1960s, enriching or deforming them according to one's prejudices. This happened partly because some of those who had taken up the unilateralist cause decided that other causes had a prior claim on their energies and could, in some way, relate to the furthering of their unilateralist goals; partly, too, because for many who were caught up in the fervour of the Aldermaston marches and other unilateralist demonstrations, style was at least as important as policy. Thus the impact of the early unilateralist movement on British politics, the Left, the peace movement, methods of protest, ethical debate, the performing arts and the youth culture was, in each case, very considerable. Authors as various as Christopher Driver (*The Disarmers*), Peggy Duff (*Left, Left, Left*) and Jeff Nuttall (*Bomb Culture*) have described some part of this gradual diffusion into British society, which has nothing *directly* to do with the pursuit of disarmament. This makes it very difficult to determine how far the present bibliography should seek to encompass the cultural offshoots and sociological ramifications of what began, after all, as a position of principle on disarmament: the line has to be drawn somewhere, but it has been thought worth while to list some of the more important writing in this category, under the heading, 'CND: aspects other than unilateral nuclear disarmament – political and sociological', in Section 58.

9

After 1965 the pattern of the literature changes, as its volume diminishes. Despite the renewed growth of CND, very little specifically unilateralist writing has appeared. (There has, however, been a mild flurry of biographies, memoirs and reminiscences in which the solipsistic fallacy that CND disappeared as soon as the individual in question left it is sometimes evident, although less so probably than on radio and television where it would appear to be almost *de rigueur*.) CND's concerns have broadened, as have those of other groups, and among the areas to which they have most significantly extended are weapon delivery systems (the Tornado multi-role combat aircraft, the MIRV, the cruise missile and so on), military expenditure and industrial conversion (i.e. switching from military to other, less objectionable projects), and the dangers of civil nuclear energy programmes.

Above all, in the 1970s, there has been a rapid growth in the literature on the arms trade, generally critical of Britain's part in it. This proliferation parallels the actual expansion in the scale of Britain's arms exports since the later 1960s, with the arousal of concern about the ethics of this trade and with the emergence of an active and widespread campaign to stop it.

The United Nations Association and the Friends Peace and International Relations Committee remained the most prolific publishers on disarmament, apart from CND itself, in Britain during this period. Together with other groups on occasion, they constituted a small but persistent and generally well-informed 'lobby' in an era when disarmament was fast becoming unfashionable (save in the UN General Assembly, where by contrast it loomed ever larger in the counsels of the nations).

The preoccupations of the disarmament negotiators at Geneva and New York continued to be reflected in British writing. The Partial Test Ban Treaty (1963) was succeeded by difficult negotiations for the Non-Proliferation Treaty (1968) and this transition was paralleled in the literature. Indeed, writing on the dangers of nuclear-weapon proliferation proved even more popular an occupation than writing on the dangers of nuclear-weapon testing had done. The signing of the Treaty, and its entry into force in 1970, reduced the flow of articles and pamphlets somewhat, but it perked up again before and after the First Review Conference of states parties to the Treaty, in 1975. To a much lesser extent, the Geneva diplomacy leading to the Seabed Arms

Control Treaty (1971) and the Convention on Biological and Toxin Weapons (1972) was reflected in British writing on these subjects. Two other major concerns of the Geneva Conference — general and complete disarmament (GCD) and the banning of chemical weapons — have received some sporadic attention.

Since 1969 the Strategic Arms Limitation Talks between the USA and USSR have generated a fair amount of British comment; the Vienna talks[9] on central Europe, in which Britain has participated since 1973, rather less (a fact which has not gone unremarked abroad).

In 1966 the Swedish Parliament decided to mark the achievement of 150 years of unbroken peace (for Sweden) by setting up a generously funded and genuinely independent institute. This was the Stockholm International Peace Research Institute (SIPRI), which rapidly made itself indispensable to governments and disarmament campaigners alike by the sheer extent, and deservedly high repute, of its publications on armaments and disarmament, including in particular the dangers of nuclear proliferation, military research and development programmes, arms sales to Third World countries, chemical and biological weapons, and the technical aspects of negotiating disarmament agreements. Although its staff has always comprised many different nationalities, it so happens that the first two Directors of SIPRI have both been British — Professor Robert Neild, an economist, and Dr. Frank Barnaby, a nuclear physicist and science journalist — as have several of SIPRI's leading researchers, including Frank Blackaby, Mary Kaldor and Julian Perry Robinson who are to be found in this bibliography. Four of the five were members of the United Nations Association's Disarmament Committee in London in the early 1970s.

So in 1978 the *corpus* of British writing on disarmament could be said to embrace some SIPRI publications and other writers' and organisations' books, articles and pamphlets as varied — if not plentiful — as ever. Among the politicians making their contribution were Lord Noel-Baker (b. 1889) and Robin F. Cook, M.P. (b. 1947); outside politics, too, in the academic and ecumenical worlds, in institutes and associations and committees ranged across a wide spectrum of opinion, pacifist and non-pacifist, committed and cautious, young and old alike found a place, all adding to the discourse of disarmament.

Looking back over the years surveyed in this bibliography, one gains

[9] The Negotiations on Mutual Reduction of Forces and Armaments and Associated measures in Central Europe, or M(B)FR negotiations, in which some nineteen countries are involved.

a strong impression of *plus ça change, plus c'est la même chose*. The disarmers' sense of outrage at the magnitude of the forces ranged against them is a constant theme; Butler's fifteen-page pamphlet entitled *The Enormous Evils of Military Establishments and Standing Armies* was published in Manchester in 1881 but it finds a powerful echo in the title of a recent pamphlet by an M.P. in next-door Salford, Frank Allaun's *The Wasted £30,000,000,000 Spent on False Security*.

Another constant theme is the attraction of unilateralism, which so far from being a phenomenon unique to our generation in fact has its roots deep in the past. When Wayland Young wrote in 1958

> Conditional diarmament seems unobtainable. Nations must disarm unconditionally.[10]

he was expressing in a different way the same thought as George Bairstow had had in 1931:

> Disarmament by example would undoubtedly create a new international outlook. . . . The way of righteousness is the only practical way.[11]

Despite occasional attacks on the patriotism of disarmers, they themselves have often openly avowed their patriotism, as in the slogan printed on the colourful banner of York CND which was carried in so many marches from Aldermaston to London: 'Britain's unilateral action ended the slave trade: let Britain lead again.'

The debates among the advocates of disarmament likewise have a perennial quality. Take the age-old question of whether gradualism helps or hinders the achievement of large-scale disarmament in the end. The Vice-President of the Peace Society, preaching a sermon in 1904, declared that

> Any steps we can take in the reduction of armaments are steps in the direction of lessening the probability of war.[12]

[10] Wayland Young, 'An Abolitionist's Position', *Encounter*, November 1958.

[11] George Bairstow, 'Accepting the Risks of Peace: Why a Quaker Desires Disarmament', *Halifax Courier and Guardian*, 8 October 1931; reprinted in *Disarmament Campaign* (Rawdon, nr. Leeds: Northern Friends Peace Board, 1931), p. 4.

[12] The Rev. B. F. Horton, *Peace on Earth* (London: Peace Society, 1904), p. 11.

Yet only eleven years later, contemplating post-war arrangements for international order, the Friends Peace Committee wrote

> It may be that a complete reform is easier than a partial one in this very unusual, indeed unique case.[13]

'Piecemeal Disarmament No Longer Possible!', declared an article in *The Observer* of 22 November 1925, under the title, 'Why War Is Hell':

> If you want to abolish the submarine you must abolish war altogether. The greater includes the less. The idea of war on limited liability is the most pathetic of human delusions.

But this contention did not deter some advocates of disarmament from focusing attention (with the necessary disclaimers, doubtless) on a particular weapon, then as now. In 1930 you could buy for 1s. 9d. a batch of 100 copies of *Poison Gas*, 'a leaflet dealing with the animal experiments carried out on Salisbury Plain'.[14] (The research establishments at Porton Down were even then arousing the opposition of the animal welfare and anti-vivisectionist lobbies as well as that of opponents of chemical warfare.) Over the next four years, the issue of whether it was right to select certain disarmament items for special pressure, and the corresponding weapons for special obloquy, can be traced through the literature of such disarmament-committed bodies as the Friends Peace Committee, the Northern Friends Peace Board and the National Council for the Prevention of War (which in 1934 reverted to its earlier name of National Peace Council). This argument over the permissibility of campaigns for limited, short-term objectives is still a lively one within peace organisations.

Then again, one finds different emphases when the discussion turns to deterrence. Is disarmament merely a means of avoiding war, or would it still be imperative even if deterrence diminished the risk of war to near zero? At the beginning of the century it was closely bound up with concepts of arbitration and war avoidance, but it was not long before a new kind of case for disarmament was making itself heard. E. Vipont Brown prepared a memorandum in 1902 for a Quaker Peace Deputation, in which he wrote:

[13] *Looking Towards Peace* (London: Headley, 1915), p. 14.

[14] London: Friends Peace Committee, 1930, pp. 4.

13

To me an armed peace seems little, if at all, less immoral than a condition of actual warfare. The dogs of war are as little in harmony with the spirit of Christ's life and teaching when they are chained as when they are let loose, and morally, there is but little to choose between England spending her millions in preparation for war, and England spending her lifeblood on the battlefield.[15]

Compare the stirring declaration made by a (predominantly non-pacifist) working party on defence and disarmament in its report to the British Council of Churches, exactly seventy years later:

We believe it our duty to pursue disarmament not just as a means to enhance security, or to effect economies, but as a clear Christian obligation, by which we mean that to use the human and material resources of God's creation to prepare for destruction is contrary to God's will for the human family.[16]

Over against that view of disarmament stands a powerful tradition of thinking which regards it still as simply a means to the particular end of making war less likely, and which accordingly accepts it as being on a moral par with military deterrence, both being susceptible to intelligent use for broadly the same purpose. That tradition too is amply represented in this bibliography.

Lastly, we find a recurring disagreement over the utility of international organisation and diplomacy as approaches to disarmament. Some believe them to be useless for this task and fear that the appearance of limited progress may delude the public into thinking that something of substance has occurred and that disarmament can be achieved that way. Others continue to see signs of hope in the United Nations and the Geneva disarmament conference (the Conference of the Committee on Disarmament), believing that good will may yet overcome cynical inertia. When the League of Nations was still young, a gifted observer who was to work for disarmament until his death in 1973 reported:

[15] E. Vipont Brown, *Christianity and War*, 3rd edition (London: Friends Peace Committee, 1915 — having been first published by Morland of Birmingham in 1904), p. 34.

[16] Report of a Working Party on Defence and Disarmament (Chairman, the Rev. Edward Rogers) appointed by the Department of International Affairs of the British Council of Churches and the Conference of British Missionary Societies. The Working Party met from 1969 to 1972 and its report was subsequently published as *The Search for Security: A Christian Appraisal* (London: SCM Press, 1973). The quotation is from p. 104.

It is impossible to be in Geneva, even for a week, and to come away without hope. The crystalline summit of Mont Blanc spells hope every time it emerges from the encompassing clouds.[17]

It is equally impossible not to be impressed by the sincerity and dedication of those who, over the years, have pursued what has often seemed at best a distant ideal, at worst a lost cause. Their watchwords, adapted and requoted over the years, have been Philip Noel-Baker's dictum:

Disarmament has not been 'fully carried out'; it has not even begun.[18]

and Arthur Henderson's assurance to his audience at the Queen's Hall, London, in February 1931:

At the Disarmament Conference the Governments will do what the peoples want. If the peoples want disarmament they can have it. If they exert their will they can compel results.[19]

In the face of repeated disappointments, the disarmament enterprise persists. Some might regard this as proof only of human folly, or of obstinacy in the teeth of certain unalterable facts of international life. We prefer to see in it something altogether more positive, rational and hopeful.

Nicholas A. Sims

[17] Bertram Pickard, 'The Sixth Assembly of the League of Nations', *The Friend*, 18 September 1925 (Article reprinted by Friends Peace Committee as a pamphlet, 1925).

[18] P. J. Noel-Baker, *The End of a Myth* (Rawdon, nr. Leeds: Northern Friends Peace Board, 1933), p. 4. (reprinted from *Headway*).

[19] Quoted in a Northern Friends Peace Board leaflet, *Disarm! Why?* (1931).

PART ONE

1. General: pre-1914

Angell, Norman. THE GREAT ILLUSION: A STUDY OF THE
RELATION OF MILITARY POWER IN NATIONS TO THEIR
ECONOMIC AND SOCIAL ADVANTAGE. London: W. Heinemann.
1911. pp. xv + 335. (The present work is the outcome of a large
pamphlet published towards the end of 1909 under the title
'Europe's Optical Illusion'. Preface to 1910 edn. See also review in
Spectator (1910))

Angell, Norman. THE GREAT ILLUSION: A STUDY OF THE
RELATION OF MILITARY POWER TO NATIONAL
ADVANTAGE. London. 1914 (another edn 1913). pp. xix + 374

Angell, Norman. THE POLICY BEHIND ARMAMENTS. 1911.
Pamphlet. pp. 8

Angell, N[orman]. DREAM OF PERPETUAL PEACE. Spectator. Vol.
108. 6 January 1912. pp. 12–13

Angell, Norman. WAR AND THE WORKERS. London. 1912.
Pamphlet. pp. 63

Angell, Norman. COMMERCIAL SECURITY. CAN IT BE OBTAINED
BY ARMAMENTS? London: The 'War and Peace' Publishing Co. for
the Garton Foundation. ?1913. Pamphlet. pp. 15

Barclay, Sir Thomas. HAGUE AND OTHER WAR CONVENTIONS
IN SPIRIT AND IN PRACTICE. 19th Century. May 1915. pp. 1203–
11

Butler, E. THE ENORMOUS EVILS OF MILITARY ESTABLISH-
MENTS AND STANDING ARMIES. Manchester. 1881. Pamphlet.
pp. 15

Cobden Club. THE BURDEN OF ARMAMENTS: A PLEA FOR
RETRENCHMENT. London. 1905. pp. 228

Hayward, C. W. WAR, CONSCRIPTION, ARMAMENTS AND SANITY.
1913. Pamphlet. pp. 28

Headlam-Morley, (Sir) James. PROPOSALS FOR THE REDUCTION OF
ARMAMENTS. Chapter IX of his book STUDIES IN DIPLOMATIC
HISTORY. London: Methuen. 1930. (History of nineteenth-century
thinking on disarmament)

Hirst, Francis W[rigley]. A LETTER ON TAXATION AND ARMA-
MENTS. London. 1910. Pamphlet. pp. 8

Hirst, Francis W[rigley]. THE SIX PANICS AND OTHER ESSAYS.
London. 1913. pp. vii + 271

Hirst, Francis W[rigley]. THE FIFTH OR DREADNOUGHT PANIC.
Reprinted from THE SIX PANICS, AND OTHER ESSAYS. London.
n.d. Pamphlet. pp. 46

Newbold, J. T. W. THE WAR TRUST EXPOSED. London. ?1913.
Pamphlet. pp. 19

Novikoff, Olga. ANOTHER LEAGUE OF NATIONS. Asiatic Review.
April 1919. pp. 243-8. (The Tsar's proposal in 1898 and Germany's
wrecking of the scheme)

Perris, G. H. FOR AN ARREST OF ARMAMENTS. London. 1906.
Pamphlet. pp. 24

Richardson, Lewis F. THE ARMS RACE OF 1909-13. Nature. 29
October 1938. pp. 792-3

Rowntree, J. JUSTICE NOT FORCE. London. 1913. Pamphlet. pp. 8

Russell, B[ertrand] A. W. WAR: THE OFFSPRING OF FEAR. London.
?1914. Pamphlet. pp. 14

Spectator. DISARMAMENT AND FACTS. Vol. 99. 24 August 1907.
pp. 250-1.

Spectator. Review of ANGELL (1911), q.v. Vol. 105. 26 November
1910. pp. 908-10

Tate, M. THE DISARMAMENT ILLUSION. New York: The Macmillan
Company. 1942. (negotiations to 1907)

Webster, Professor C[harles] K[ingsley]. DISARMAMENT PROPO-
SALS IN 1810. The Contemporary Review. Vol. CXXI. November
1922. pp. 621-7

Wilson, W. E. CHRIST AND WAR: THE REASONABLENESS OF
DISARMAMENT. London. 1913. pp. 212

2. General: 1914-1919

Angell, Norman. PRUSSIANISM AND ITS DESTRUCTION (with
which is reprinted Part 2 of THE GREAT ILLUSION). London.
1915. pp. xx + 240

Bolton, D. J. THE FULFILMENT OF THE LAW. International Journal
of Ethics. January 1917. pp. 200-12. (Disarmament is the only
practical politics, and we shall have war just so long as we prepare
for it)

Bracher, S. V. THE SHORT WAY TO A LONG PEACE. Manchester.

?1915. Pamphlet. pp. 15

Bracher, S. V. INITIATIVE IN DISARMAMENT. Socialist Review. May 1915. pp. 527–36

Brailsford, H[enry] N[oel]. THE WAR OF STEEL AND GOLD: A STUDY OF THE ARMED PEACE. London: G. Bell & Sons Ltd. 1914, 1915. pp. 340

Burns, C[ecil] Delisle. WHEN PEACE BREAKS OUT. International Journal of Ethics. October 1915. pp. 82–91. (The State, just as other institutions, will cease to be armed)

Clarke, J. H. THE CALL OF THE SWORD. Financial News. 1917. Pamphlet. pp. 65

Crosby, Gerda Richards. DISARMAMENT AND PEACE IN BRITISH POLITICS, 1914–1919. Cambridge, Massachusetts: Harvard University Press. 1957. Harvard Historical Monographs, No. 32. pp. ix + 192

Dickinson, Goldsworthy Lowes. RIGHT AND WRONG OF MODERN WARFARE. Tokyo (in Japanese). 1915. pp. v + 134

Dickinson, Goldsworthy Lowes. (1) DISARMAMENT (2 papers) (2) THE PROBLEM OF ARMAMENTS AND THE LEAGUE OF NATIONS. Friends Quarterly Examiner. No. 202. 1917. pp. 182–97

Dickinson, W[illoughby] H[yett]. DISARMAMENT AND A LEAGUE OF NATIONS. 1918. Pamphlet. pp. 12

Foster, T. A LASTING PEACE BY DISARMAMENT. Manchester. 1918. Pamphlet. pp. 15

Friends Peace Committee. LOOKING TOWARDS PEACE. London: Headley. 1915. Pamphlet. pp. 16

Fry, Sir Edward. LIMITATION OF ARMAMENTS. Nation. 6 November 1915. pp. 211–12

Jacks, L. P. PUNISHMENT AND RECONSTRUCTION. Hibbert Journal. April 1917. pp. 373–81. (All dreams of a peaceful and regenerated Europe are worthless unless they have as their starting point the condemnation and final removal of the military autocracies)

Jacks, L. P. THE WAR-MADE EMPIRES AND THE MARTIAL RACES OF THE WESTERN WORLD. Hibbert Journal. October 1917. pp. 1–18. Note by E. Lyttelton. January 1918. pp. 324–5. (All our states and empires have been built up by and for war)

Jacks, L. P. ARMS AND MEN: A STUDY IN HABIT. Hibbert Journal. Vol. 17. October 1918. pp. 21–38. (Sequel to 'War-made Empires', etc.)

Johnston, R. M. ARMS AND THE RACE: THE DIFFICULTIES IN

THE WAY OF DISARMAMENT. Century Magazine. March 1915.
pp. 648-58.

Jordan, D. S. WAR AND WASTE: A SERIES OF DISCUSSIONS OF
WAR AND WAR ACCESSORIES. London. 1914. pp. xi + 296

Laidlaw, Sir Robert. INTERNATIONAL CONTROL OF ARMA-
MENTS. Contemporary Review. April 1915. pp. 457-63

Lloyd George, David. Chapter XIII: DISARMAMENT, pp. 583-603
in THE TRUTH ABOUT THE PEACE TREATIES. Vol. I. London:
Gollancz. 1938. pp. 735

MacDonald, James Ramsay. WAR AND THE WORKERS: A PLEA
FOR DEMOCRATIC CONTROL. London. ?1915. Pamphlet. pp. 17

Marshall, Henry Rutgers. MEN AND ARMS: A STUDY OF INSTINCT.
Hibbert Journal. Vol. 17. April 1919. pp. 504-14.

Ponsonby, A[rthur] A. H., M.P. WHY WE SHOULD THINK ABOUT
PEACE. London. 1915. Pamphlet. pp. 4

Sydenham of Combe, Lord [George Sydenham Clarke]. WAR AND
ILLUSION. Edinburgh Review. January 1915. pp. 178-203. (In
controversion of the theories of Mr. Norman Angell and other
pacifists)

Unwin, E. E. 'AS A MAN THINKETH . . .': the personal problem of
militarism. London. 1919. pp. 120

Walsh, W. THE THINKER AND THE FIGHTER. Manchester. 1916.
pp. 184

Whyte, A. F. DISARMAMENT ACCORDING TO DELBRÜCK. New
Europe. 28 March 1918. pp. 321-7.

Review of Reviews. HOW TO INSURE CIVILIZATION. THE HAGUE
TRIBUNAL AWAITS THE NATIONS. June 1915. pp. 476-7

3. General: 1920-1925

Angell, Norman. THE FRUITS OF VICTORY: A SEQUEL TO THE
GREAT ILLUSION. London: Collins. 1921. pp. xviii + 338

Angell, N[orman]. PUBLIC AND THE GENEVA MINIMUM. Nation.
Vol. 37. 30 May 1925. pp. 259-60

Baker, P[hilip] J[ohn]. REAL PLAN TO OUTLAW WAR. Our World.
Vol. 5. June 1924. pp. 19-25

Baker, P[hilip] J[ohn]. MENACE OF ARMAMENTS. Nation. Vol. 35.
16 August 1924. pp. 613-14

Bullard, Arthur. ARMS AND THE INSTINCT. Harper's Magazine.

January 1922. pp. 167-74. (Human nature changes rapidly)

Cambridge Union Society. THE LEAGUE OF NATIONS IN RELA-
TION TO THE REDUCTION OF ARMAMENTS. Report of a
Committee to the Cambridge Union Society. 1924. Pamphlet

Carlton, David. DISARMAMENT WITH GUARANTEES: LORD
CECIL 1922-1927. Disarmament and Arms Control. Vol. 3.
Autumn 1965. pp. 143-64

Cecil, R. A. T. G. (3rd Marquis of Salisbury). DISARMAMENT AND
THE LEAGUE OF NATIONS. New York: Foreign Policy Association. 1923. Pamphlet. pp. 19

Cecil, Lord Robert, M.P. AMERICAN ADDRESSES BY LORD
ROBERT CECIL. World Peace Foundation. 1923. Pamphlet. Vol. 5.
No. 6

Coit, S. FOUR PATHS TO WORLD PEACE. London. 1924. Pamphlet.
pp. 16

Davids, C. A. F. Rhys. THE WILL TO PEACE. London: Fisher Unwin.
1923. pp. 160

Davies, M. L. DEATH OR LIFE. London. ?1924. Pamphlet. pp. 15

Dell, R[obert]. PEACE, DISARMAMENT AND THE LEAGUE. New
Statesman. Vol. 23. 2 August 1924. pp. 485-6.

Dickinson, Goldsworthy Lowes. WAR: ITS NATURE, CAUSE AND
CURE. London: G. Allen & Unwin Ltd. 1923. pp. 155

Dickinson, Goldsworthy Lowes. KRIGET, FREDEN OCH FRAM-
TIDEN. Uppsala. 1924. pp. 160

Dickinson, Goldsworthy Lowes. KRIGEN, FREDEN OG FREM-
TIDEN. København. 1923. pp. 151

Enock, A[rthur] G[uy]. THE PROBLEM OF ARMAMENTS. London:
Macmillan. 1923. pp. xii + 199

Grant, J. E. THE PROBLEM OF WAR AND ITS SOLUTION. London:
Allen & Unwin. 1922. pp. 384

Harris, W. LORD ROBERT CECIL'S FIGHT FOR DISARMAMENT.
Our World. Vol. 4. February 1924. pp. 16-21.

Hobson, J[ohn] A[tkinson]. ARMS AND MAN. Nation. Vol. 38. 5
December 1925. pp. 350-1

International Council of Women. THE PREVENTION OF THE
CAUSES OF WAR. Addresses delivered at the conference held at
the British Empire Exhibition, 1924. Tarland. ?1924. pp. iii + 327

Joint Disarmament Committee. THE PROBLEM OF DISARMAMENT.
London. 1921. Disarmament pamphlets. No. 1. Pamphlet. pp. 11

Kerr, P[hilip] H[enry]. THE PREVENTION OF WAR. New Haven.
1923. Institute of Politics Publications. pp. 170

League of Nations Union. FINAL REPORT OF THE COMMITTEE ON
THE LIMITATION OF ARMAMENTS. London. 1921. Pamphlet.
pp. 15

Lodge, Sir O. CIVILISED WARFARE. 1922. Pamphlet. pp. 8

MacDonald, James Ramsay, M.P. THE WAY TO PEACE. London.
1924. Pamphlet. pp. 12

Maurice, Sir Frederick [Barton] (Major-General). THE LEAGUE OF
NATIONS AND THE REDUCTION OF ARMAMENTS. New World.
February 1920. pp. 197-203

Maurice, Sir F[rederick Barton] (Major-General). THE LIMITATION
OF ARMAMENTS. The Contemporary Review. Vol. CXX. October
1921. pp. 433-40

Maurice, Sir Frederick [Barton] (Major-General). LORD ESHER'S
PROPOSAL FOR THE LIMITATION OF ARMAMENTS. International Affairs. July 1922. pp. 101-12

Maurice, Sir Frederick Barton (Major-General). DISARMAMENT, BY
MAJOR GENERAL SIR FREDERICK MAURICE. London: The
Daily News Ltd. 1924. The New Way series. Pamphlet. pp. 32

Maurice, (Sir) Frederick [Barton] (Major-General). ARMIES OF
EUROPE IN 1925. Foreign Affairs. Vol. 3. July 1925. pp. 611-23

Morgan, J[ohn] H[artman] [Brigadier-General]. THE DISARMA-
MENT OF GERMANY AND AFTER. Quarterly Review. Vol. 242.
August 1924. pp. 415-57

National Council for the Prevention of War. MEMORANDUM ON
MILITARISM AND EDUCATION. London. 1924. Pamphlet. pp. 4

Noyes, W. A. BUILDING FOR PEACE. Cambridge. 1924. Pamphlet.
pp. 78

Page, K. WAR: ITS CAUSES, CONSEQUENCE AND CURE. London:
Allen & Unwin. 1924. pp. 215

Pickard, Bertram. THE SIXTH ASSEMBLY OF THE LEAGUE. Friends
Peace Committee. 1925. Pamphlet. pp. 7. (Reprinted from THE
FRIEND. 18 September 1925)

Pollard, F. E. THE MEANING OF DISARMAMENT. Pilgrim. January
1922. pp. 134-44

Ponsonby, A[rthur, A. W. H.], M.P. NOW IS THE TIME. AN APPEAL
FOR PEACE. London: Parsons. 1925. pp. 191

Ponsonby, Arthur (A. W. H.), M.P. DISARMAMENT BY EXAMPLE.
The Contemporary Review. Vol. CXXXII. December 1927.

pp. 687–93

Ponsonby, Arthur [A. W. H.], M.P. DISARMAMENT BY EXAMPLE. International Affairs. Vol. 7. July 1928. pp. 225–40

Raglan, Lord. ARMAMENTS AND FRONTIERS. 19th Century. July 1922. pp. 17–24

Ranjitsinhji, H. H. Prince. Chapter on the disarmament question in Fry, Charles Burgess. KEY-BOOK OF THE LEAGUE OF NATIONS. London: Hodder & Stoughton. 1923.

Rose, F. H. SWORD-BLADES OR PLOUGH SHARES? THE INFLUENCE OF STEEL ON WAR AND PEACE. Labour Party. 1923. Pamphlet. pp. 12

Singh, Sr. N. NATIONAL STATES AND THE WORLD AFFAIRS. London Quarterly Review. Vol. 136. October 1921. pp. 241–50

Sykes, Sir F [rederick] H[ugh] (Major-General), M.P. REDUCTION OF ARMAMENTS, ECONOMIC AND IMPERIAL DEFENCE. London. 1926. Pamphlet. pp. 16

Thurtle, E. MILITARY DISCIPLINE AND DEMOCRACY. London. 1920. pp. xviii + 82

Wheeler-Bennett, John W(heeler). INFORMATION ON THE REDUCTION OF ARMAMENTS. London: Allen & Unwin. Information Service on International Affairs, Information Series, No. 2. 1925. pp. 216

Woolf, Leonard. REDUCTION OF ARMAMENTS. Contemporary Review. November 1922

Wright, Q. LIMITATION OF ARMAMENT. London. 1921. Pamphlet. pp. 39

English Review. THERE SHALL BE NO WAR? Vol. 39. October 1924. pp. 466–71

Nation. NEW RACE IN ARMAMENTS. Vol. 32. 31 March 1923. pp. 974–5

Nation. DISARMAMENT, EVACUATION AND SECURITY. Vol. 37. 6 June 1925. pp. 286–7

New Statesman. FINE WORDS AND COLD FACTS. Vol. 18. 8 October 1921. pp. 7–8

New Statesman. DISARMAMENT AND GUARANTEES. Vol. 19. 23 September 1922. pp. 653–4

New Statesman. ARMED CAMP. Vol. 21. 28 July 1923. pp. 460–1

New Statesman. MR. MACDONALD AND THE LEAGUE. Vol. 23. 26 July 1924. pp. 456–7

Outlook (London). DISARMAMENT ILLUSION. Vol. 52. 28 July

1923. pp. 65-6

Saturday Review. PACTS, DEBTS AND DISARMAMENT. Vol. 140. 19 September 1925. pp. 303-4

4. General: 1926-1930

Arnold-Forster, W[illiam] and Murray, G(ilbert). SECURITY AND DISARMAMENT. Nation. Vol. 41. 10 September 1927. p. 742. Discussion: Vol. 41. 17 September – 1 October 1927. pp. 770-1, 792-800

Aston, Sir George (Major-General), [ed.]. THE STUDY OF WAR. London: Longmans, Green. 1927. pp. 205

Austin, F. B. THE WAR-GOD WALKS AGAIN. London: Williams & Norgate. 1926. pp. 247

Barnes, Rt. Hon. George N[icoll]. SECURITY, DISARMAMENT AND AMERICA. The Contemporary Review. Vol. CXXXIII. March 1928. pp. 289-93

Bartlett, V[ernon]. WHAT DISARMAMENT MEANS. London. 1930. Pamphlet. pp. 11

Brock, C. J. L. PEACE AND DISARMAMENT. London. 1928. Pamphlet. pp. 24

Brockway, A. Fenner. CAN BRITAIN DISARM? No More War Movement. ?1929. Pamphlet

Cecil, Robert (1st Viscount Cecil of Chelwood). DISARMAMENT AND THE LEAGUE. Address delivered before the Foreign Policy Association, Hotel Astor, New York, 1923, in THE WAY OF PEACE. London: Philip Allan & Co. Ltd. 1928. pp. 211-32

Cecil, Robert (1st Viscount Cecil of Chelwood). CASE FOR DIS- ARMAMENT. Nation. Vol. 45. 27 April 1929. pp. 99-100

Chamberlain, W. J. FIGHTING FOR PEACE. THE STORY OF THE WAR RESISTANCE MOVEMENT. No More War Movement. 1929. pp. 155

Cushendun, Lord. DISARMAMENT. International Affairs. Vol. 7. March 1928. pp. 77-93

Dalton, Hugh, M.P. TOWARDS THE PEACE OF NATIONS: A STUDY IN INTERNATIONAL POLITICS. Ch. VII: Disarmament; The General Question, pp. 141-166. Ch. VIII: Disarmament; Technical Questions, pp. 167-207. London: George Routledge & Sons, Ltd. 1928. pp. xi + 316

Davies, Major David, M.P. THE PROBLEM OF DISARMAMENT. The
Contemporary Review. Vol. CXXX. August 1926. pp. 152-60

Dawson, W. H. THE FUTURE OF EMPIRE AND THE WORLD PRICE
OF PEACE. London: Williams & Norgate. 1930. pp. 285

De Watteville, H. PROBLEM OF DISARMAMENT. Journal of Royal
Artillery. Vol. 54. January 1928. pp. 563-75

Dickinson, Sir W(illoughby) H(yett). INTERNATIONAL PEACE.
SPCK. 1929. Major Issues of the Day. No. 1. Pamphlet. pp. 7

Galsworthy, J. THE WAY TO PREPARE PEACE. Harrot. 1927.
Pamphlet. pp. 9

Hall, W. G. Carlton. DISARMAMENT. English Review. Vol. 42.
February 1926. pp. 182-9

Hall, W. G. Carlton. REGULATION OF WARFARE BY TREATY.
English Review. March 1927. pp. 322-30

Hall, W. G. C[arlton]. WAR AND THE MAN IN THE STREET.
English Review. January 1930. pp. 61-71

Hall, W. G. C[arlton]. MILLENNIUM OR MIRAGE. English Review.
Vol. 50. March 1930. pp. 288-91

Harley, J. H. MAIN ISSUE IN DISARMAMENT. Fortnightly Review.
June 1930. pp. 751-60

Harris, H[enry] W[ilson]. BRITISH POLICY AND DISARMAMENT.
Academy of Political Science Proceedings. Vol. 12. July 1926.
pp. 27-34

Harris, H[enry] Wilson. DISARMAMENT PROGRESS. The Contemporary Review. Vol. CXXXI. June 1927. pp. 699-703

Harris, H[enry] Wilson. ARMS OR ARBITRATION? London: Hogarth
Press. 1928. pp. 93

Harris, H[enry] Wilson. WILL DISARMAMENT COME? The Contemporary Review. Vol. XXXIII. May 1928. pp. 572-9

Harris, Lilian. DISARMAMENT AND SECURITY. London: Women's
Co-operative Guild. n.d. Pamphlet. pp. 15

Hart, B. H. L. PARIS: OR, THE FUTURE OF WAR. London: Kegan
Paul. 1925. pp. 92

Huddleston, Sisley. FOGS, HOGS, BOGS AND ALL. New Statesman.
Vol. 28. 12 March 1927. pp. 657-9

Huddleston, Sisley. DISARMAMENT – A WARNING. New Republic.
22 June 1927. pp. 114-6

Huddleston, Sisley. LEAGUE'S FAILURE. New Statesman. Vol. 29.
23 August 1927. pp. 33-4

Huddleston, S[isley]. TEN YEARS LATE. New Statesman. Vol. 36.

15 November 1930. pp. 169-70

Hyde, H. E. THE PRICE OF NATIONAL SECURITY. London: P. S. King. 1930. pp. xvii + 289

Keen, F. N. REAL SECURITY AGAINST WAR. London: Williams & Norgate. 1929. Pamphlet. pp. 32

Kerr, P[hilip]. PACT OR WAR – NO OTHER ALTERNATIVE. Christian Century. Vol. 46. 3 January 1929. pp. 9-10

Kerr, Philip. EUROPE AND USA: THE PROBLEM OF SANCTIONS. International Affairs. Vol. 9. 1930. pp. 288-324

Kerr, Philip. NAVIES AND PEACE: A BRITISH VIEW. Foreign Affairs (New York). October 1929. pp. 20-9

King-Hall, Stephen. IMPERIAL DEFENCE. A BOOK FOR TAX-PAYERS. London: Fisher Unwin. 1926. pp. 204. (Difficulty of reducing armaments in present unsatisfactory state of security)

League of Nations Union. ARMAMENTS: THEIR REDUCTION AND LIMITATION. London. 1926. Pamphlet No. 198. pp. 42

League of Nations Union. SPEAKERS NOTES ON INTERNATIONAL DISARMAMENT. London. 1927. Pamphlet. pp. 16

League of Nations Union. NOTES ON RECENT PROGRESS WITH REGARD TO THE REDUCTION AND LIMITATION OF ARMA-MENTS. London. 1927. Pamphlet. pp. 22

League of Nations Union. DISARMAMENT. London. 1927. Pamphlet No. 210. pp. 40

League of Nations Union. LAW NOT WAR: ARBITRATION NOT ARMAMENTS: LEARN OR PERISH. London. 1927. Pamphlet. pp. 31

League of Nations Union. INTERNATIONAL DISARMAMENT, SECURITY AND ARBITRATION. London. 1928. Pamphlet. pp. 22

League of Nations Union. ARMAMENTS. THEIR REDUCTION AND LIMITATION. London. October 1928. Pamphlet No. 198. pp. 42 Pamphlet No. 198. pp. 42

Lefebure, Major Victor. SCIENTIFIC DISARMAMENT. London. 1930. pp. 320. (See also review in NATURE (1931) q.v.)

MacDonald, J[ames] R[amsay], M.P. THE RISKS OF PEACE. New York. 1929. pp. 13. (Supplement to FOREIGN AFFAIRS, Vol. 8, No. 1)

MacDonald, James Ramsay, M.P. AMERICAN SPEECHES. London: Cape. 1930. pp. 158

McDougall, William. JANUS: THE CONQUEST OF WAR. A PSYCHO-

LOGICAL INQUIRY. London: Kegan Paul. 1927. pp. 140

MacKenzie, N. A. DISARMAMENT. No place of publication. 1929.
Pamphlet. pp. 7

Madariaga, Salvador de. DISARMAMENT. Oxford: Oxford University
Press. 1929

Madariaga, S[alvador] de. DISARMAMENT: THE ROLE OF THE
ANGLO-SAXON NATIONS, pp. 51–74 in Geneva Institute of
International Relations, PROBLEMS OF PEACE, third series,
lectures delivered August 1928. London: Humphrey Milford
(OUP). 1929

Madariaga, Salvador de. DISARMAMENT – AMERICAN PLAN.
Atlantic Monthly. April 1929. pp. 525–38

Maurice, Sir Frederick Barton (Major-General). DISARMAMENT.
International Affairs. May 1926. pp. 117–33

Nearing, Scott. HOOVER AND MACDONALD. Labour Monthly.
December 1929. pp. 753–6

Noel-Baker, Philip [John]. DISARMAMENT. London: Hogarth Press.
1926. pp. xiv + 352. (See also review in NATION (1926) *q.v.*)

MacCabe, J. IS WAR INEVITABLE? Girard. 1930. Pamphlet. pp. 32

National Council for the Prevention of War. DISARMAMENT:
BRITAIN MUST GIVE A LEAD. 1926. Pamphlet. pp. 8

Norwood, Rev. F. W. DISARMAMENT: THE DESIRE AND FEAR
OF NATIONS. London: Brotherhood Movement. 1928. Pamphlet.
pp. 43 (John Clifford Lecture, 1928)

Ponsonby, Arthur (M.P.). DISARMAMENT BY EXAMPLE. Contemporary Review. December 1927. pp. 687–93

Reilly, Henry J. OUR CRUMBLING NATIONAL DEFENCE. Century
Magazine. January 1927. pp. 271–80. March 1927. pp. 513–22.
April 1927. pp. 748–56

Reilly, Henry J. WORLD STILL UNDER ARMS. World Today. Vol. 50.
June 1927. pp. 27–37

Smith, Rennie (M.P.). GENERAL DISARMAMENT OR WAR? London:
Allen & Unwin. 1927. pp. 111

Spanner, Edward Frank. ARMAMENTS AND THE NON-COMBATANT:
TO THE 'FRONT-LINE' TROOPS OF THE FUTURE. London:
Williams & Norgate. 1927. pp. xiv + 303

Spender, Hugh F. DIFFICULTIES OF DISARMAMENT. Fortnightly
Review. May 1927. pp. 610–17

Spender, Hugh F. DISARMAMENT CRISIS. Fortnightly Review.
February 1928. pp. 162–70

Steed, H. Wickham. WHITHER? LORD CECIL AND THE GOVERN-
MENT. Review of Reviews. September 1927. pp. 205-12

Steed, H. Wickham. DO WE WANT PEACE? Review of Reviews.
October 1928. pp. 198-207

Villarr, L. PROBLEM OF DISARMAMENT. Quarterly Review. July
1927. pp. 81-99

Webster, C[harles] K[ingsley]. NINTH ASSEMBLY. Welsh Outlook.
October 1928. pp. 296-8

Webster, C[harles] K[ingsley]. ANGLO-AMERICAN OPPORTUNITY.
Nation. 29 June 1929. pp. 423-4

Wheeler-Bennett, J[ohn]. INFORMATION ON THE RENUNCIATION
OF WAR. London: G. Allen & Unwin. 1928. pp. 191

Wheeler-Bennett, J[ohn]. DISARMAMENT AND SECURITY SINCE
LOCARNO, 1925-31 (being the political and technical background
of the General Disarmament Conference, 1932). London: Information
Service on International Affairs, Information Series, No. 7. George
Allen & Unwin Ltd. 1932. pp. 383

Wilkinson, Spenser. SECURITY. 19th Century. April 1927. pp. 465-75

Williams, Rhys. WAR AND ARMAMENTS. Millgate Monthly. January
1934. pp. 203-4

Women's Peace Crusade. WOMEN AND DISARMAMENT. London. 1930.
Pamphlet. pp. 17

Army Quarterly. WHY ARE NATIONS ARMED? WHY SHOULD THEY
DISARM? WHY DO NOT THEY? Vol. 17. January 1929. pp. 342-8

Economist. ARMAMENTS SUPPLEMENT. 19 October 1929. pp. 8

English Review. BUYING PEACE — A VISION OF 1950. September
1930. pp. 348-56

Nation. Lord Cecil's Crusade. Vol. 41. 3 September 1927. pp. 710-11

Nation. DISARMAMENT AND DISTRACTIONS. Vol. 41. 10
September 1927. pp. 738-9

Nation. FULL TEXT OF THE RESOLUTION OF THE 8TH
ASSEMBLY. Vol. 42. 8 October 1927. pp. 11-12

Nation. LORD CECIL'S CRUSADE. Vol. 41. 3 September 1927.
pp. 710-11

Nation. Review of Philip Noel-Baker: DISARMAMENT (1926, q.v.).
Vol. 39. 29 May 1926. pp. 200-1

Nation. CABINET AND DISARMAMENT. Vol. 42. 26 November 1927.
pp. 306-7

Nature. Review of Major Victor Lefebure: SCIENTIFIC DISARMA-
MENT (1931, q.v.). 4 April 1931. pp. 153-5

New Statesman. PROSPECTS OF DISARMAMENT. Vol. 30. 26
November 1927. pp. 196-7
New Statesman. DISARMAMENT. Vol. 30. 31 March 1928. pp. 784-5
New Statesman. DISARMAMENT TANGLE. Vol. 33. 22 June 1929.
pp. 330-1
New Statesman. ARMS AND MEN. Vol. 33. 28 September 1929.
pp. 732-3
Outlook. PROBLEM OF DISARMAMENT. Vol. 59. 7 May 1927.
pp. 474-5
Outlook. SECURITY OF DISARMAMENT? Vol. 60. 3 December
1927. pp. 721-2
Review of Reviews. SPECTRE OF WAR IN EUROPE. January 1931.
pp. 8-12
Saturday Review. PROBLEM OF DISARMAMENT. Vol. 143. 29
January 1927. pp. 144-6
Saturday Review. LIMITS OF LIMITATION. Vol. 143. 25 June 1927.
pp. 964-5
Socialist Review. FAILURE TO DISARM. December 1930. pp. 63-8
Spectator. CHOICE OF RISKS. Vol. 139. 29 October 1927. pp. 701-2
Spectator. CRUX OF DISARMAMENT. Vol. 145. 29 November 1930.
pp. 830-1
Times. FACTS AND THE PROBLEM. 24 November 1927. pp. 15-16

5. General: 1931-1933

Angell, Sir Norman and Bliven, B. WHAT CAUSES WAR? ?New York.
1932. Pamphlet. pp. 27
Angell, Sir Norman. THE GREAT ILLUSION, 1933. London: Heine-
mann. 1933. pp. xiii + 397
Angell, Sir Norman. Chapter on the choice between arming the litigants
and arming the judge, in George Peabody Gooch (ed.): IN PURSUIT
OF PEACE. Addresses delivered at the National Peace Congress,
Oxford, 7-10 July 1933. London: Methuen. 1933. pp. xi + 134
Angell, [Sir] Norman. MAN CAN ABOLISH WAR. Spectator. Vol. 150.
17 February 1933. pp. 207-8. Reply by J. Yeats-Brown. Vol. 150.
24 February 1933. p. 251
Arnold-Forster, William E. PRINCIPLE OF EQUALITY IN DIS-
ARMAMENT. New Statesman and Nation. Vol. 3. 30 January

1932. pp. 136-7

Arnold-Forster, W[illiam E.] THE DISARMAMENT CRISIS: LEVEL UP OR LEVEL DOWN? National Peace Council. 1932. Pamphlet. pp. 4

Bairstow, George. DISARMAMENT CAMPAIGN (Accepting the risks of peace. Why a Quaker desires disarmament). Northern Friends Peace Board. 1931. Pamphlet. pp. 4. (Reprinted from the HALIFAX COURIER AND GUARDIAN, 8 October 1931)

Bellerby, J. R. WORLD ORDER WITHOUT ARMS. London: Richard Clay for Education Services. 1933. World Commonwealth Series II. Pamphlet. pp. 16

Brailsford, H[enry] N[oel]. IF WE WANT PEACE. London: Woolf. Day to Day Pamphlets, No. 11. 1932. Pamphlet. pp. 64

Broad, C. D. WAR-THOUGHTS IN PEACE-TIME. London. 1931. Pamphlet. pp. 44

Brown, A. J. DISARMAMENT OR DISASTER. London. 1932. Pamphlet. pp. 18

Cadogan, H. 'WHY DO THE NATIONS . . .?' London: A. H. Stockwell. 1933. pp. 90. (on the prevention of war)

Carter, W. H. THE TRIPOD OF PEACE. 19th Century. March 1933. pp. 298-311

Cecil, Robert (1st Viscount Cecil of Chelwood). A LETTER TO AN M.P. ON DISARMAMENT. London: Leonard and Virginia Woolf at the Hogarth Press. 1931. Hogarth Letters, No. 2. Pamphlet. pp. 40

Cecil, Robert (1st Viscount Cecil of Chelwood). WILL THE WORLD DISARM IN 1932? Spectator. Vol. 146. 28 March 1931. pp. 495-6

Cecil, Robert (1st Viscount Cecil of Chelwood). ZUR ABRÜSTUNGS-FRAGE. Neue Europa. Vol. 17. July—August 1931. pp. 7-15

Cecil, Robert (1st Viscount Cecil of Chelwood). PEACE ON EARTH. Spectator. Vol. 147. 21 November 1931. pp. 665-6

Cecil, Robert (1st Viscount Cecil of Chelwood) and Davis, Norman H. DISARMAMENT (articles by Cecil and Davis and texts of official documents). Worcester, Mass, New York City: Carnegie Endowment. 1932. pp. 74

Day, J. W. WOLF IN SHEEP'S CLOTHING: MR. BALDWIN, THE DOPE PEDDLAR OF CONSERVATISM. Saturday Review. Vol. 156. 21 October 1933. pp. 410-11

Dickinson, Willoughby (Lord Dickinson of Painswick). DIS-ARM OR RE-ARM? 19th Century. February 1932. pp. 129-39

Fanshawe, Maurice. WORLD DISARMAMENT: A HANDBOOK ON THE REDUCTION AND LIMITATION OF ARMAMENTS. London: League of Nations Union. 1931. pp. 142. (Epilogue by Viscount Cecil of Chelwood analysing draft convention)

Fitzgerald, W. G. ARMAMENTS AND BRITISH PRESTIGE. Quarterly Review. January 1933. pp. 124-40

Franklyn, J. E. CULTURE, PEACE AND PROGRESS. Dexter. 1934. Pamphlet. pp. 15

Fuller, A. C. FACT VERSUS FANCY IN DISARMAMENT. National Review. November 1932. pp. 625-30

Fuller, John Frederick Charles (Major-General). THE DRAGON'S TEETH: A STUDY OF WAR AND PEACE. London: Constable. 1932. pp. xi + 337

Fuller, J[ohn] F[rederick] Ch[arles] Major-General. WHAT IS AN AGGRESSIVE WEAPON? English Review. Vol. 54. June 1932. pp. 601-5

Garnett, J. C. M. THE ORGANISATION OF PEACE. London: Kegan Paul. 1933. Psyche Miniatures, General Series No. 53. pp. 123

Gwynn, C. W. THE ARMY AND THE AIR FORCE. Quarterly Review. October 1932. pp. 285-98

Haestier, R. E. GILT-EDGED INSECURITY (the peace farce played by the world's diplomatists). Jarrolds. 1932. pp. 191

Harper, J. E. T. DISARMAMENT AND PEACE MACHINES. National Review. February 1932. pp. 202-6

Harris, H[enry] Wilson. TOWARDS DISARMAMENT. Contemporary Review. Vol. CXXXIX. February 1931. pp. 147-53

Harris, H[enry] Wilson. DISARMAMENT — AND NOW? Contemporary Review. Vol. CXLII. September 1932. pp. 274-81

Hart, Heber Leonidas. THE BULWARKS OF PEACE AND INTER-NATIONAL JUSTICE. London: Methuen. 1933. pp. 240

Henderson, Arthur (M.P.). CONSOLIDATING WORLD PEACE (the Burge Memorial Lecture for the year 1931). Oxford: Clarendon Press. 1931. Pamphlet. pp. 27

Henderson, Arthur (M.P.). LABOUR OUTLAWS WAR. London. 1933. Pamphlet. pp. 11

Howell, M. O. FOUNDATIONS OF PEACE FOR A NEW WORLD ORDER. The Author. 1932. Pamphlet. pp. 10

Huddleston, S[isley]. TWO DOCTRINES OF PEACE. New Statesman. Vol. 34. 5 April 1930. pp. 830-2

Hutt, Allen. 'DISARMAMENT' AND THE COMING WAR. Labour Monthly. Vol. 13. May 1931. pp. 292-9

Innes, G. A. DISARMAMENT, THE QUESTION OF THE DAY.
London: League of Nations Union. 1931. Pamphlet. pp. 30

Innes, K[athleen] E. Chapter on disarmament in THE PREVENTION
OF WAR. London: The Friends Peace Committee. 1932. pp. 93

Jackson, J. A SIMPLE PLAN FOR THE REDUCTION OF ARMA-
MENTS. Glasgow: R. Gibson & Sons. 1931. Pamphlet. pp. 48

Jacobs, A. N. WORLD PEACE AND ARMAMENTS. THE PROBLEM
RE-EXAMINED. London: Hutchinson. 1931. pp. 183

Joad, C. E. M. 'PACIFISTS' ESCAPE FROM DILEMMA. New Statesman. 25 November 1933. pp. 653-4

King-Hall, S[tephen]. NOW OR NEVER. 19th Century. November
1932. pp. 513-24

King-Hall, Stephen. THE DRIVE FOR PEACE. Fortnightly Review.
December 1933. pp. 641-54

Kirchhoff, Dr H. REAL DISARMAMENT. London: King. ?1931

Knebworth, Viscount. PEACE AND PIETY. English Review. Vol. 55.
December 1932. pp. 627-34

Labour Party. DISARM? 1931. Pamphlet. pp. 24

League of Nations Union. ARMS AND THE PEOPLE. London. 1931.
Pamphlet. pp. 4

Lefebure, (Major) Victor. SCIENTIFIC DISARMAMENT (a treatise
based on the facts of armament). London. Mundanus (Gollancz).
1931. pp. 318

Lefebure, (Major) Victor. THE DECISIVE AGGRESSIVE VALUE OF
THE NEW AGENCIES OF WAR. pp. 96-117 in INTER-
PARLIAMENTARY UNIONS: WHAT WOULD BE THE CHARAC-
TER OF A NEW WAR? London: P. S. King & Son. 1931

Lefebure, (Major) Victor. COMMON SENSE ABOUT DISARMAMENT.
London: V. Gollancz Ltd. 1932. pp. 176

Liddell-Hart, Basil. AGGRESSION AND THE PROBLEM OF
WEAPONS: REPLY TO J. F. C. FULLER. English Review. Vol. 55.
July 1932. pp. 71-8

de Ligt, Bart. DIRECT ACTION FOR IMMEDIATE TOTAL DIS-
ARMAMENT. Socialist Review. Vol. 4. 1932. pp. 175-9

Madariaga, Salvador de. THE DIFFICULTY OF DISARMING. pp. 284-
303 in Geneva Institute of International Relations, PROBLEMS OF
PEACE, fifth series, lectures delivered August 1930. London:
Humphrey Milford (OUP). 1931

Madariaga, S[alvador] de. LE DÉSARMEMENT NÉCESSAIRE.
L'Europe Nouvelle (Paris). Vol. 14. 26 September 1931. pp. 1305-8

Marvin, F. S. (ed.). THE EVOLUTION OF WORLD PEACE. London: OUP. 1933. United Series, No. 4. pp. 209

Money, Sir L. G. Chiozza. CAN WAR BE AVERTED? London: T. Butterworth. 1931. pp. 293

Murray, Gilbert. WORK FOR PEACE. Times. 2 September 1932. pp. 13-14

National Council for the Prevention of War. PEACE YEAR BOOK, 1931. London: NCPW. 1931. pp. 145

National Council for the Prevention of War. OURSELVES AND DIS-ARMAMENT: WHERE DO WE STAND? London. 1931. Pamphlet No. 20. pp. 12

National Council for the Prevention of War. TOWARDS DISARMA-MENT. CAMPAIGN NOTES. 1931. Pamphlet.

National Council for the Prevention of War. 1932 – A VITAL YEAR. 1931. Pamphlet. pp. 4

Nemo. WAR AGAIN TOMORROW! BY NEMO. London: Modern Books. 1933. Pamphlet. pp. 31

Newbold, J. T. W. DEMOCRACY, DEBTS AND DISARMAMENT. London: Methuen. 1933. pp. 343

Nichols, Beverley. CRY HAVOC! London: Jonathan Cape. 1933. pp. 254

Nickerson, H. CAN WE LIMIT WAR? London; Arrowsmith. 1933. pp. 256

Noel-Baker, P[hilip] J[ohn]. THE END OF A MYTH. Northern Friends Peace Board. 1933. Pamphlet. pp. 4. (Reprinted from HEADWAY)

No More War Movement. YOUR COUNTRY IS IN DANGER. London(?). 1932. Pamphlet. pp. 4

Pennington, Richard. THE PACIFIST PROBLEM. Week-End Review. November 1933. pp. 493-4

Petrie, C[harles]. PROBLEM OF DISARMAMENT. Saturday Review. Vol. 151. 21 February–14 March 1931. pp. 257-8, 295-6, 331-2, 368-9

Ponsonby Arthur (Baron Ponsonby of Shulbrede). DISARMAMENT: A DISCUSSION. London: Hogarth Press. 1932. Pamphlet. pp. 45. (Day to Day Pamphlets No. 14)

Powell, W. A. WHY DISARMAMENT FAILS. Week-End Review. 7 January 1933. pp. 6-7

Powell, W. A. DISARMAMENT AND ITS PROBLEMS. Saturday Review. Vol. 155. 8 April 1933. pp. 332-3

Rajagopalan, S. S. DISARMAMENT, PAST, PRESENT AND FUTURE.

Modern Review. November 1931. pp. 536-8

Robbins, George Norman. SECURITY BY DISARMAMENT. London: Williams & Norgate. 1932. pp. 127

Robert the Peeler (pseudonym). LETTERS TO JOHN BULL AND OTHERS. London: William & Norgate. 1931. pp. 141

Rowntree, J. [Stevenson]. SOME POINTERS ON PEACE, WAR AND DISARMAMENT. Northern Friends Peace Board: Rawdon near Leeds. 1931. Pamphlet. pp. 4

Rowntree, J. [Stevenson]. FRIENDS AND PEACE IN 1933. Northern Friends Peace Board. 1933. Pamphlet. pp. 4. (Reprinted from THE FRIEND)

Salter, Arthur et al. CREATION OF PEACE; BASED ON CAUSES OF WAR: ECONOMIC, INDUSTRIAL, RACIAL, RELIGIOUS, SCIENTIFIC AND POLITICAL. Quarterly Review. Vol. 259. October 1932. pp. 331-43

Salter, Arthur et al. DISARMAMENT. The Listener. 26 October 1932. pp. 577-9, 623-5. 2 November 1932. pp. 636. Correspondence 9-23 November 1932. pp. 679, 719-20, 762

de Sélincourt, B. TOWARDS PEACE, AND OTHER ESSAYS CRITICAL OR CONSTRUCTIVE. London: OUP. 1932. pp. 119

Smith, A. Baird. DISARMAMENT. Army Quarterly. October 1931. pp. 121-8

Smith, Professor H. A. THE PROBLEM OF DISARMAMENT IN THE LIGHT OF HISTORY. International Affairs. Vol. X, 1931. pp. 600-21

Smith, Pitt C. THE CASE FOR PACIFISM (defence of the No fight resolution recently passed at the Oxford Union Society). London: White Owl Press. 1933. Pamphlet. pp. 26

Smuts, Jan Christian. THE DISARMED PEACE (the Basil Hicks Lecture delivered to the University of Sheffield). Sheffield. 1931. Pamphlet. pp. 26

Spaull, H[ebe]. PIONEERING FOR PEACE. London: Sheldon Press. 1931. pp. 152

Spaull, Hebe. THE WORLD'S WEAPONS. London: Ivor Nicolson & Watson Ltd. 1932. Pamphlet. pp. 48

Steed, H. Wickham. ARMAMENTS AND DISARMAMENT SINCE 1918. Journal of Royal United Services Institute. November 1931. pp. 824-42

Steed, H. Wickham. THE DRIFT TOWARDS WAR. Fortnightly Review. November 1933. pp. 513-21

Stratford, E. C. W. THEY THAT TAKE THE SWORD. London:

Routledge. 1932. pp. 422

Thorne, Christopher. THE QUEST FOR ARMS EMBARGOES: FAILURE IN 1933. Journal of Contemporary History. October 1970. pp. 129-49

Wade, D. A. L. DISARMAMENT. Army Quarterly. October 1932. pp. 55-64

Walmsley, R. G. TREATY REVISION AND ITS RELATION TO DISARMAMENT. Liverpool. 1931. pp. 20

Wingfeld-Stratford, Esmé. THEY THAT TAKE THE SWORD. London: George Routledge & Sons Ltd. 1932.

Wintringham, T. H. WAR! – AND THE WAY TO FIGHT AGAINST IT. London: Communist Party of Great Britain. 1932. Pamphlet. pp. 23

Women. WORKING WOMEN! WAR IS COMING! (a Communist pamphlet). London: Modern Books. 1931. Pamphlet. pp. 15

Woolf, Leonard (ed.). THE INTELLIGENT MAN'S WAY TO PREVENT WAR. London: Gollancz. 1933. pp. 569. (with chapters by: Norman Angell; W. Arnold-Forster; Viscount Cecil of Chelwood; Gilbert Murray; Charles Buxton; Harold Laski)

Zangwill, E. A. THE STORY OF THE DISARMAMENT DECLARATION. Saffron Walden. 1932. Pamphlet. pp. 16

Zimmern, A[lfred]. PROBLEM OF DISARMAMENT; EXCERPTS. Review of Reviews. Vol. 82. December 1932. pp. 41-3

Zimmern, Alfred. DISARMAMENT: THE DECISIVE PHASE. Fortnightly Review. December 1932. pp. 681-91

Economist. DISARMAMENT OR WAR? Vol. 113. 18 July 1931. pp. 105-6

Listener. WAR OR PEACE? (articles and discussion – 7 articles). 18 November–30 December 1931

New Statesman and Nation. MORE SCRAPS OF PAPER. Vol. 2. 28 November 1931. pp. 664-5

New Statesman and Nation. MILITARY CONSEQUENCES OF THE PEACE. Vol. 5. 18 March 1933. pp. 312-13

New Statesman and Nation. TWILIGHT OF PEACE. Vol. 6. 18 November 1933. pp. 623-4

Review of Reviews. BRITAIN LEADS THE WAY. August 1931. p. 20

Review of Reviews. IF BRITAIN RE-ARMS, EXCERPTS. Vol. 86. November 1935. pp. 36-8

Round Table. POLITICAL FOUNDATION FOR DISARMAMENT.

Vol. 21. September 1931. pp. 713-37

Round Table. FOUNDATION FOR DISARMAMENT. Vol. 23. December 1932. pp. 1-20

Spectator. DISARMAMENT. Vol. 147. 4 July 1931. pp. 5-6

Spectator. DISARMAMENT: ALL PARTIES AGREED. Vol. 147. 18 July 1931. pp. 73-4.

World Today. MEN, GUNS AND SHIPS. (quick reference guide to the world's armaments). March 1932. pp. 285-91

6. General: 1934-1935

Allen, R. C. (1st Baron). WHAT IS THE REALY DIFFICULTY IN THE WORLD CRISIS? Farnham. 1934. Pamphlet. pp. 16

Angell, Sir Norman. WHY THE DISARMAMENT DEADLOCK? 19th Century. July 1934. pp. 16-28

Angell, Sir Norman. PREFACE TO PEACE. A GUIDE FOR THE PLAIN MAN. London: H. Hamilton. 1935. pp. 312

Arnold-Forster, W[illiam] E. THE PRICE OF PEACE: DISARMA-MENT AND WORLD GOVERNMENT. Chapter 3 in C. E. M. Joad (ed.), MANIFESTO. London. 1934

Arnold-Forster, W[illiam] E. NEW DISARMAMENT RESOLUTION. Contemporary Review. July 1934. pp. 11-20

Bailey, J. DISARMAMENT AND THE WAR DANGER. Millgate Monthly. July 1934. pp. 554-6

Bauer, L. WAR AGAIN TOMORROW. London: Faber. 1932. pp. 314 pp. 314

Brailsford, H[enry] N[oel]. PROPERTY OR PEACE? London: Gollancz. 1934

BRITAIN AND WORLD PEACE. Burrup, Mathieson. 1935. pp. 101. (An account of the National Government's efforts to provide disarmament and to ensure world peace)

Brown, Francis C. C. Y. DOGS OF WAR! London: P. Davies. 1934. pp. 223. (A repiy to CRY HAVOC! by J. B. Nichols)

Calthrop, E. E. WEAPONS OR WAR? Journal of Royal United Services Institute. May 1934. pp. 280-8

Catlin, George E. G. DYING PEACE? Contemporary Review. April 1934. pp. 404-10

Chaput, Rolland A. DISARMAMENT IN BRITISH FOREIGN POLICY. London: Allen & Unwin. 1935. pp. 432 (bibliography pp. 379-423)

Cohen, C. HUMANITY AND WAR. Pioneer Press. 1935. Pamphlet.
pp. 40

Cornwall, J. H. M. GEOGRAPHIC DISARMAMENT (a study of
regional demilitarization). London: RIIA. 1935. pp. 207

Davies, Major David Davies (1st Baron Davies). FORCE AND THE
FUTURE. London. 1934. Pamphlet. pp. 54

Davies, Major David Davies (1st Baron Davies). THE PROBLEMS OF
THE TWENTIETH CENTURY. London: Benn. 1934. pp. 819.
(See also reviews by Ivan Jones (1934) *q.v.* and F. S. Marvin (1934)
q.v.)

Farrar, Stanley C. SECURITY OR PEACE? Rawdon for Northern
Friends Peace Board. 1935. Pamphlet. pp. 12

Finch, H. A. THE PROSPECTS FOR PEACE. Military Engineer.
September 1934. pp. 395-6

Fuller, J[ohn] F[rederick] C[harles] (Major-General). WAR AND
PEACE. English Review. February 1934. pp. 184-9

Gorman, J. DEATH'S JAMBOREE (an anti-war pamphlet addressed to
the Scout Movement). London: J. Gorman. 1934. Pamphlet

Grane, W. L. WAR: ITS CURSE AND CURE. London: Allen & Unwin.
1935. pp. 164

Greaves, H. R. G. THE PREVENTION OF WAR, OR LABOUR AND
THE LEAGUE OF NATIONS. London: Gollancz. 1934. Pamphlet.
pp. 36. (New Fabian Research Bureau Publications)

Griffen, Jonathan. ALTERNATIVE TO REARMAMENT. New
Statesman. 19 October 1935. pp. 549-50

Groves, (General) P. R. C. BEHIND THE SMOKE SCREEN. London:
Faber. 1934. pp. 239. (On National Security and Disarmament, with
a criticism of the British Policy in air armament after the European
war of 1914-19)

Harris, H[enry] Wilson. DISARMAMENT IN 1934. Listener. 9 January
1935. pp. 75-6

Heath, C. ARMED FORCE 1917-1934. London: Friends Book Centre.
1934. Pamphlet. pp. 19

Henderson, Arthur. ARBITRATION, SECURITY AND DISARMA-
MENT. Labour Party. 1934. Pamphlet. pp. 15

Henderson, Arthur. PURSUIT OF PEACE. 19th Century. January
1934. pp. 1-14

Henderson, Arthur. LABOUR'S WAY TO PEACE. London: Methuen.
1935. pp. viii + 120. (Labour shows the way)

Inge, Dean *et al.* THE CAUSES OF WAR. London: Allen & Unwin.
1935. pp. 105. (Chapter by G. D. H. Cole; (also contains chapters
by Norman Angell, Beaverbrook, Huxley, Major Douglas, Sir
Josiah Stamp))

Innes, Kathleen E. WOMEN AND WAR. Friends Peace Committee.
1934. Pamphlet. pp. 8

Jones, Ivan. Review of David Davies: PROBLEM OF THE 20TH
CENTURY (1934, *q.v.*). Welsh Outlook. October 1934. pp. 255-7

Kerr, Philip H[enry] (11th Marquis of Lothian). PACIFISM IS NOT
ENOUGH, NOR PATRIOTISM EITHER (Burge Memorial Lecture,
1935). Oxford: Clarendon Press. 1935. pp. 57

Krishna Menon Vengalil Krishnan. YOUNG OXFORD AND WAR.
Selwyn & Blount. 1934. pp. 256

Kypa, J. P. BRITISH ATTITUDES TOWARDS DISARMAMENT AND
REARMAMENT 1932-5. Ph.D. Thesis No. 723, London School of
Economics, 1966-7

Labour Party. DISARM (3rd edn). 1934. Pamphlet. pp. 24

Labour Party. FOR SOCIALISM AND PEACE (the agenda for the
Annual Conference of the Party in 1934). London. 1934. Pamphlet.
pp. 83

Labour Party. FOR SOCIALISM AND PEACE (the Labour Party's
programme of action as adopted by the Annual Conference of the
Party held at Southport in October 1934). London. 1934. Pamphlet.
pp. 32

Labour Party. 'NATIONAL' GOVERNMENT'S DISARMAMENT
RECORD. 1935. Pamphlet. pp. 17

Livingstone, Dame Adelaide L. THE PEACE BALLOT (i.e. the
National Declaration on the League of Nations and Armaments).
The official history. London: Gollancz. 1935. pp. 64

London Trades Council. THE WAR MENACE. London. 1935.
Pamphlet. pp. 8

MacLean, N. HOW SHALL WE ESCAPE? LEARN OR PERISH.
London. 1934. pp. xxii + 232

Macmunn, Sir G. F. BRITAIN, THE WORLD AND THE WAR GOD.
London: Sampson Low. 1934. pp. 166

Madariaga, Salvador de. THE PRICE OF PEACE (Richard Cobden
Lecture, 1935). London: Cobden-Sanderson. 1935. Pamphlet. pp. 27

Marshall-Cornwall, Major-General James Handyside. GEOGRAPHIC
DISARMAMENT: A STUDY OF REGIONAL DEMILITARIZA-
TION. London: Humphrey Milford (OUP) for RIIA. 1935. pp. xii +

Martin, Kingsley. ARMAMENT RAMP. Political Quarterly. Vol. 5.
   January 1934. pp. 123-9

Marvin, F. S. Review of David Davies: PROBLEM OF THE 20TH
   CENTURY (*q.v.* 1934). Nature. 17 January 1934. pp. 83-5

National Declaration Committee. PEACE OR WAR (Peace Ballot).
   London. 1934/5. 11 pamphlets

National Declaration Committee. THE BALLOT WORKER. 1935.
   Pamphlet

National Declaration Committee. WAR OR PEACE? (the worker's
   guide to the National Declaration on the League of Nations and
   Armaments). 1934. Pamphlet. pp. 51

National Declaration Committee. THE NATIONAL DECLARATION
   ON THE LEAGUE OF NATIONS AND ARMAMENTS (results
   in each constituency in the United Kingdom). 1935. Pamphlet.
   pp. 43

Noel-Baker Philip [John]. Chapter on DISARMAMENT in Storm
   Jameson (ed.): CHALLENGE TO DEATH. London: Constable. 1934

Noel-Baker, Philip John. DISARMAMENT, WITH DISCUSSION
   (address delivered 21 November 1933). International Affairs.
   Vol. 13. January 1934. pp. 3-25

Pearson, D. and Brown, C. THE DIPLOMATIC GAME. London. 1935.
   pp. 381

Pollard, Francis E. PEACE-MAKING: A CONTRIBUTION TO
   THEORY AND PRACTICE. Friends Peace Committee. 1935.
   Pamphlet. pp. 7

Pollitt, H[arry]. LABOUR AND WAR. Communist Party of Great
   Britain. 1934. Pamphlet. pp. 24

Shaw, G[eorge] B[ernard]. ARE WE HEADING FOR WAR? London:
   Labour Party. 1934. Pamphlet. pp. 11

Smith, W. Compton. HISTORICAL EXAMPLES OF THE RESULTS OF
   DISARMAMENT. National Review. January 1935. pp. 76-9

Smuts, General Jan Christian. THE KEY TO PEACE OR WAR. Far
   East Review. December 1934. pp. 532-4

Stenning, H. J. (ed.). THE CAUSES OF WAR. London: Allen &
   Unwin. 1935. pp. 105

Tomlinson, H. M. MARS HIS IDIOT. London. 1935. pp. 298

Trades Union Congress. PEACE OR WAR? London. 1935. Pamphlet.
   pp. 31

Watts, A. THE PARISH PUMP AND TOTAL DISARMAMENT.

Halifax. 1935. pp. 93

Webster, C[harles] K[ingsley]. SURVEY OF 1933. Listener. 24 January 1934. pp. 162-3

Wheeler-Bennett, John W[heeler]. THE DISARMAMENT DEADLOCK. London: Routledge. 1934. pp. xii + 302

Wheeler-Bennett, John W[heeler]. THE PIPE DREAM OF PEACE. New York: Morrow. 1935. pp. 302

White, Freda. DEADLOCK IN DISARMAMENT. 19th Century. May 1934. pp. 485-95

WORKING FOR PEACE (a review of Great Britain's efforts to promote world peace, 1931-35). Foreword by Rt. Hon. Stanley Baldwin (M.P.). Introduction by Rt. Hon. Anthony Eden (M.P.). London: Durrup, Mathieson & Co. Ltd. 1935. Pamphlet. pp. 31

Zimmern, Alfred. ORGANIZE THE PEACE WORLD! Political Quarterly. Vol. 5. April 1934. pp. 153-66

New Statesman and Nation. ARMS SCANDAL. Vol. 7. 22 August 1934. pp. 348-9

New Statesman and Nation. POLICY AND ARMAMENTS. Vol. 9. 16 March 1935. pp. 372-3

New Statesman and Nation. MUDDLE, MUDDLE, TOIL AND TROUBLE. Vol. 7. 10 March 1934. pp. 332-3

7. General: 1936-1940

Allen, R[eginald] C[lifford] (Baron Allen of Hurtwood). PEACE IN OUR TIME. Chatto & Windus. 1936. Pamphlet. pp. 20. (Appeal to the International Peace Conference of 16 June 1936)

Angell, [Sir] Norman. PEACE WITH THE DICTATORS? London. 1938. pp. 328

Angell, Sir Norman. THE GREAT ILLUSION — NOW. Middlesex, England: Harmondsworth, Penguin Books Ltd. 1938. pp. xii, 11, 15-282. (On cover: A Penguin Special. An abridged version of THE GREAT ILLUSION, first published in 1908, with material defending its theme as applied to present-day conditions)

Atkinson, Henry Avery. PRELUDE TO PEACE (a realistic view of international relations). New York and London: Harper & Brothers. 1937. pp. vii, 11, 222

Ball, W. M. POSSIBLE PEACE. Melbourne. 1936. pp. 199

Ballance, E. R. THE CHALLENGE OF WAR — AND OF PEACE.

Sanderstead. 1937. pp. 43

Bill, A. C. THE COVENANT OF HUMANITY TO MAINTAIN WORLD PEACE. Beauchamp. 1936. Pamphlet. pp. 28

Boulding, K. PATHS OF GLORY (a new way with war). NFPB. Leeds, FPC. London. 1937. Pamphlet. pp. 32

Booth, M. PEACE AND POWER (a political pamphlet). Letchworth. 1937. Pamphlet. pp. 53

Bowyer, E. FOUR WAYS TO PEACE. London: A. H. Stockwell. 1938. Pamphlet. pp. 44

Brailsford, H[enry] N[oel]. WHY CAPITALISM MEANS WAR. London: Gollancz. 1938. pp. 95. (New People's Library)

Buchanan, M. DISARMAMENT. RAMSAY MACDONALD'S GREAT ACHIEVEMENT. Saturday Review. Vol. 161. 25 January 1936. pp. 110-12

Buxton, Charles Roden. THE ALTERNATIVE TO WAR. A PRO-GRAMME FOR STATESMEN. London: Allen & Unwin. 1936. pp. 176

Capper-Johnson, Karlin. LOOKING TOWARDS PEACE. London: Friends Peace Committee. n.d. [1940]. Pamphlet. pp. 15

Cecil, Robert (1st Viscount Cecil of Chelwood). AN OPEN LETTER . . . ON FORCE BEHIND THE LAW. London. 1937. Pamphlet. pp. 12

Cecil, Robert (1st Viscount Cecil of Chelwood). PEACE AND PACIFISM. Clarendon Press. 1938. Pamphlet. pp. 33

Covenanter (pseudonym). LABOUR AND WAR RESISTANCE. Gollancz. 1936. pp. 40. (New Fabian Research Bureau Publication)

Cripps, Sir R[ichard] S[trafford] (M.P.). THE STRUGGLE FOR PEACE. London. 1936. pp. 287

Davies, Major David [Davies] (1st Baron Davies). ANARCHY OR PEACE. London. 1936. Pamphlet. pp. 17

Davies, Major David [Davies] (1st Baron Davies). THE DRIFT TO WAR AND HOW TO MEET IT. Swansea. 1937. Pamphlet. pp. 24

Dawson, A. M. P. HOW CAN THE PEOPLE OF THE WORLD ACHIEVE UNIVERSAL DISARMAMENT? Friends Quarterly Examiner. July 1938. pp. 242-9

Dollan, Sir P. J. LIMITS OF REARMAMENT PROSPERITY. London. 1937. pp. 25-32. (Eleventh-hour questions)

Douglas, C. E. THE COVENANT OF PEACE (a study of man's mission of civilization and its relation to war). Faith Press. 1939. pp. 60

Dupays, P. and Catlin, G[eorge] E. G. WAR AND DEMOCRACY (essays on the causes and prevention of war). London: Kegan Paul.

1938. pp. viii + 360

Durbin, E. F. M. and Bowlby, J. M. PERSONAL AGGRESSIVENESS AND WAR. London: Kegan Paul. 1939. pp. 154

Engelbrecht, H. C. REVOLT AGAINST WAR. London: Werner Laurie. 1938. pp. 367

Fielding, R. J. THE ELIMINATION OF WAR (an examination of the work of Sir Norman Angell). Ph.D. Thesis, Sussex University, 1966-7

Friends' Anti-War Group. THE ROOTS OF WAR (a pamphlet on war and the social order). Woolf. 1936. Pamphlet. pp. 72

Fry, A. R. THE WHIRLPOOL OF WAR (collected addresses). Peace Book Co. 1939. pp. 134

Goldstein, R. THE ELIMINATION OF WAR (a study of the writings of Sir Norman Angell on International Affairs 1903-39). Ph.D. Thesis, Swansea. 1966-7

Greaves, H. R. G. THE PREVENTION OF WAR. League of Nations. International Institute for Intellectual Co-operation, International Studies Conference. 1936

Hart, B. H. L. EUROPE IN ARMS. London: Faber. 1937. pp. 362

Historicus. BALDWIN TURNS KINGS EVIDENCE: THE NEMESIS OF MACDONALD. Saturday Review. Vol. 162. 21 November 1936. pp. 656-7

Howe, Q. BLOOD IS CHEAPER THAN WATER: THE PRESENT CITIZEN'S GUIDE TO PEACE AND WAR. R. Hale. 1939. p. 223

Huxley, A[ldous] L. WHAT ARE YOU GOING TO DO ABOUT IT? THE CASE FOR CONSTRUCTIVE PEACE. London. 1936. Pamphlet. pp. 34

Jerrold, D. THEY THAT TAKE THE SWORD: THE FUTURE OF THE LEAGUE OF NATIONS. London. 1936. pp. viii + 247

Joad, C[yril] E[dwin] M[itchinson]. WHY WAR? Harmondsworth. 1939. pp. 247. (Penguin special)

Kier, D. L. DEFENCE AND DISARMAMENT (a plain guide). London: News Chronicle Publications Dept. 1936. pp. 77

Lansbury, G[eorge] (M.P.). MY QUEST FOR PEACE. M. Joseph. 1938. pp. 286

Lewis, C. P. WE'RE NOT GOING TO DO NOTHING: . . . A REPLY TO MR. ALDOUS HUXLEY'S PAMPHLET, WHAT ARE YOU GOING TO DO ABOUT IT? London. 1936. Pamphlet. pp. 31

de Ligt, Bart. PLAN OF CAMPAIGN AGAINST ALL WAR AND ALL PREPARATION FOR WAR. London: Peace Pledge Union. 1939.

Pamphlet. pp. 20

London Trades Council. THE MENACE OF WAR. London. 1936.
Pamphlet. pp. 7

Martin, J. PEACE ADVENTURE. London: Hodge. 1937. pp. 212

Morgan, L. P. A POSSIBLE TECHNIQUE OF DISARMAMENT
CONTROL. Geneva Studies. Vol. 11, No. 7. 1940

Mousley, E. O. MAN OR LEVIATHAN (a twentieth-century enquiry
into war and peace). London. 1939. pp. 470

M.P. LABOUR AND ARMAMENTS. The Labour Monthly. Vol. 19,
No. 10. October 1937. pp. 624-33

Nicolson, H[arold]. POLICY AND ARMAMENTS. New Statesman and
Nation. Vol. 11. 15 February 1936. p. 223. Discussion. Vol. 11.
22-29 February 1936. pp. 259-60, 303

Noel-Baker, Philip J[ohn] (M.P.). THE FUTURE OF THE COLLEC-
TIVE SYSTEM. Geneva Institute of International Relations,
PROBLEMS OF PEACE, 10th series. 1936. pp. 178-98

Norven, S. FREEDOM FROM WAR. Croydon. 1936. Pamphlet. pp. 31

Nordon, C. L. INTERNATIONAL RELATIONS AND THE ELIMINA-
TION OF WAR. London: Caledonian Press. 1937. Pamphlet. pp. 23

Plumb, C. PARADISE REJECTED (a study in war and society today).
A. Maclehose. 1937. pp. 104

Pollard, Robert S. W. THE STRUGGLE FOR DISARMAMENT.
London: Friends Peace Committee. n.d. [1949]. Pamphlet. pp. 36

Rowntree, M. L. MANKIND SET FREE. London. 1939. pp. 349

Russell, Bertrand A. W. (3rd Earl Russell). WHICH WAY TO PEACE.
London. 1936. pp. 224

Steed, H[enry] W[ickham]. VITAL PEACE: A STUDY OF RISKS.
London: Constable. 1939. pp. vii + 346

Swanwick, H. M. COLLECTIVE INSECURITY. London. 1937. pp. 285

Swanwick, H. M. THE ROOTS OF PEACE (a sequel to COLLECTIVE
INSECURITY, being an essay on some of the uses, conditions and
limitations on compulsive force in the prevention of war). London:
Cape. 1938. pp. 192

Walters, Frank *et al.* WAR IS NOT INEVITABLE. New York: OUP
for Geneva Institute of International Relations. 1939. pp. 299

Wells, H[erbert] G[eorge]. THE COMMON SENSE OF WAR AND
PEACE: WORLD REVOLUTION OR WAR UNENDING.
Harmondsworth. 1940. pp. 116

Woolf, Leonard [S]. IDEAL OF THE LEAGUE REMAINS. Political
Quarterly. Vol. 7. July 1936. pp. 330-45

Woolf, Leonard [S] . ARMS AND PEACE. Political Quarterly. Vol. 8. January 1937. pp. 21-35

Woolf, L[eonard] S. THE WAR FOR PEACE. London. 1940. pp. ix + 244

Labour Monthly. LABOUR AND ARMAMENTS. October 1937. pp. 624-33

New Statesman and Nation. ARMAMENTS AND POLICY. 15 February 1936. pp. 216-17

New Statesman and Nation. LABOUR AND THE ARMS RACE. Vol. 11. 22 February 1936. pp. 252-3. Reply by S. Mumford. Vol. 11. 29 February 1936. pp. 364

8. Naval Aspects (see also under: 29. HMSO Publications; 23. Other Countries; 21. Air Aspects; 20. Disarmament Conference, Geneva, 1932-1934; 16. London Naval Treaty, 1936; 15. London Naval Conference, 1935-1936; 14. Anglo-German Naval Agreement, 1935; 13. London Naval Treaty, 1930; 12. London Naval Conference, 1930; 11. Anglo-French Project for Limiting Armaments, 1928; 10. Three-power Naval Conference, Geneva, 1927; 9. Washington Conference 1921-1922)

Ackworth, Bernard. Chapter with critical analysis of various methods of naval disarmament in THE NAVIES OF TODAY AND TOMORROW. A STUDY OF THE NAVAL CRISIS FROM WITHIN. London: Eyre & Spottiswoode. 1930. pp. 277

Ackworth, B[ernard] . SEA POWER SURRENDERED. English Review. Vol. 60. February 1935. pp. 195-200

Altham, E. SEA, AIR AND EMPIRE. Quarterly Review. July 1934. pp. 1-15

Angell, (Sir) Norman. PARITY OR REDUCTION. Nation (New York). 5 March 1930. pp. 266-8

Bell, A. C. SEA POWER AND THE NEXT WAR. London. 1938. pp. viii + 184

Brailsford, H[enry] N[oel] . SCRAP BATTLESHIPS! London. ?1930. Pamphlet. pp. 7

Bridgeman, Rt. Hon. W[illiam] . NAVAL DISARMAMENT. International Affairs. November 1927. pp. 335-49

Bruce, Sir C[larence Napier] . THE ENGLISH NAVY AND THE PEACE OF THE WORLD. London. 1912. Pamphlet. pp. 12

Bywater, H[ector] C. SEA-POWER IN THE PACIFIC. Boston: Houghton

Mifflin. 1921

Bywater, Hector C. AMERICA AND BRITAIN: THE NAVAL ISSUE. FORUM. January 1927. pp. 96-106

Bywater, H[ector] C. NAVIES AND NATIONS: A REVIEW OF NAVAL DEVELOPMENTS SINCE THE GREAT WAR. London: Constable. 1927. pp. viii + 285. (Favour's naval restriction. Translated into French: LES MARINES DE GUERRE ET LA POUTIQUE NAVALE DES NATIONS DEPUIS LA GUERRE. Paris. Payot. 1930. pp. 287)

Bywater, Hector C. THE FRANCO-ITALIAN NAVAL SITUATION. 19th Century. March 1931. pp. 305-16

Cecil, Robert (1st Viscount Cecil of Chelwood) and Arnold-Foster, W[illiam] E. THE FREEDOM OF THE SEAS. International Affairs. March 1929. pp. 89-116

Chirol, Sir Valentine and Elliston, H. B. ANGLO-AMERICAN RELATIONS AND SEA-POWER. 19th Century. November 1929. pp. 577-97

Churchill, Winston [L]. Spencer (M.P.). THE NAVY LEAGUE. London. 1930. Pamphlet. pp. 7

Clark, John J. ANGLO-GERMAN NAVAL NEGOTIATIONS, 1898 TO 1914 AND 1933 TO 1938: A STUDY IN ARMS CONTROL. Journal of the RUSI. No. 108. November 1963. pp. 349-53

Cobb, Sir Cyril. NAVY AND DISARMAMENT. Empire Review. November 1929. pp. 329-34

Cunninghame, Sir T. M. DISARMAMENT. EUROPEAN DIFFICULTIES. 19th Century. January 1932. pp. 35-60

Dewar, Alfred [Charles]. PEACE TREATY AND AFTER. Brassey's Naval Annual. 1930. pp. 61-74

Dewar, Alfred C[harles]. DISARMAMENT AND NAVAL PARITY. Brassey's Naval Annual. 1935. pp. 61-73

Dewar, Alfred C[harles]. THE END OF DISARMAMENT. Brassey's Naval Annual. 1936. pp. 58-69

Drage, G. SEA POWER. London: J. Murray. 1931. pp. xiv + 318. (Series of articles and letters regretting existing naval agreements hinder development of Great Britain's navy)

Engely, G. THE POLITICS OF NAVAL DISARMAMENT. London: Williams & Norgate. 1932. pp. xvi + 301

Fayle, C. Ernest. CRUISERS AND DISARMAMENT. Nation. Vol. 42. 26 February 1927. pp. 715-16

Gardiner, William Howard. NAVAL PARITY? Harper's. January 1928. pp. 211-19

Kerr, P[hilip] Ratcliffe, S. K. and Garner, J. W. THE RIDDLE OF THE SEAS: AN ANGLO-AMERICAN DISCUSSION (Liberal Summer School. August 1929). London: Nation. 1929. Pamphlet. pp. 39

Glasgow, George. NAVAL DISARMAMENT. Contemporary Review. March 1927. pp. 386-

Gwynn, C. W. DISARMAMENT: THE NAVAL ASPECT. Quarterly Review. October 1932. pp. 273-84

Hall, W. G. Carlton. SEA LAW AND THE UNITED STATES NAVY. English Review. May 1929. pp. 567-75

Hard, W. DOLLARS AND SENSE OF NAVAL REDUCTION. World Today. February 1930. pp. 226-32

Hard, W. CONTINUOUS NAVAL PARLEYS (PLEA FOR). World Today. April 1931. pp. 429-35

Harper, J. E. T. ESTIMATES AND DISARMAMENT. National Review. April 1932. pp. 450-7. (With special reference to the British navy)

Harris, H[enry] W[ilson]. NAVAL DISARMAMENT. London: G. Allen & Unwin. 1930. pp. 124

Higgins, A. Pearce. SUBMARINE WARFARE. British Yearbook of International Law. 1920-21. pp. 149-66

Hovgaard, W. REDUCTION OF NAVAL ARMAMENTS. Engineering. 26 July 1929. pp. 116-17

Huddleston, S[isley]. ANGLO-AMERICAN ACCORD. New Statesman. Vol. 33. 5 October 1929. pp. 769-70

Hurd, (Sir) A[rchibald]. NAVY LEAGUE'S RENUNCIATION. Fortnightly Review. August 1921

Hurd, Sir Archibald. BANKRUPTS AND BATTLESHIPS. Spectator. 10 August 1934. pp. 184-5

Kenworthy, (Commander) J. M. (M.P.). INTERNATIONAL NAVAL RACE. Nation (New York). 23 February 1927. pp. 203-4

Kenworthy, (Commander) J. M. (M.P.) and Young, George. FREEDOM OF THE SEAS. London: Hutchinson. 1928. pp. 283. (The question before and after the war favours naval disarmament followed by conference for reorganizing laws of naval warfare)

Kenworthy, (Commander) J. M. (M.P.). NEW WARS: NEW WEAPONS. London: Matthews & Marrot. 1930. pp. 160. (Chiefly from standpoint of naval and air defence)

Kenworthy, (Commander) J. M. (M.P.). DISARMAMENT. FREEDOM OF THE SEAS. 19th Century. January 1932. pp. 35-60

Kerr, M. REDUCTION OF NAVAL ARMAMENTS. Outlook. Vol. 60. 20 August 1927. pp. 242-3

Kimball, J. H. SEA POWER AND SUBMARINES. English Review. Vol.
46

42. March 1926. pp. 340-4

Latimer, Hugh. NAVAL DISARMAMENT (a brief record from the Washington Naval Conference to date). London: Humphrey Millford (RIIA). 1930. pp. x + 112. (Chatham House Monographs, No. 3)

Latimer, Hugh. THE FRANCO-ITALIAN NAVAL NEGOTIATIONS. Bulletin of International News. April 1931. pp. 3-10

Moore, Frederick. AMERICAN VIEW OF NAVAL REDUCTION; BASED ON AMERICA'S NAVAL CHALLENGE. Spectator. Vol. 143. 5 October 1929. pp. 429-30

Richmond, (Admiral) Sir H[erbert] W[illiam]. NATIONAL POLICY AND NAVAL STRENGTH, AND OTHER ESSAYS. London: Longmans, Green. 1928. pp. xvii + 355

Richmond, Admiral Sir Herbert William. NAVAL WARFARE. London: E. Benn Ltd. 1930. pp. 96

Richmond, (Admiral) Sir Herbert William. ECONOMY AND NAVAL SECURITY. London: E. Benn Ltd. 1931. pp. 227. (A plea for the examination of the problem of the reduction in the cost of naval armaments on the lines of strategy and policy)

Richmond, (Admiral) Sir Herbert W[illiam]. IMMEDIATE PROBLEMS OF NAVAL REDUCTION. Foreign Affairs (New York). Vol. 9. April 1931. pp. 371-88

Richmond, (Admiral) Sir Herbert [William]. BIG SHIPS. Times. 10 November 1932. pp. 15-16. 12 November 1932. pp. 13-14

Richmond, (Admiral) Sir H[erbert] W[illiam]. SEA POWER IN THE MODERN WORLD. London. 1934. pp. iv + 266

Richmond, (Admiral) Sir Herbert [William]. NAVAL DISARMAMENT. 19th Century. December 1934. pp. 640-50. (Is size an essential factor in the efficiency of warships?)

Richmond, Admiral Sir Herbert William. NAVAL REARMAMENT. 19th Century. January 1936. pp. 38-46

Stein, Leonard. NAVAL DISARMAMENT. Nation. 19 March 1927. pp. 844-6

Talbot, Melvin F. A YOUNGER OFFICER VIEWS THE NAVY. Scribner's. October 1927. pp. 439-43. (Against limitation)

Watt, Donald. HISTORICAL LIGHT ON SALT: PARALLELS WITH INTER-WAR NAVAL ARMS CONTROL. The Round Table. Vol. 245. January 1972. pp. 29-35

Young, George. ANGLO-AMERICAN COMMAND OF THE SEAS. Contemporary Review. March 1928. pp. 294-302

Economist. PROSPECTS FOR THE DISARMAMENT CONFERENCE. Vol. 112. 21 March 1931. pp. 600-1. (Development of question of naval disarmament since Treaty of London)

Engineer. LIMITATION OF NAVAL ARMAMENT. 5 October 1928. pp. 377-8

Engineer. NAVAL DISARMAMENT PROSPECTS (Editorial). 10 May 1929. pp. 519-20. 20 June 1929. pp. 683-4

Engineer. NAVAL DISARMAMENT: THE LATEST PHASE (Editorial). 20 September 1929. pp. 305-6

Engineering. NAVAL ESTIMATES AND THE ONE POWER STANDARD. 25 March 1927. pp. 359-60

Engineering. PROBLEM OF CRUISER AND DESTROYER LIMITA-TION (Editorial). 24 January 1930. pp. 111-13

International Affairs (RIIA). CANADA AND THE PROBLEM OF NAVAL DISARMAMENT. Vol. 8. September 1928. pp. 433-44

Nation. NAVAL LIMITATION AND THE FRENCH PROGRAMME. Vol. 36. 31 January 1925. pp. 603-4

Nation. NAVAL EXPERT IN SPITE OF HIMSELF. Vol. 45. 28 September 1929. pp. 819-20

National Review. ONE-POWER STANDARD AND THE NEW DIPLOMACY. January 1930. pp. 686-99

Quarterly Review. NAVAL REALITIES. January 1930. pp. 1-14

Quarterly Review. SOME NAVAL HERESIES. July 1931. pp. 1-14. (Reduction in size of capital ships)

Quarterly Review. DISARMAMENT: THE NAVAL ASPECT. Vol. 259. October 1932. pp. 273-84

Round Table. NAVAL PROBLEM. Vol. 18. March 1928. pp. 223-55

Round Table. NAVAL DISARMAMENT. Vol. 19. June 1929. pp. 447-64

Saturday Review. PROBLEM OF THE SUBMARINE. Vol. 140. 21 November 1925. pp. 587-8

Spectator. FUTURE OF NAVIES. Vol. 126. 1 January 1921. pp. 5-7

Spectator. SEA POLITICS. Vol. 140. 24 March 1928. pp. 444-5

Spectator. HOW TO DEFEAT YOUR OWN PURPOSE. Vol. 141. 29 September 1928. pp. 388-9

Spectator. FRESH HOPE FOR NAVAL DISARMAMENT. Vol. 142. 27 April 1929. pp. 640-1

9. Washington Conference, 1921-1922 (see also under: 29. HMSO
Publications; 13. London Naval Treaty, 1930; 8. Naval Aspects)

Abbott, A. H. THE LEAGUE'S DISARMAMENT ACTIVITIES, AND
THE WASHINGTON CONFERENCE. Political Science Quarterly.
March 1922. pp. 1-24

Arnot, R. Page. THE NAVAL CONVERSATIONS. Labour Monthly.
Vol. 17. February 1935. pp. 88-94

Berry, Sir William J. CAPITAL SHIPS AND CRUISERS: EFFECTS OF
THE TREATIES OF WASHINGTON AND LONDON ON DESIGN.
Brassey's Naval Annual. 1931. pp. 104-12

Bruce, C. D. PROGRESS AT WASHINGTON. Asiatic Review. January
1922. pp. 1-8. (The peaceful development of China the key to
general disarmament)

Bryce, James (Viscount) and Cecil, Lord Robert. WASHINGTON.
Contemporary Review. Vol. CXX. December 1921. pp. 721-6

Bull, Hedley. STRATEGIC ARMS LIMITATION: THE PRECEDENT
OF THE WASHINGTON AND LONDON NAVAL TREATIES in
Morton A. Kaplan (ed.): SALT: PROBLEMS AND PROSPECTS,
Morristown, N.J.: General Learning Press. 1973. (Papers presented
to the University of Chicago Arms Control and Foreign Policy
Seminar, Winter 1970-1)

Bywater, Hector C. THE LIMITATION OF NAVAL ARMAMENTS.
Atlantic Monthly. February 1922. pp. 259-69

Chirol, Sir Valentine. THE WASHINGTON CONFERENCE AND THE
PACIFIC PROBLEM. The Contemporary Review. Vol. CXXI.
February 1922. pp. 147-56

Dewar, Alfred C[harles]. THE NAVY AND THE WASHINGTON
CONFERENCE. Quarterly Review. January 1922. pp. 177-87

Dillon, E. J. (Introd.). PRESIDENT OBREGÓN AT WASHINGTON.
English Review. January 1922. pp. 68-76

Douglas, C. H. WORLD AFTER WASHINGTON. English Review. Vol.
34. March–April 1922. pp. 260-5, 367-71

Gardiner, William Howard. A NAVAL VIEW OF THE [WASHINGTON]
CONFERENCE: FLEET AND BASE LIMITATIONS. Atlantic
Monthly. April 1922. pp. 521-39

Harris, H[enry] Wilson. WASHINGTON IMPRESSIONS. Contemporary
Review. Vol. CXXI. January 1922. pp. 8-15

Harrison, A. GREAT PROSPECTS. English Review. Vol. 33. August
1921. pp. 158-64

Harrison, A. WASHINGTON CONFERENCE. English Review. Vol. 33. November 1921. pp. 414-25

Hurd, Archibald. THE WASHINGTON NAVAL STANDARDS: WAR FLEETS OF FOUR MILLION TONS. Fortnightly Review. January 1922. pp. 106-21

Hurd, A[rchibald]. IS THE WASHINGTON CONFERENCE DOOMED? Fortnightly Review. January 1923.

Lee, Arthur Hamilton (Lord Lee of Fareham). THE WASHINGTON CONFERENCE. United Empire. June 1922. pp. 378-85

McCall, Samuel W. THE WASHINGTON CONFERENCE. Atlantic Monthly. March 1922. pp. 386-94

Malkin, H[erbert] W[illiam]. [NOTES] WASHINGTON CONFE-RENCE. British Yearbook of International Law. 1922-3 (1922). pp. 179-82

Ponsonby, Arthur and Watney, Charles. WASHINGTON CONFERENCE. CONFERENCE. Nation. Vol. 30. 8 October 1921. pp. 49-50

ROADS TO PEACE: A HANDBOOK TO THE WASHINGTON CONFERENCE. New York: The Republic Pub. Co. 1921. pp. 64. (Contains the following chapters: G. Glasgow, The British View; S. Huddleston, What France wants)

Roxburgh, Ronald F. SUBMARINES AT THE WASHINGTON CONFERENCE. British Yearbook of International Law, (1922). pp. 1!

Russell, H. BRITISH SEA-POWER BY PERMISSION. English Review. Vol. 40. March 1925. pp. 335-40

Shaw, B. LIMITATION CONFERENCE. Nation. Vol. 30. 12-26 November 1921. pp. 244-5, 302-4, 339-41

Sullivan, A. WHAT WE WANT AMERICA TO KNOW. English Review. Vol. 33. December 1921. pp. 508-13

Sullivan, M. THE GREAT ADVANCE AT WASHINGTON: THE STORY OF THE CONFERENCE. London: Heinemann. 1922. pp. xiii + 290

Wells, H[erbert] G[eorge]. WASHINGTON AND THE HOPE OF PEACE. London: Collins. 1922. pp. vii + 272

Wester-Wemyss (1st Baron Rosslyn). WASHINGTON: AND AFTER. 19th Century. March 1922. pp. 405-16. (Translation: Revue de Paris. 1 March 1922. pp. 143-56)

Wickersham, George W. HAS THE CONFERENCE SUCCEEDED? Forum. January 1922. pp. 54-63

Engineer. POINTS FROM THE NAVAL TREATY. 24 February 1922. pp. 201. (Editorial pp. 215-16)

Nation. WILL THE WORLD DISARM? Vol. 30. 29 October 1921.
  pp. 170-1

Nation. TRIUMPH OF OPEN DIPLOMACY. Vol. 30. 19 November
  1921. p. 300-1

Nation. FROM FORCE TO CONFERENCE. Vol. 30. 17 December
  1921. pp. 458-9

Nation. EMPIRE, THE FLEET AND JAPAN. Vol. 29. 25 June 1921.
  pp. 459-60

New Statesman. PROBABLE FAILURE OF THE WASHINGTON
  CONFERENCE. Vol. 17. 23 July 1921. pp. 432-3

New Statesman. POSSIBILITIES OF WASHINGTON. Vol. 18. 22
  October 1921. pp. 64-6

New Statesman. RAINBOW ACROSS THE SKIES. Vol. 18. 12
  November 1921. pp. 156-7

New Statesman. SPIRIT OF WASHINGTON. Vol. 18. 19 November
  1921. pp. 188-9

New Statesman. NEXT WASHINGTON CONFERENCE. Vol. 18.
  26 November 1921. pp. 216-17

New Statesman. LESSONS FROM WASHINGTON. Vol. 18. 17
  December 1921. pp. 308-9

New Statesman. COMPARISON OF CANNES AND WASHINGTON.
  Vol. 18. 14 January 1922. pp. 408-10

Round Table. WASHINGTON RESULTS; WITH TEXTS. Vol. 12.
  March 1922. pp. 294-302

Round Table. AMERICAN REFLECTIONS. Vol. 12. March 1922.
  pp. 279-85

Round Table. AMERICA AND THE CONFERENCE. Vol. 12.
  December 1921. pp. 115-32.

Round Table. THE WASHINGTON RESULTS. March 1922. pp. 294-
  302

Round Table. END OF THE WASHINGTON TREATIES. March 1936.
  pp. 253-65

Spectator. NAVAL CONFERENCE. Vol. 126. 4 June 1921. pp. 705-6

Spectator. PRESIDENT HARDING'S INVITATIONS. Vol. 127. 16
  July 1921. pp. 70-1

Spectator. ONE THING AT A TIME. Vol. 127. 17 September 1921.
  pp. 353-4

Spectator. MR LLOYD GEORGE AND WASHINGTON. Vol. 127.
  22 October 1921. pp. 516-17

Spectator. SUPPORT THE AMERICANS. Vol. 127. 5 November 1921.
pp. 587-8

Spectator. WASHINGTON CONFERENCE. Vol. 127. 19 November
1921. pp. 657-8

Spectator. JAPAN AND THE WASHINGTON CONFERENCE. Vol.
127. 26 November 1921. pp. 692-3

Spectator. HONOUR TO WHOM HONOUR IS DUE. Vol. 128. 1 April
1922. pp. 389-90

10. Three-power Naval Conference, Geneva, 1927 (see also under: 29. HMSO Publications; 8. Naval Aspects)

Atkins, J. B. UNITED STATES AFTER THIRTY YEARS; NAVAL
MISUNDERSTANDINGS. Spectator. Vol. 140. 12 May 1928.
pp. 706-7

Arnold-Forster, W[illiam]. WHY HAVE WE FAILED TO DISARM?
THE LEAGUE OF NATIONS CONFERENCE AND THE
COOLIDGE CONFERENCE EXAMINED. National Council for the
Prevention of War. 1927. Pamphlet No. 7. pp. 16

Brailsford, H[enry] N[oel]. FAILURE OF 1927 CONFERENCE. New
Republic. 19 October 1927. pp. 228-30

Carlton, David. GREAT BRITAIN AND THE COOLIDGE NAVAL
DISARMAMENT CONFERENCE OF 1927. Political Science
Quarterly. Vol. 83, No. 4. 1968. pp. 573-98

Das, T. N. FAILURE OF ANGLO-AMERICAN JAPANESE NAVAL
CONFERENCE, 1927. Modern Review. November 1927.
pp. 526-9

Dewar, A[lfred Charles]. GENEVA CONFERENCE. English Review.
Vol. 45. September 1927. pp. 256-63

Dewar, A[lfred] C[harles]. GENEVA CONFERENCE (1927). Brassey's
Naval Annual. 1928. pp. 60-8

Dewar, A[lfred] C[harles]. GENEVA CONFERENCE AND AFTER.
Brassey's Naval Annual. 1929. pp. 80-91

Glasgow, George. NAVAL LIMITATION CONFERENCE. Contemporary Review. Summer 1927. pp. 373-85

Noel-Baker, Philip [John]. DISARMAMENT AND THE COOLIDGE
CONFERENCE. London: Hogarth Press. 1927. pp. 53

Smith, Rennie (M.P.). THE BREAKDOWN OF THE COOLIDGE
CONFERENCE. The Contemporary Review. Vol. CXXXII.

September 1927. pp. 290-5

Smith, Rennie (M.P.). THE NAVAL CONFERENCE. Round Table.
September 1927

Spender, H[ugh] F. THE NAVAL CONFERENCE. Fortnightly Review.
No. 728. August 1927. pp. 180-9

Spender, Hugh F. RIDDLE OF THE CRUISERS. Fortnightly Review.
September 1927. pp. 317-25

Spender, Hugh F. CROSS CURRENTS AT GENEVA. Fortnightly
Review. November 1927. pp. 600-9

Stein, L[eonard]. NAVAL DISARMAMENT THROUGH AMERICAN
EYES. Nation. Vol. 41. 16 July 1927. pp. 503-5

Stein, L[eonard]. AMERICAN OPINION ON THE DISARMAMENT
FAILURE. Nation. Vol. 41. 1 October 1927. pp. 829-30

Stein, L[eonard]. NAVAL DISARMAMENT CONFERENCE – AND
AFTER. Nation. Vol. 43. 26 May 1928. pp. 243-5

Engineering. NAVAL POLICIES AT GENEVA. 1 July 1927. pp. 17-19

Engineering. GENEVA CONFERENCE AND SUBMARINES. 22 July
1927. pp. 112-13

Engineering. GENEVA CONFERENCE AND BRITISH NAVAL
POLICY. 12 August 1927. pp. 207-8

Nation. DISARMAMENT CRISIS. Vol. 41. 16 July 1927. pp. 502-3

Nation. FIASCO AT GENEVA? Vol. 41. 6 August 1927. pp. 598-9

Round Table. NAVAL CONFERENCE. Vol. 17. September 1927.
pp. 659-83

Saturday Review. SHIPS AND COMMON SENSE. Vol. 144. 16 July
1927. pp. 81-2

Saturday Review. ANGLO-AMERICAN NAVAL RIVALRY. Vol. 144.
30 July 1927. pp. 152-3

11. Anglo-French Project for Limiting Armaments, 1928 (see also
    under: 8. Naval Aspects)

Carlton, David. THE ANGLO-FRENCH COMPROMISE ON ARMS
LIMITATION, 1928. Journal of British Studies. Vol. 8, No. 2.
1969. pp. 141-62

Dell, Robert. ANGLO-FRENCH NAVAL AGREEMENT. Nation. Vol.
43. 1 September 1928. pp. 698-9

Ewer, W. N. PACT AND ENTENTE. Labour Monthly. Vol. 10. October
1928. pp. 619-25

Huddleston, S[isley]. EUROPE'S TWO PILLARS. New Statesman. Vol. 32. 13 October 1928. pp. 5–6

Kenworthy, (Commander) J. M. (M.P.). ANGLO-FRENCH COMPRO-MISE. Review of Reviews. November 1928. pp. 336–41

Kerr, P[hilip Henry]. ESCAPE FROM A GREAT DISASTER. Christian Century. Vol. 45. 1 November 1928. pp. 1323–6

Stein, Leonard. NAVAL AGREEMENT THROUGH AMERICAN EYES. Nation. Vol. 44. 27 October 1928. pp. 131–2

Nation. IS THERE A NEW ENTENTE? Vol. 43. 18 August 1928. pp. 638–9

Nation. ANTAGONIZING AMERICA; FRANCO-BRITISH NAVAL COMPROMISE. Vol. 43. 29 September 1928. pp. 810–11

Nation. TRUE NAVAL COMPROMISE. Vol. 44. 6 October 1928. pp. 6–7

Nation. HEADING FOR WAR; FRANCO-BRITISH NAVAL/ MILITARY DEAL. Vol. 44. 20 October 1928. pp. 98–9

Nation. WHITE PAPER; FRANCO-BRITISH COMPROMISE. Vol. 44. 27 October 1928. pp. 130–1

Saturday Review. NEW NAVAL AGREEMENT. Vol. 146. 11 August 1928. pp. 172–3

Spectator. ANGLO-FRENCH COMPROMISE AND AMERICA. Vol. 141. 8 September 1928. p. 285

12. London Naval Conference, 1930 (see also under: 29. HMSO Publications; 13. London Naval Treaty, 1930; 8. Naval Aspects)

Angell, (Sir) Norman (M.P.). LONDON NAVAL CONFERENCE. Contemporary Review. 1930. pp. 273–80

Arnold-Forster, D. NAVAL CONFERENCE: BASIS OF DISCUSSION. Fortnightly Review. March 1930. pp. 289–97

Bridgeman, William S. (1st Viscount). LONDON NAVAL CONFER-ENCE. Empire Review. February 1930. pp. 91–6

Buell, R. L. LONDON NAVAL CONFERENCE. Forum. June 1930. pp. 358–62

Bywater, Hector C. and Kawakami, K. K. LONDON NAVAL CON-FERENCE: EUROPEAN AND JAPANESE VIEWS. 19th Century. December 1929. pp. 717–42

Dewar, A[lfred] C[harles]. LONDON NAVAL CONFERENCE. 19th Century. March 1930. pp. 285-99

Dewar, A[lfred] C[harles]. THE END OF THE NAVAL CONFERENCE. 19th Century. Vol. 107. May 1930. pp. 606-19

Drury-Lowe, S. R. LONDON NAVAL CONFERENCE. Contemporary Review. May 1930. pp. 545-54

Drury-Lowe, S. R. PROSPECTS OF THE FIVE-POWER NAVAL CONFERENCE. Contemporary Review. January 1930. pp. 7-12

Glasgow, George. LONDON NAVAL CONFERENCE. Queens Quarterly. April 1930. pp. 225-45

Huddleston, S[isley]. THREE OR FIVE. New Statesman. Vol. 34. 11 January 1930. pp. 433-4

Huddleston, S[isley]. CONFERENCE OPENS. New Statesman. Vol. 34. 25 January 1930. pp. 493-4

Huddleston, S[isley]. PUBLICITY AND PRIVACY. New Statesman. Vol. 34. 8 February 1930. pp. 561-2

Kenworthy, (Commander) J. M. (M.P.). LEGEND OF PARITY: TECHNICAL ASPECTS OF THE NAVAL CONFERENCE. Review of Reviews. March 1930. pp. 199-206

Kumarappa, J. M. LONDON NAVAL CONFERENCE. Modern Review. February 1930. pp. 185-9

MacDonald, James Ramsay (M.P.). THE LONDON NAVAL CON-FERENCE, 1930. International Affairs. Vol. 9. July 1930. pp. 429-51. (Abridged version in INTERNATIONAL DIGEST. Vol. VI. October 1930. pp. 1-4)

MacDonald, J[ames] R[amsay] (M.P.) and Stimson, H. L. THE LONDON NAVAL CONFERENCE, 1930. London: Encyclopaedia Britannica. 1931. p. 10

Mackay, R. A. POLITICAL IMPLICATIONS OF THE LONDON CONFERENCE. Queens Quarterly. July 1930. pp. 532-42

Martin, W. NAVAL CONFERENCE SEEN FROM GENEVA. Spectator. Vol. 144. 22 February 1930. p. 272

Poseidon. WORD TO THE NAVAL CONFERENCE. English Review. Vol. 50. February 1930. pp. 152-8

Roberts, Chalmers. PRESIDENT HOOVER AND THE NAVAL CON-FERENCE. World Today. January 1930. pp. 108-10

Roberts, C[halmers]. PHASES OF THE NAVAL CONFERENCE; AN INTERIM COMMENTARY. World Today. Vol. 55. March 1930. pp. 331-4.

Roberts, C[halmers]. CAN FRANCE EVER BE PLACATED? World

Today. Vol. 55. April 1930. pp. 434-8

Steed, H[enry] Wickham. THE NAVAL CONFERENCE – POSSIBILI-
TIES AND PROSPECTS. Review of Reviews. January 1930. pp. 18-
29. WHY CUT DOWN OUR NAVY? MUSINGS ON THE CONFER-
ENCE. Op. cit. February 1930. pp. 102-11. LESSONS OF THE
CONFERENCE. Op. cit. April 1930. pp. 275-82. THE CHANCES
OF THE NAVAL TREATY. Op. cit. May 1930. pp. 361-72

Taylor, E. A. LONDON NAVAL CONFERENCE. Empire Review. Vol.
50. March 1930. pp. 176-82

Taylor, E. A. CRITICISM OF THE NAVAL CONFERENCE. English
Review. Vol. 50. June 1930. pp. 681-8

English Review. WORD TO THE NAVAL CONFERENCE. Vol. 50.
February 1930. pp. 152-8. (Against limitation)

Fortnightly Review. NAVAL CONFERENCE: THE POLITICAL
BYWAYS. March 1930. pp. 298-304

Fortnightly Review. LONDON NAVAL CONFERENCE. March 1930.
pp. 305-9

Journal of Royal United Services Institute. AFTERMATH OF THE
LONDON NAVAL CONFERENCE. August 1930. pp. 594-9

Nation. ISSUES OF THE CONFERENCE. Vol. 46. 18 January 1930.
pp. 530-1

Nation. NAVAL CONFERENCE SUPPLEMENT. Vol. 46. 18 January
1930. pp. 553-60

Nation. PROGRESS OF THE CONFERENCE. Vol. 46. 15 February
1930. pp. 662-3

Nation. LEAD TO THE CONFERENCE. Vol. 46. 22 March 1930.
pp. 850-1

Nation. ARTICLE SIXTEEN AND THE MEDITERRANEAN. Vol. 47.
12 April 1930. pp. 38-9

Nation. PROGRESS. Vol. 47. 26 April 1930. pp. 102-3

Nation. BALANCE-SHEET OF THE CONFERENCE. Vol. 47. 26
April 1930. pp. 103-5

New Statesman. SHIPS AND MEN. Vol. 34. 18 January 1930.
pp. 460-1

New Statesman. JOURNALISTS DREAM. Vol. 34. 8 February 1930.
pp. 562-3

New Statesman. BELLING THE CAT; FRANCE DEMANDS
SECURITY. Vol. 34. 15 March 1930. pp. 728-9

New Statesman. END OF A CHAPTER. Vol. 35. 26 April 1930.
pp. 72-3

Review of Reviews. A SUCCESS FOR BRITISH STATESMANSHIP.
March 1931. pp. 15-18
Round Table. LONDON CONFERENCE. Vol. 20. December1929.
pp. 1-21
Saturday Review. NAVAL CONFERENCE. Vol. 148. 28 December
1929. pp. 771-2
Saturday Review. NAVAL CONFERENCE. Vol. 149. 18 January
1930. pp. 65-6
Saturday Review. CONFERENCE CLOSE-UP. Vol. 149. 25 January
1930. pp. 97-8
Saturday Review. CONFERENCE SO FAR. Vol. 149. 15 February
1930. pp. 184-5
Socialist Review. LONDON NAVAL CONFERENCE. February 1930.
pp. 179-84
World Today. PRESIDENT HOOVER AND THE NAVAL CON-
FERENCE. Vol. 55. January 1930. pp. 108-11

13. London Naval Treaty, 1930 (see also under: **29. HMSO Publications; 12. London Naval Conference, 1930; 8. Naval Aspects**)

Berry, Sir William J. CAPITAL SHIPS AND CRUISERS: EFFECTS OF
THE TREATIES OF WASHINGTON AND LONDON ON DESIGN.
Brassey's Naval Annual. 1931. pp. 104-12
Bull, Hedley. STRATEGIC ARMS LIMITATION: THE PRECEDENT
OF THE WASHINGTON AND LONDON NAVAL TREATIES in
Morton A. Kaplan (ed.): SALT: PROBLEMS AND PROSPECTS.
Morristown, New Jersey: General Learning Press. 1973. pp. 26-52.
(Papers presented to the University of Chicago Arms Control and
Foreign Policy Seminar, Winter 1970-1)
Dewar, Alfred C[harles]. LONDON NAVAL TREATY. Brassey's Naval
Annual. 1931. pp. 69-84
Dewar, Alfred C[harles]. AFTER THE TREATY OF LONDON, 1931.
Brassey's Naval Annual. 1932. pp. 63-72
Dorling, T. THE NAVAL TREATY AND AFTER. 19th Century.
April 1931. pp. 414-28
Kim. SCRAP THE TREATY OF LONDON NOW! Saturday Review.
Vol. 157. 14 April 1934. pp. 398-9
Sidebotham, H. NAVAL LIMITATION TREATY. 19th Century. Vol.
107. June 1930. pp. 754-62

Engineer. NAVAL LIMITATION TREATY. 25 April 1930. pp. 463-4

Engineering. NAVAL LIMITATION TREATY. 2 May 1930. pp. 575-7

Nation. TORIES AND THE TREATY. Vol. 47. 24 May 1930. pp. 238-9

National Review. WHAT OF OUR NAVY NOW? June 1930. pp. 183-91

Saturday Review. NAVAL AGREEMENT. Vol. 151. 14 March 1931. pp. 365-6

Spectator. UNIONIST PARTY AND THE NAVY. Vol. 144. 7 June 1930. pp. 929-30

Tablet. BRITANNIA SHARES THE WAVES. 18 January 1930. pp. 69-70

14. Anglo-German Naval Agreement, 1935 (see also under: **29. HMSO Publications; 8. Naval Aspects**)

Bywater, H[ector] C. COMING STRUGGLE FOR SEA-POWER. Far East Review. Vol. 30. November 1934. pp. 481-3

Harper, J. E. T. THE ANGLO-GERMAN AGREEMENT. National Review. July 1935. pp. 41-4

Hines, H. Hau. THE FOREIGN POLICY-MAKING PROCESS IN BRITAIN 1934-1935, AND THE ORIGINS OF THE ANGLO-GERMAN NAVAL AGREEMENT. Historical Journal. Vol. 19. June 1976. pp. 477-99

Mitter, Karuna. NAVAL TALKS. Modern Review. January 1935. pp. 103-6

Prendergast, M. WARSHIP CONSTRUCTION UNDER THE NAVAL TREATIES. Journal of Royal United Services Institute. February 1935. pp. 93-103

Richmond, (Admiral) Sir Herbert [William]. THE NAVAL CONFERENCE: PRESTIGE OR COMMON SENSE? Fortnightly Review. December 1935. pp. 661-9

New Statesman and Nation. NAVAL BALANCE OF POWER. Vol. 8. 20 October 1934. pp. 536-7

15. London Naval Conference, 1935-1936 (see also under: **29. HMSO Publications; 8. Naval Aspects**)

Kerr, Mark. JAPANESE VIEWS OF THE NAVAL CONFERENCE. Empire Review. February 1936. pp. 77-83

'Periscope'. NAVAL CONFERENCE DANGERS. Saturday Review.
Vol. 161. 15 February 1936. pp. 202–3
Thursfield, H. G. THE NAVAL CONFERENCE, 1935–6. 19th Century.
June 1936. pp. 734–47
Asiatic Review. THE NAVAL CONFERENCE. April 1936. pp. 330–
40
Round Table. NAVAL CONFERENCE. Vol. 26. December 1935.
pp. 44–55
Spectator. NAVAL CONFERENCE. Vol. 155. 13 December 1935.
pp. 975–6

16. London Naval Treaty, 1936 (see also under: 29. HMSO Publications; 8. Naval Aspects)

Altham, E. WHAT THE LONDON NAVAL TREATY MEANS.
Listener. 13 January 1937. pp. 75–6
Clark, John J. ANGLO-GERMAN NAVAL NEGOTIATIONS, 1898
TO 1914 AND 1933 TO 1938: A STUDY IN ARMS CONTROL.
Journal of the RUSI. Vol. 108. November 1963. pp. 349–53
Round Table. NEW NAVAL TREATY. Vol. 26. June 1936. pp. 518–
27
Times. NAVAL TREATY READY. 23 March 1936. pp. 13–14
Times. NAVAL TREATY SIGNED [BY BRITAIN, FRANCE AND
USA]. 26 March 1936. pp. 14, 15, 18, 19

17. Draft Treaty of Mutual Assistance, 1923; Geneva Protocol, 1924 (see also under: 29. HMSO Publications)

Barnes, George N. THE PROTOCOL AND DISARMAMENT. Review of
Reviews. November 1927. pp. 412–15
Buxton, Charles Roden. LABOUR'S WORK FOR PEACE AT GENEVA
(with full text of Draft Protocol for the pacific settlement of inter-
national disputes). London: Labour Publications Dept. 1924.
Pamphlet. pp. 15
Cecil, Robert (1st Viscount Cecil of Chelwood). THE DRAFT TREATY
OF MUTUAL ASSISTANCE. International Affairs. March 1924.
pp. 45–82
Henderson, Arthur (M.P.). THE NEW PEACE PLAN (Labour's work at

the League of Nations Assembly). London. 1924. Pamphlet. pp. 15

Henderson, Arthur (M.P.). LABOUR AND THE GENEVA PROTOCOL. Labour Party. 1925. Pamphlet. pp. 16

[Noel-] Baker, P[hilip] J[ohn]. M. HERRIOT'S OFFER. Nation. Vol. 35. 5 July 1924. pp. 431-2

Noel-Baker, Philip [John]. THE GENEVA PROTOCOL FOR THE PACIFIC SETTLEMENT OF INTERNATIONAL DISPUTES. London: P. S. King & Son. 1925. pp. x + 228. (Discusses disarmament in relation to the protocol)

Webster, C[harles] K[ingsley]. 5TH ASSEMBLY: SECURITY, DISARMAMENT, ARBITRATION. Nation. Vol. 35. 13 September 1924. pp. 711-13

Wheeler-Bennett, J[ohn] and Langerman, F. E. INFORMATION ON THE PROBLEM OF SECURITY (1917-1926). Part III (ii): THE TREATY OF MUTUAL ASSISTANCE. London: Allen & Unwin. 1927. pp. 272

Williams, Sir John Fischer. THE GENEVA PROTOCOL OF 1924. London: G. Allen & Unwin Ltd. 1925. Pamphlet. pp. 18. (Reprinted from INTERNATIONAL AFFAIRS)

International Affairs. THE DRAFT TREATY OF MUTUAL ASSISTANCE (record of a meeting of the Royal Institute of International Affairs, held 19 February 1924). RIIA. March 1924. pp. 45-82

Manchester Guardian. AN EXAMINATION OF THE GENEVA PROTOCOL, BY A STUDENT OF FOREIGN AFFAIRS. Manchester: Manchester Guardian. 1925. Pamphlet. pp. 43. (Reprinted from the Manchester Guardian of 26, 27, 28 and 29 January 1925)

Nation. LORD CECIL'S TREATY. Vol. 34. 8 March 1924. pp. 786-7. Discussion. Vol. 34. 15-19 March 1924. pp. 828-9, 883-4, 916-17

Nation. SECURITY AND GUARANTEES. Vol. 35. 2 August 1924. pp. 554-5

Outlook. TWO VOICES AT GENEVA. Vol. 54. 13 September 1924. pp. 183-4

18. **Preparatory Commission for the Disarmament Conference** (see also under: **29: HMSO Publications; 20. Disarmament Conference, Geneva, 1932-1934; 19. Preparatory Commission: Draft Convention**)

Churchill, W[inston Spencer]. LES ÉTATS DÉSUNIS D'EUROPE. Les

Annales Politiques et Littéraires. Vol. 96. 1 March 1931. pp. 199–200

Spender, Hugh F. AMERICAN PEACE MESSAGE. Fortnightly Review. June 1929. pp. 743–52. (6th Session of Preparatory Disarmament Commission)

Whiteford, D. G. RECENT WORK OF THE LEAGUE PREPARATORY COMMISSION FOR A CONFERENCE FOR THE LIMITATION OF ARMAMENTS. Army Quarterly. July 1927. pp. 288–305

Nation. PRESIDENT HOOVER MOVES. Vol. 45. 27 April 1929. pp. 98–9

19. Preparatory Commission: Draft Convention (see also under: 29. HMSO Publications; 20. Disarmament Conference, Geneva, 1932–1934; 18. Preparatory Commission for the Disarmament Conference)

Arnold-Forster, W[illiam E]. LAND MATERIAL: ARTILLERY. Towards Disarmament. 9 September 1931. pp. 1–3

Bernhard, G. THE CRUX OF THE DISARMAMENT QUESTION. Nation. Vol. 48. 27 December 1930. p. 430. (Criticism of draft convention for disarmament conference by preparatory commission, German viewpoint)

20. Disarmament Conference, Geneva, 1932–1934 (see also under: 29. HMSO Publications; 23. Other Countries; 19. Preparatory Commission: Draft Convention; 18. Preparatory Commission for the Disarmament Conference)

Arnold-Forster, W[illiam E]. THE DISARMAMENT CONFERENCE. London: National Peace Council 1931. Pamphlet. pp. 91

Arnold-Forster, W[illiam E]. A POLICY FOR THE DISARMAMENT CONFERENCE. Political Quarterly. Vol. 2. July–September 1931. pp. 378–93. (Analysis of resolution in favour of disarmament adopted by Federation of League of Nations Societies at Budapest Congress, May 1931)

Arnold-Forster, William [E]. THE FIRST STAGE IN DISARMAMENT; A COMMENTARY ON THE CONTINUING PROGRAMME OF THE CONFERENCE. Geneva: Geneva Research Centre. 1932. Pamphlet.

pp. 54. (Report of ideas discussed by members of an international group who closely followed 1932 disarmament conference)

Arnold-Forster, W[illiam E]. BRITISH POLICY AT THE DISARMAMENT CONFERENCE. Political Quarterly. Vol. 3. July 1932. pp. 365-80

Arnold-Forster, W[illiam E]. LECTURE ON THE BRITISH DRAFT CONVENTION in PROBLEMS OF PEACE, Eighth series. Lectures delivered at the Geneva Institute of International Relations, August 1933. London: Allen & Unwin. 1933. pp. xvi + 291

Arnold-Forster, W[illiam E]. HOW SHOULD WE ANSWER HITLER? London. 1933. Pamphlet. pp. 4

Ashby, M. C. THE FAILURE IN LEADERSHIP AT THE DISARMAMENT CONFERENCE. London. 1935. Pamphlet. pp. 8

Cecil, Robert (1st Viscount Cecil of Chelwood). PUBLIC OPINION AND DISARMAMENT (reply to G. Bernhard). Nation. Vol. 48. 3 January 1931. pp. 451-2

Cecil, Robert (1st Viscount Cecil of Chelwood). LORD CECIL DESCRIBES THE WORK OF THE PREPARATORY COMMISSION FOR THE DISARMAMENT CONFERENCE. London: League of Nations Union. 1931. Pamphlet No. 290. pp. 32

Cecil, Robert (1st Viscount Cecil of Chelwood). THE CONFERENCE MUST SUCCEED. Nation. (New York). Vol. 132. 25 March 1931. pp. 319-20

Cecil, Robert (1st Viscount Cecil of Chelwood). GENEVA MUST BRING DISARMAMENT. Nation (New York). 29 July 1931. pp. 107-8

Cecil, Robert (1st Viscount Cecil of Chelwood). FACING THE WORLD DISARMAMENT CONFERENCE. Foreign Affairs (New York). October 1931. pp. 13-22

Cecil, Robert (1st Viscount Cecil of Chelwood). RIDDLE OF THE AIR. New Statesman and Nation. Vol. 3. 7 May 1932. pp. 579-80

Chilton, C. B. BELIEVE IT AND ACT, OR — PERISH (the Truth about the Disarmament Conference as seen by a world citizen, showing a practical plan to end the war menace). Geneva. 1933. Pamphlet. pp. 32

Davies, David [Davies] (1st Baron Davies of Llandinam). SUICIDE OR SANITY?
(an examination of the proposals before the Geneva Disarmament Conference: the case for an international police force). London: Williams & Norgate Ltd. 1932. Pamphlet. pp. v + 55

Davies, David [Davies] (1st Baron Davies of Llandinam). FRENCH

PLAN. Contemporary Review. January 1933. pp. 1-10

Davies, David [Davies] (1st Baron Davies of Llandinam). THE REIGN OF LAW: LESSONS OF GENEVA'S FAILURE. Review of Reviews. Vol. 85. 7 July 1934. pp. 54-7

Dewar, Alfred C[harles]. THE DISARMAMENT CONFERENCE, 1932. Brassey's Naval Annual. 1933. pp. 57-70

Dewar, Alfred C[harles]. THE DISARMAMENT CONFERENCE, 1933. Brassey's Naval Annual. 1934. pp. 60-72

Dickinson, Willoughby (Lord Dickinson of Painswick). PROBLEM OF DISARMAMENT (1) IS DISARMAMENT POSSIBLE? 19th Century. September 1932. pp. 272-88. (For second article see Richmond (1932))

Dutt, R. P. LAUSANNE, GENEVA AND THE WAR CRISIS. Labour Monthly. Vol. 14. August 1932. pp. 470-5

Garnett, Dr Maxwell. THE WORLD CRISIS AND THE DISARMA-MENT CONFERENCE. The Contemporary Review. Vol. CXLI. February 1932. pp. 144-53

Gillow, P. J. THE DISARMAMENT CONFERENCE. Financial Review of Reviews. June 1934. pp. 5-7

Harris, H[enry] W[ilson]. TOWARDS DISARMAMENT. Contemporary Review. Vol. 139. February 1931. pp. 147-53

Harris, H[enry] W[ilson]. WORLD FROM GENEVA. Spectator. Vol. 150. 2 June 1933. pp. 796-7

Harris, L[ilian]. NOTES ON THE DRAFT DISARMAMENT CONVENTION. London: Women's Co-operative Guild. Vol. 2. 1931. Pamphlet. pp. 12

Heald, S. A. MEMORANDUM ON THE PROGRESS OF DISARMA-MENT, 1919-1932; WITH AN ANALYSIS OF THE DRAFT DISARMAMENT CONVENTION. London: RIIA Information Department Memoranda No. 1. 1932. Pamphlet. pp. 68

Ibbotson, E. SO FAR AT GENEVA. World Today. Vol. 59. March 1932. pp. 279-84

Ibbotson, E. DEBTS AND DISARMAMENT. World Today. Vol. 59. May 1932. pp. 456-8

Ibbotson, E. PREMIERS' PARLEY; BEHIND THE SCENES AT GENEVA. World Today. Vol. 60. June 1932. pp. 23-6

Kennedy, J. R. DISARMAMENT AND THE BRITISH PLAN. 19th Century. May 1933. pp. 568-75

Kim. REAL CAUSE OF WORLD UNSETTLEMENT. Saturday Review. Vol. 155. 3 June 1933. pp. 532-3

Labour Party. DISARM! DISARM! DISARM! (world labour's demands to the Disarmament Conference). London. 1931. Pamphlet. pp. 4

Latimer, Hugh. THE DRAFT CONVENTION FOR DISARMAMENT. Bulletin of International News. 18 December 1930. pp. 3-11

League of Nations Union. THE NATIONAL DEMONSTRATION OF JULY 11, 1931 TO PROMOTE THE SUCCESS OF THE WORLD DISARMAMENT CONFERENCE. London: LNU. July 1931. Pamphlet. pp. 36

Lippay, F. BEHIND THE SCENES OF THE 'DISARMAMENT' CONFERENCE. London: Modern Books Ltd. 1932. Pamphlet. pp. 58

Lloyd George, David (M.P.). LA FRANCE A SES RAISONS. Annales Politiques et littéraires. Vol. 100. 7 April 1933. pp. 383-4. (See also: LES RAISONS DE LA FRANCE; reply L. BARTHOU 14 April 1933, pp. 413-14)

Martin, K[ingsley]. DISARMAMENT CONFERENCE AND THE RUSSIAN PLAN. Political Quarterly. Vol. 5. July 1934. pp. 413-21

No More War Movement. REAL COWARDS (a talk about the Disarmament Conference). London(?) ?1931. Pamphlet. pp. 4

Richmond, Admiral Sir Herbert [William]. PROBLEM OF DISARMAMENT (2) GENEVA AND THE NAVIES. 19th Century. September 1932. pp. 272-88

Royal Institute of International Affairs. THE PROGRESS OF DISARMAMENT, 1930-2 (with analysis of draft convention). RIIA. ?1932. Pamphlet

Salter, A[rthur]. CONFERENCES OF THIS YEAR: GENEVA, LAUSANNE, OTTAWA, LONDON. Political Quarterly. Vol. 3. October 1932. pp. 467-88

Temple, William (Archbishop of York). SERMON ON THE OCCASION OF THE DISARMAMENT CONFERENCE (preached on 31 January 1932). London: League of Nations Union. 1933. Pamphlet

Trampler, Kurt. BACKGROUND OF THE CONFERENCE; PROBLEM OF GENERAL DISARMAMENT. Modern Review. February 1932. pp. 130-6

Turner, G. C. GENEVA IN THE AIR. National Review. October 1933. pp. 455-62

Wheeler-Bennett, John W[heeler]. DISARMAMENT AND SECURITY SINCE LOCARNO, 1925-1931 (being the political and technical background of the general Disarmament Conference, 1932). London: Information Service on International Affairs, Information Series,

No. 7. G. Allen & Unwin Ltd. 1932. pp. 383

Wheeler-Bennett, John W[heeler]. THE DISARMAMENT CON-
FERENCE. London: Routledge. 1934

Economist. THE DRAFT DISARMAMENT CONVENTION. 20
December 1930. pp. 1160-1

Economist. MORIBUND PEACE. 9 June 1934. pp. 1239-40

Journal of Royal United Services Institution. DISARMAMENT CON-
FERENCE. February 1933. pp. 160-3. May 1933. pp. 398-402.
August 1933. pp. 618-22

New Statesman and Nation. DISARMAMENT SUPPLEMENT. Vol. 3.
30 January 1932. pp. 131-46. (Issues of the Conference. pp. 132-4)

New Statesman and Nation. END OF A TABOO. Vol. 5. 25 March
1933. pp. 376-7

New Statesman and Nation. ROOSEVELT AND HITLER. Vol. 5. 20
May 1933. pp. 620-1

New Statesman and Nation. UPS AND DOWNS AT GENEVA. Vol. 5.
27 May 1933. pp. 676-7

New Statesman and Nation. GERMAN CHALLENGE. Vol. 6. 14
October 1933. pp. 436-7

Quarterly Review. SOME ASPECTS OF DISARMAMENT. Vol. 261.
October 1933. pp. 347-65

Review of Reviews. GERMANY AND DISARMAMENT, HOPES AND
FEARS FOR THE CONFERENCE. Vol. 82. November 1932.
pp. 11-14

Review of Reviews. DISARMAMENT AND SECURITY: COMMENTS
ON THE NEW FRENCH PLAN. Vol. 82. December 1932. pp. 12-17

Review of Reviews. GENEVA-ROME EXPRESS. Vol. 83. April 1933.
pp. 13-16

Review of Reviews. INTERLUDE AT GENEVA; DISARMAMENT
MOUNTAIN AND FOUR-POWER PACT MOUSE. Vol. 83. June
1933. pp. 21-4

Review of Reviews. BACK TO ARMS? Vol. 85. June 1934. pp. 18-20

Review of Reviews. RETROSPECT AND PROSPECT. Vol. 85. June
1934. pp. 21-36. (Disarmament Conference 1934 in cartoons)

Round Table. DISARMAMENT. Vol. 22. June 1932. pp. 532-51

Spectator. DISARMAMENT ISSUES. Vol. 148. 30 January 1932.
pp. 133-4

Spectator. VOICES AT GENEVA. Vol. 148. 6 February 1932. pp. 169-
70

Times. GERMANY AND GENEVA. 21 October 1932. pp. 15-16

World Today. MEN, GUNS AND SHIPS. Vol. 59. March 1932.
pp. 285-91. (A quick reference guide with a graphic chart showing comparative strengths)

21. Air Aspects (see also under: **20. Disarmament Conference, Geneva, 1932-1934**)

Altham, E. SEA, AIR AND EMPIRE. Quarterly Review. July 1934.
pp. 1-5
Cable, B. AIR 'DISARMAMENT' MYTH. Saturday Review. 20 January 1934. pp. 65-6
Chamier, J. A. AIR BOMBING AND AIR DISARMAMENT. Army Quarterly. October 1933. pp. 93-8. Bookman. August 1933.
pp. 233-4
Chamier, J. A. AIR BOMBING AND AIR DISARMAMENT. Army Quarterly. January 1934. pp. 284-8
Charlton, L. E. O. THE MENACE OF THE CLOUDS. Hodge. 1937.
pp. 295. (On aerial warfare and its possible implications)
Garnett, Dr Maxwell. FREEDOM OF THE AIR: AERIAL DEFENCE. Contemporary Review. May 1933. pp. 542-51
Groves, Brigadier-General P. R. C. THE INFLUENCE OF AVIATION ON INTERNATIONAL RELATIONS. International Affairs. May 1927. pp. 133-52. July 1929. pp. 289-317
Groves, (Brigadier-)General P. R. C. THE RELATIONS BETWEEN CIVIL AND MILITARY AVIATION. League of Nations Publications. 1930. VIII. 6. C. 339. M. 139. 1930. VIII. pp. 84-93.
(Enquiries into the economic, administrative and legal situation of International Air Navigation)
Ide, J. J. TWO YEARS OF THE FRENCH AIR MINISTRY. 19th Century. February 1931. pp. 149-61
Innes, G. A. THE ABC OF AIR DISARMAMENT (an account of the efforts made to abolish military and naval aircraft). London: League of Nations Union. 1935. Pamphlet. pp. 47
Joad, C[yril] E[dwin] M[itchinson]. 'DEFENCE' THAT IS NO DEFENCE: A MESSAGE TO EVERY CITIZEN. National Peace Council. 1937. Pamphlet. pp. 8
Kenworthy, (Commander) L. J. M. (M.P.). NEW WARS: NEW WEAPONS. London: Matthews & Marrot. 1930. pp. 160. (Chiefly from standpoint of naval and air defence)

MacCloughry, E. J. K. WINGED WARFARE (air problems of peace and war). London: Cape. 1937. pp. 286

Martin, K[ingsley]. PUBLIC OPINION: THE AIR PACT AND THE BRITISH PRESS. Political Quarterly. Vol. 6. April 1935. pp. 269–76

Mumford, P. S. HUMANITY, AIR POWER AND WAR (an essay upon international relations). Jarrolds. 1936. pp. 252

Murphy, P. ARMADAS OF THE SKY (the problem of armaments). London. 1931. pp. 120

Neon, Ackworth M. THE GREAT DELUSION (a study of aircraft in peace and war). London: E. Benn Ltd. 1927. pp. 288. (Importance of aviation overestimated and expenditure out of proportion to results obtained; should renounce as means of attack. For reply see Rear-Admiral Sueter (1928)).

Noel-Baker, P[hilip] J[ohn]. WAR IN THE AIR? THE ATTITUDE OF THE GOVERNMENT. National Peace Council. 1934. Pamphlet. pp. 4

Smith, Edward G. BOMBING FOR PEACE; OR, THE GREATEST ILLUSION. London: The Author. 1933. Pamphlet. pp. 7

Spaight, J. M. THE BEGINNINGS OF ORGANISED AIR POWER. London: Longmans, Green. 1927. pp. 323

Spaight, J. M. AIR POWER AND THE CITIES. London: Longmans, Green & Co. 1930. pp. ix + 244

Spaight, J. M. AN INTERNATIONAL AIR FORCE. Gale & Polden. 1932. pp. 115

Sueter, Rear-Admiral M. F. AIR MEN OR NOAHS (fair play for our airmen. The great 'Neon' air myth exposed). London: Pitman & Sons. 1928. pp. 448. (Reply to NEON (1927), q.v.)

Swanwick, H. M. L. FRANKENSTEIN AND HIS MONSTER. AVIATION FOR WORLD SERVICE (a sequel to NEW WARS FOR OLD). London: Women's International League. 1934. Pamphlet. pp. 22

Thomson, Christopher B. (1st Lord Thomson). AIR FACTS AND PROBLEMS. London: J. Murray. 1927. Pamphlet. pp. 55

Warner, Edward P. CAN AIRCRAFT BE LIMITED? Foreign Affairs (New York). April 1932. pp. 431–43

Review of Reviews. AERIAL DISARMAMENT; THE QUESTION OF POLICE BOMBING. Vol. 84. July 1933. pp. 20–4

22. Chemical Disarmament (see also under: **29. HMSO Publications**)

Carlton, David and Sims, Nicholas. THE CS GAS CONTROVERSY:

GREAT BRITAIN AND THE GENEVA PROTOCOL OF 1925.
Survival. Vol. 13. October 1971. pp. 333-40
Friends Peace Committee. POISON GAS. 1930. Pamphlet. pp. 4. (A
leaflet dealing with the animal experiments carried out on Salisbury
Plain)
Joad, C[yril] E[dwin] M[itchinson]. 'DEFENCE' THAT IS NO
DEFENCE: A MESSAGE TO EVERY CITIZEN. National Peace
Council. 1937. Pamphlet. pp. 8
League of Nations Union. CHEMICAL WARFARE. London. 1925.
Pamphlet No. 171. pp. 20
Lefebure, Major V[ictor]. THE RIDDLE OF THE RHINE (chemical
strategy in peace and war). London: Collins Sons & Co. 1921.
pp. 279. (Deals with chemical disarmament among other aspects)
Lockhart, Dr L. P. CHEMICAL WARFARE AS A BRANCH OF
NATIONAL DEFENCE. National Review. January 1929. pp. 705-
25
Manisty, H. F. THE USE OF POISON GAS IN WAR. Grotius Society.
Vol. IX. pp. 17-28
Nature. CHEMICAL WARFARE AND DISARMAMENT. Vol. 129.
4 June 1932. pp. 809-11
Nature. CHEMICAL DISARMAMENT. Vol. 131. 25 March 1933.
pp. 413-15

23. Other Countries (see also under: 29. HMSO Publications; 20. Disarmament Conference, Geneva, 1932-1934; 17. Draft Treaty of
Mutual Assistance, Geneva Protocol; 12. London Naval Conference,
1930; 11. Anglo-French Project for Limiting Armaments, 1928;
10. Three-Power Naval Conference, Geneva, 1927; 9. Washington
Conference, 1921-1922; 8. Naval Aspects)

Arnold-Forster, W[illiam] E. HOW SHOULD WE ANSWER HITLER?
National Council for the Prevention of War. 1933. Pamphlet. pp. 4
Arnold-Forster, W[illiam E]. DISARM — SOON, OR REARM —
PRESENTLY. New Statesman and Nation. Vol. 6. 28 October
1933. pp. 510-11. (Germany)
Bell, J. FRANCE AND HER PROBLEMS. English Review. Vol. 58.
May 1934. pp. 580-6
Brailsford, H[enry] N[oel]. SHOULD WE COERCE GERMANY? New
Statesman and Nation. Vol. 6. 21 October 1933. pp. 478-9

Bruce, C. D. DISARMAMENT IN THE FAR EAST. Army Quarterly. July 1933. pp. 293-9

Charques, R. D. THE SOVIETS AND THE NEXT WAR (the present case for disarmament). London: M. Secker. 1932. pp. 94

Davray, Henry D. DISILLUSIONMENT OF FRANCE. Spectator. Vol. 128. 14 January 1922. pp. 44-5

Hurd, Archibald. AMERICA'S INCREASING ARMAMENTS. Fortnightly Review. March 1927. pp. 364-75

Fitzgerald, W. G. AMERICA AND DISARMAMENT. Quarterly Review. Vol. 258. January 1932. pp. 121-38

Friends of Europe. GERMANY RE-ARMING (a study of the actual situation in Germany). London: Friends of Europe Publication No. 5. 1933. Pamphlet. pp. 10

Friends of Europe. THE MILITARY PREPAREDNESS OF GERMAN INDUSTRY. London: Friends of Europe Publication No. 6. 1933. Pamphlet. pp. 24

Garvin, James Louis. HITLER AND ARMS. London: Friends of Europe Publication No. 1. 1933. Pamphlet. pp. 7

Germains, V. W. SOME ASPECTS OF THE PRESENT MILITARY SITUATION BETWEEN FRANCE AND GERMANY. English Review. Vol. 57. December 1933. pp. 609-16

Grey, Edward (Viscount Grey of Fallodon). IL FAUT EMPÊCHER L'ALLEMAGNE DE RÉARMER. Annales politiques et littéraires. Vol. 101. 15 September 1933. pp. 294-5

Kennedy, M. D. SOME ASPECTS OF JAPAN AND HER DEFENCE FORCES. London: Kegan, Paul, Trench, Trübner & Co. 1928. pp. 243. (One chapter devoted to Japanese attitude towards disarmament)

Kennedy, M. D. TRIANGULAR RELATIONS. Empire Review. October 1935. pp. 215-20. (Between Britain, USA, Japan)

Ratcliffe, S. K. PRESIDENT HOOVER AND EUROPE. Contemporary Review. August 1929. pp. 137-45

Remnant, E. GERMAN PERIL. Saturday Review. Vol. 156. 8 July 1933. pp. 37-8

Roberts, Chalmers. CAN FRANCE EVER BE PLACATED? World Today. April 1930. pp. 434-8

Stone, F. G. THE SOVIET AND DISARMAMENT AT GENEVA. 19th Century. May 1928. pp. 577-89

Twiss, W. L. O. DISARMAMENT WITH SPECIAL REFERENCE TO ASIA. Journal of the Central Asian Society. Vol. 19. 1932. pp. 447-

Villard, Oswald G. FRANCE AGAINST THE WORLD. Nation (New York). 12 August 1931. pp. 149-51

Wheeler-Bennett, John W[heeler]. MEMORANDUM ON GERMANY AND DISARMAMENT, 1918-1932. London: RIIA. 1933. Information Department Memorandum No. 8. Pamphlet. pp. 36

New Statesman and Nation. RUSSIA AND MR CHURCHILL. Vol. 2. 4 July 1931. pp. 4-5

Quarterly Review. SOME ASPECTS OF DISARMAMENT. Vol. 261. October 1933. pp. 347-65. (Germany)

Review of Reviews. GERMANY DEMANDS EQUALITY; DISARMAMENT AND THE LEAGUE AT STAKE. Vol. 82. October 1932. pp. 13-18

Review of Reviews. FRANCE; A NATIONALIST VIEW OF DISARMAMENT. Vol. 82. November 1932. pp. 41-2

Saturday Review. WAY TO WAR. Vol. 155. 20 May 1933. pp. 481-2. (Germany)

Spectator. TRAMPING ARMIES. Vol. 149. 10 September 1932. pp. 304-5. (Germany)

Spectator. SOPHISTRY AND STATESMANSHIP. Vol. 149. 24 September 1932. pp. 360-1. (Germany)

Spectator. REAL CRISIS. Vol. 150. 3 March 1933. pp. 276-7. (Germany)

Times. ARMS AND THE GERMANS. 13 October 1932. p. 15. 14 October 1932. pp. 13-14

Times. ACROSS THE RHINE: DISARMAMENT IN FRANCE. 9 December 1932. pp. 15-16. 10 December 1932. p. 11

24. Christian Churches

Booth, The Rev. Alan. CHRISTIANS AND POWER POLITICS. London: SCM Press, Living Church Books. 1961. Paperback. pp. 126

Burroughs, [Bishop] E. A. THE CHRISTIAN CHURCH AND WAR. London: Nisbet. 1931. Lambeth Series. Pamphlet. pp. 45

Chichester (The Rt. Rev. Dr George Bell, 97th) Bishop of. CHRISTIANITY AND WORLD ORDER. Harmondsworth Penguin. 1940. Paperback. pp. 156

Conference of Bishops of the Anglican Communion, 1930. PEACE AND WAR. (Extracts from the work of a committee of the Lambeth Conference, 1930, on the life and witness of the Christian Community, with a part of the encyclical letter and the resolutions based upon them). London: SPCK. 1930. Pamphlet. pp. 16

Connery, D. P. THE CHURCH OR THE GATES OF HELL? (brief reflections on the Church's attitude to war). London: A. H. Stockwell. 1931. Pamphlet. pp. 48

Council of Christian Pacifist Groups. A PEACE CALL TO CHRISTIANS (the manifesto of the Christian pacifist groups). London: Council of Christian Pacifist Groups. 1935

Dickinson, Sir W[illoughby H]. THE CHURCHES AND DISARMAMENT in H. W. Fox *et al.* : THE RELIGIOUS BASIS OF WORLD PEACE. London: Williams & Norgate. 1929. pp. 167

Goff, E. N. P. THE CHRISTIAN AND THE NEXT WAR. London: P. Allan. 1933. pp. 118. (Germany)

Johnston, A. A. CHRISTIANITY AND WAR. London: Clarke. 1931. pp. 115

Jones, Ernest N. THE RIGHT USE OF FORCE (a call to the Churches; being a correspondence between E. N. Jones and Lord Davies). London: New Commonwealth Pamphlets. Series C, No. 1. 1934. Pamphlet. pp. 30

Keating, Joseph. CATHOLICS AND DISARMAMENT. Month. December 1931. pp. 509-21

League of Nations Union. ARMS AND THE CHURCHES. London. 1931. Pamphlet No. 304. pp. 15

Norwood, (Rev). F. W. THE FREE CHURCHES AND THE MILITARY STATE. London: City Temple. 1935. Pamphlet. pp. 16. (Presidential address at the assembly of the National Council of the Evangelical Free Churches)

Norwood, (Rev). F. W. TOWARDS A CONSTRUCTIVE PEACE POLICY FOR THE CHURCHES. London: Independent Press. 1935. Pamphlet. pp. 24

Quail, J. Arnold. DISARMAMENT AND THE CHURCHES. Congregational Quarterly. April 1927. pp. 174-8

Raven, C. E. IS WAR OBSOLETE? (a study of the conflicting claims of religion and citizenship). London: Allen & Unwin. 1935. pp. 186. (Halley Steward Lecture, 1934)

Richards, L. P. THE CHRISTIAN'S ALTERNATIVE TO WAR. London: Student Christian Movement. 1935. pp. 125

Richards, L. P. THE CHRISTIAN'S CONTRIBUTION TO PEACE (a constructive approach to international relationships). London: Student Christian Movement. 1935. pp. 160

Robinson, W. CHRISTIANITY IS PACIFISM. London: Allen &

Unwin. 1933. pp. 126

Stevenson, J. W. A DISARMED CHURCH IN AN ARMED WORLD.
London: Fellowship of Reconciliation. 1935. pp. 32

Temple, William (Archbishop of York). CHRIST AND THE WAY TO
PEACE. London: Student Christian Movement. 1935. Pamphlet.
pp. 31

Thorning, J. F. THE CHURCH LOOKS AT DISARMAMENT.
Ecclesiastical Review. August 1932. pp. 124-9

25. Arms Trade and Manufacture of Armaments (see also under:
29. HMSO Publications; 26. Economic Aspects of Disarmament)

Abad, C. H. MUNITIONS INDUSTRY IN WORLD AFFAIRS. Scribners.
September 1933. pp. 176-9

Adams, Vyvyan. THE PRIVATE MANUFACTURE OF ARMAMENTS.
Spectator. 16 October 1936. pp. 640-2. (Review of NOEL-BAKER
(1936) *q.v.*)

Angell, (Sir) Norman. THE UNSEEN ASSASSINS. London: H.
Hamilton. 1932. pp. 283

Borrill, L. THE GOVERNMENT AND THE ARMAMENT
INDUSTRIES. Millgate. May 1936. pp. 437-8

Angell, Ernest. SHALL WE NATIONALISE MUNITIONS? Harpers.
March 1935. pp. 407-17

Arnold-Forster, W[illiam E]. THE ARMAMENTS RACKET. 19th
Century. November 1934. pp. 520-34

Brockway, Archibald Fenner. THE BLOODY TRAFFIC (an account of
the armaments industry). London: Gollancz. 1933. pp. 288

Carnegie, Colonel David. THE PRIVATE MANUFACTURE OF ARMS,
AMMUNITION AND IMPLEMENTS OF WAR. International Affairs.
Vol. X, No. 4. July 1931. pp. 504-23

Dennison, Warwick. SINEWS OF WAR; AN EXPOSURE OF ARMS
TRAFFIC. Review of Reviews. April 1935. pp. 20-3

Engelbrecht, H. C. and Hanighen, F. MERCHANTS OF DEATH. A
STUDY OF THE INTERNATIONAL ARMAMENTS INDUSTRY.
London: Routledge. 1934. pp. 312

Engelbrecht, H. C. CONTROLLING THE ARMS MAKERS. Nation
(New York). 13 November 1935. pp. 559-61

Eppstein, John. THE REAPERS OF DEATH. Month. July 1934.
pp. 13-23

Eppstein, John. THE HARVEST OF FEAR. THE ETHICS OF ARMA-
MENTS MANUFACTURE. Oxford. 1935. Pamphlet. pp. 16

Eppstein, John. TRAFFIC IN ARMS: THE TASK OF THE ROYAL
COMMISSION. Contemporary Review. April 1935. pp. 416–22

Friend, Vita and Joseph. HOW THE ARMS MAKERS WORK. Forum.
November 1933. pp. 278–84

Fuller, J. V. GENESIS OF THE MUNITIONS TRAFFIC. Journal of
Modern History. September 1934. pp. 280–93

Good, E. T. THE ARMAMENTS INDUSTRY: ITS WIDE RAMIFICA-
TIONS. Financial Review of Reviews. April 1936. pp. 6–10

Gunther, John. SLAUGHTER FOR SALE. Harper's. May 1934.
pp. 649–59

Hill, J. W. NATIONALIZATION OR CONTROL. Spectator. 21
December 1934. pp. 953–4

Innes, Kathleen E. SAFEGUARDING THE WAR INDUSTRY. Friends
Peace Committee. 1928. Pamphlet. pp. 4. (Reprinted from FOREIGN
AFFAIRS, February 1928)

League of Nations Union. TRAFFIC IN ARMS. London. 1928.
Pamphlet. pp. 20

Morgan, J. H. TRAFFIC IN ARMS. New Statesman and Nation. Vol. 4.
26 November 1932. pp. 653–4

Noel-Baker, Philip [John] (M.P.). HAWKERS OF DEATH: THE
PRIVATE MANUFACTURE AND TRADE IN ARMS. London.
1934. Pamphlet. pp. 28

Noel-Baker, Philip [John]. SUPPRESSING THE PRIVATE MANUFAC-
TURE OF ARMAMENTS: THE OBJECTIONS ANSWERED.
National Peace Council. 1934. Pamphlet. pp. 8

Noel-Baker, Philip [John] (M.P.). THE PRIVATE MANUFACTURE
OF ARMAMENTS, Volume One (no Volume Two). London: Victor
Gollancz. 1936. pp. 574. (See also review by V. Adams (1936))

Perris, G. H. THE WAR TRADERS. London: National Peace Council.
1913. Pamphlet. pp. 32

Perris, G. H. THE WAR TRADERS. London: National Peace Council.
1914. pp. viii + 168

Pickard, Irene et al. THE WAR TRADE AND THE CHRISTIAN CON-
SCIENCE. Friends' Peace Committee. 1933. Pamphlet. pp. 32

Slater, G. WAR OR PEACE? (the national control of armaments).
Woolwich typescript. ?1922. ?1923. Pamphlet. pp. 36. (Advocates nationalisation)

Snowden, Philip. DREADNOUGHTS AND DIVIDENDS: AN EX-

POSURE OF THE ARMAMENTS RING. Labour Party Pamplet.
1914. pp. 22

Spender, J. A. ARMS AND THE STATE. Fortnightly Review. December
1936. pp. 651-60. (Whether to nationalize the manufacture of
armaments)

Stone, William T. EXPOSING THE DEATH BUSINESS. Nation (New
York). 3 October 1934. pp. 376-8

Trebilcock, Clive. LEGENDS OF THE BRITISH ARMAMENT
INDUSTRY 1890-1914: A REVISION. Journal of Contemporary
History. Vol. 5, No. 4. 1970. pp. 3-19

Union of Democratic Control. THE INTERNATIONAL INDUSTRY OF
WAR. London. ?1915. Pamphlet. pp. 14

Union of Democratic Control. THE SECRET INTERNATIONAL
(armament firms at work). London: Union of Democratic Control.
1932. Pamphlet. pp. 47

Union of Democratic Control. PATRIOTISM LTD (an exposure of the
war machine). London: Union of Democratic Control. 1933.
Pamphlet. pp. 64

White, F. TRAFFIC IN ARMS. London: League of Nations Union.
1934. Pamphlet. pp. 83

Wild, J. VICKERS LTD: INTERNATIONALISM IN ARMS. Millgate.
December 1936. pp. 123-6

Williams, W. H. WHO'S WHO IN ARMS. London: Labour Research
Department. 1935. Pamphlet. pp. 47

Wohlforth, Robert. ARMAMENT PROFITEERS, 1934. Nation (New
York). 14 March 1934. pp. 299-301

Economist. THE PRIVATE ARMS TRADE. 7 November 1936.
pp. 250-1

Review of Reviews. DIVIDENDS AND DISARMAMENT: THE
SECRET INTERNATIONAL. August 1932. pp. 34-9

Times. PRIVATE TRADE IN ARMS (Government White Paper). 7
May 1937. pp. 17-18

26. Economic Aspects of Disarmament (see also under: 28. Economic
Aspects of Rearmament; 25. Arms Trade and Manufacture of Armaments; 21. Air Aspects; 20. Disarmament Conference, Geneva,
1932-1934; 8. Naval Aspects)

Angell, Sir Norman. THE REAL COST OF ARMAMENTS. National

Peace Council. 1932. Pamphlet. pp. 4

Angell, Sir Norman (M.P.). WILL DISARMAMENT INCREASE UNEMPLOYMENT? London: No More War Movement. 1931. Pamphlet. pp. 10

Benson, George. WHY BRITAIN SHOULD DISARM (the economic case for non-resistance). Manchester and London: The National Labour Press Ltd. ?1914. Pamphlet. pp. 15

Cooper, Spencer. DISARMAMENT AND TRADE PROTECTION. Socialist Review. September 1929. pp. 21-5

Davenport, E. H. ECONOMICS OF DISARMAMENT. New Statesman and Nation. Vol. 3. 30 January 1932. pp. 134-6

Dening, B. C. DISARMAMENT AND ECONOMICS. Journal of Royal United Services Institute. No. 75. November 1930. pp. 713-16

Edgeworth, F. Y. THE COST OF WAR AND WAYS OF REDUCING IT SUGGESTED BY ECONOMIC THEORY. London. 1915. Pamphlet. pp. 48

Glasgow, George. DISARMAMENT AND FINANCIAL RECOVERY. Queens Quarterly. February 1932. pp. 12-28

Jacobsson, P. ARMAMENTS EXPENDITURE OF THE WORLD. London: The Economist. 1929. Pamphlet. pp. 26

League of Nations Union. INTERNATIONAL DISARMAMENT AND UNEMPLOYMENT: WHAT WE MEAN BY DISARMAMENT. London. n.d. Pamphlet. pp. 8

League of Nations Union. THE EFFECT OF NATIONAL ARMA-MENTS UPON THE PEOPLE'S LIFE AND WORK (speeches delivered at the League of Nations Union 'Disarmament' Conference L.S.E. 24 May 1927. Sir William Beveridge: Economic Disadvantages of going to war. pp. 3-8. Sir Hilton Young: The cost of Armaments Today. pp. 8-20. Sir Josiah Stamp: Economic Aspects of Disarmament. pp. 20-32. Mr W. L. Hichens: The Wastefulness of Armaments. pp. 32-42.) London: League of Nations Union. July 1927. Pamphlet. pp. 42

League of Nations Union. INTERNATIONAL DISARMAMENT AND THE UNEMPLOYMENT PROBLEM. London. 1928. Pamphlet. pp. 20

Pigou, A. C. THE POLITICAL ECONOMY OF WAR. London: Macmillan. 1921. pp. 251

Salter, J. A[rthur]. ECONOMIC POLICIES AND PEACE. London. 1936. pp. 38

Stamp, J. Chapter on THE FINANCIAL ASPECTS OF DISARMA-

MENT in STUDIES IN CURRENT PROBLEMS IN FINANCE AND
GOVERNMENT. London: P. S. King & Son. 1925. pp. 342
Economist. ARMAMENTS AND INDUSTRY. 2 May 1936. pp. 232-3
Statist. RECESSION, REVIVAL AND REARMAMENT. 14 January
1939. pp. 39-41

27. Rearmament (see also under: 28. Economic Aspects of Rearmament)

Arnold-Forster, W[illiam E]. REARMAMENT: 1935. Contemporary
Review. July 1935. pp. 9-21
Arnold-Forster, William E. THE ARMAMENTS RACE. Contemporary
Review. June 1936. pp. 668-7
Bailey, Jack. GOVERNMENT'S ARMS PLAN. Millgate. April 1937.
pp. 373-6
Balogh, T. THE BURDEN OF REARMAMENT. Spectator. 22 April
1938. pp. 699-700
Butler, Harold. WHERE IS REARMAMENT LEADING US? Listener.
29 June 1939. pp. 1349-50, 1377
Campbell, J. R. LABOUR AND REARMAMENT. Labour Monthly.
November 1936. pp. 672-82
Clark, R. W. B. THE INTERNAL CONSEQUENCES OF REARMA-
MENT. Political Quarterly. July 1937. pp. 364-78
Cole, G[eorge] D[ouglas] H[oward]. THE TRADE UNIONS AND
REARMAMENT. Labour Monthly. May 1938. pp.284-90
Dunbabin, J. P. D. BRITISH REARMAMENT IN THE 1930s: A
CHRONOLOGY AND REVIEW. Historical Journal. Vol. 18.
September 1975. pp. 587-609
Flynn. THE WAR BOOM BEGINS. Harper's. July 1937. pp. 113-22
Hirst, Francis W[rigley]. ARMAMENTS: THE RACE AND THE
CRISIS. London: Cobden-Sanderson. 1937
Jennings, W. Ivor. BRITISH ORGANISATION FOR REARMAMENT.
Political Science Quarterly. December 1938. pp. 481-90
Joyce, J. A. RE-ARMAMENT DEBUNKED! OR PEACE-MAKING FOR
BEGINNERS. London: Herbert Joseph. 1938. Pamphlet. pp. 36
Keynes J[ohn] M[aynard]. WILL REARMAMENT CURE UNEMPLOY-
MENT? Listener. 1 June 1939. pp. 1142-3
Kypa, J. P. BRITISH ATTITUDES TOWARDS DISARMAMENT AND
REARMAMENT, 1932-5. Ph.D. Thesis No. 723. London School of

Economics. 1966-7

Laski, Harold J. BRITISH ARMS INQUIRY. Nation (New York). 4 March 1936. pp. 272-3

Lloyd, [George A.] (1st Lord Dolobran). NEED FOR THE RE-ARMAMENT OF BRITAIN: ITS JUSTIFICATION AND SCOPE. International Affairs. January 1936. pp. 57-79

Mander, Geoffrey. THE GOVERNMENT REARMAMENT PRO-GRAMME. Contemporary Review. April 1936. pp. 394-9

Morrison, Herbert (M.P.). THE GREAT SPEED-UP. Listener. 4 July 1940. pp. 3-5

Newbold, W. ARMS AND INDUSTRY. Fortnightly Review. May 1936. pp. 601-7

Papworth, A. F. et al. WAR LOANS, REARMAMENT AND LABOUR POLICY. The Labour Monthly. Vol. 19, No. 3. March–May 1937. pp. 158-164, 213-16, 277-82

Rathkey, W. A. CONDEMNED TO DEATH: A PACIFIST LOOKS AT REARMAMENT. Review of Reviews. January 1936. pp. 17-19

Saunders, A. W. THE ARMAMENTS REVIVAL. Financial Review of Reviews. November 1935. pp. 16-19

Sinclair, Sir Archibald. REARMAMENT. Contemporary Review. April 1937. pp. 385-92

Temperley, [Major-General] A. C. THE WORLD RE-ARMS: THE PROSPECTS OF WAR. World Review. January 1937. pp. 15-21

Thursfield, H. G. THE RESTORATION OF DEFENCE. Brassey's Naval Annual. 1937. pp. xi-xvi

Watson, W. F. THE SKILLED LABOUR PROBLEM. 19th Century. September 1936. pp. 354-64. (in the British armaments producing industries)

Wintringham, T. H. PRESENT PHASE OF THE ARMS RACE. Labour Monthly. Vol. 17. July 1935. pp. 411-16

Engineer. DEFENCE PROGRAMME: CONDITIONS OF CONTRACT (Memorandum of British Engineers' Association). 25 September 1936. pp. 327-8 (also in ENGINEERING. 25 September 1936. pp. 333-4)

New Statesman. THE ARMS INQUIRY. 18 January 1936. pp. 72-3. [IS THE REARMAMENT PROGRAMME] DEFENCE? 7 March 1936. pp. 332-3

Times. PLOUGHSHARES AND SWORDS: 1. ADAPTING AN INDUSTRY. 20 August 1936. pp. 13-14. 2. THE FACTORY AT NOTTINGHAM. 21 August 1936. pp. 11-12

28. Economic Aspects of Rearmament (see also under: 27. Rearmament; 26. Economic Aspects of Disarmament)

Carnegie, (Colonel) David. SOME ECONOMIC AND SOCIAL EFFECTS OF REARMAMENT. International Affairs. November 1939. pp. 784-97

Einzig, P. THE ECONOMICS OF REARMAMENT. London: Kegan Paul. 1934. pp. 179

Hall, N. F. SOME TECHNICAL ASPECTS OF THE FINANCE OF REARMAMENT. Economica. May 1937. pp. 137-42

Hirst, F[rancis] W[rigley]. ARMAMENTS BUDGET: THE DEFICIT, THE PROFITS TAX AND THE FINANCIAL FUTURE. Contemporary Review. June 1937. pp. 641-9

Hodson, H. V. PAYING FOR REARMAMENT. Spectator. 28 February 1936. pp. 338-9

Jones, J. H. ECONOMIC ASPECTS OF REARMAMENT. Accountant. 18 May 1935. pp. 703-4

Jones, J. H. ECONOMIC ASPECTS OF REARMAMENT. Accountant. 14 March 1936. pp. 402-5

Jones, J. H. FINANCING REARMAMENT. Accountant. 30 January 1937. pp. 148-50. 6 February 1937. pp. 183-5. 13 February 1937. pp. 220-2

Jones, J. H. FINANCIAL POLICY AND THE DEFENCE LOAN. Accountant. 27 February 1937. pp. 292-4

Jones, J. H. NOTES ON REARMAMENT. Accountant. 27 November 1937. pp. 719-22

Jones, J. H. ECONOMICS OF REARMAMENT. Accountant. 6 August 1938. pp. 176-8. 13 August 1938. pp. 211-13

Jones, J. H. THE BURDEN OF REARMAMENT. Accountant. 22 October 1938. pp. 553-5

Jones, J. H. REARMAMENT AND TRADE RECOVERY. Accountant. 17 June 1939. pp. 803-5

Keynes, J[ohn] M[aynard]. BORROWING FOR DEFENCE: IS IT INFLATION? Times. 11 March 1937. pp. 17-18

Knight, John. THE FINANCIAL CONSEQUENCES OF REARMAMENT. The Labour Monthly. Vol. 19, No. 6. June 1937. pp. 353-8

Knight, John. REARMAMENT AND OVERPRODUCTION. The Labour Monthly. Vol. 19, No. 7. July 1937. pp. 411-15

Knight, John. REARMAMENT, CAPITALIST PLANNING AND THE DEFORMATION OF CAPITALIST ECONOMY. The Labour

Monthly. Vol. 19, No. 8. August 1937. pp. 491-6

Knight, John. REARMAMENT AND LABOUR CONDITIONS. The Labour Monthly. Vol. 19, No. 9. September 1937. pp. 564-9

Knight, John. INTERNATIONAL CONSEQUENCES OF REARMA-MENT. The Labour Monthly. Vol. 19, No. 10. October 1937. pp. 634-8

Knight, John. ECONOMIC CRISIS AND ARMAMENTS. Labour Monthly. May 1939. pp. 290-6

Knight, John. ARMAMENTS, THE BUDGET AND UNEMPLOYMENT. Labour Monthly. June 1939. pp. 352-61

Parker, R. A. C. ECONOMICS, REARMAMENT AND FOREIGN POLICY: THE UNITED KINGDOM BEFORE 1939. A PRE-LIMINARY STUDY. Journal of Contemporary History. Vol. 10. October 1975. pp. 637-47

Phillips, W. J. REARMAMENT AND THE PREVENTION OF EXCESS PROFITS. Accountant. 25 April 1936. pp. 652-3

Restell, E. THE ECONOMIC CONSEQUENCES OF REARMAMENT. Millgate. July 1936. pp. 549-5

Sadd, C. T. A. DEBTS AND DISARMAMENT. London: Gee. 1932. The Accountant Lecture Series, No. 3. Pamphlet. pp. 11

Stokes, R. R. ACCOUNTANTS AND ARMAMENTS PROFITS. Accountant. 10 September 1938. pp. 364-8

Banker. REARMAMENT. ECONOMICS AND FINANCE. April 1937. pp. 9-14

Bankers Magazine. THE COST OF DEFENCE: RISE IN THE NATIONAL DEBT. March 1939. pp. 396-9

Bankers Magazine. AFTERTHOUGHT ON THE BUDGET. June 1939. pp. 888-94

Economist. THE BURDEN OF ARMS. 5 March 1938. pp. 485-6

Economist. THE BURDEN OF ARMS. 18 February 1939. pp. 329-30

Economist. BORROWING TO THE HILT [FOR ARMAMENTS]. 25 February 1939. pp. 381-2

Economist. THE ESTIMATES [FOR THE SERVICES]. 4 March 1939. pp. 433-4

Economist. THIS YEAR'S REVENUE. 8 April 1939. pp. 76-7

Economist. THE BUDGET ACCOUNTS. 29 April 1939. pp. 241-3

Economist. CONSCRIPTION OF WEALTH. 13 May 1939. pp. 359-61

Statist. REARMAMENT FINANCE. 22 July 1939. pp. 71-2

29. HMSO Publications

HMSO. 1922. Cmd 1627. xxiii. 689. Treaties, Resolutions, etc., of the International Conference held at Washington, 1921–2, on the Limitation of Armaments

HMSO. 1924. Cmd 2036. xxvii. 293. Treaty between the British Empire, France, Italy, Japan and the United States of America for the Limitation of Naval Armaments, signed at Washington, 6 February 1922. (Ratifications exchanged at Washington, 17 August 1923)

HMSO. 1924. Cmd 2200. Foreign Office: Correspondence between His Majesty's Government and the League of Nations respecting the proposed Treaty of Mutual Assistance

HMSO. 1926. Cmd 2681. xxx. 705. Report of the work of the First Session of the Preparatory Commission for the Disarmament Conference

HMSO. 1927. Cmd 2888. xxvi. 755. Report of the British Representative to the Secretary of State for Foreign Affairs on the work of the Third Session of the Preparatory Commission for the Disarmament Conference, 21 March–26 April 1927

HMSO. 1927. Cmd 2964. xxvi. 805. Speeches (in Plenary Session of the Geneva Conference for the Limitation of Naval Armaments, June to August 1927) by the Rt Hon. W. C. Bridgeman, First Lord of the Admiralty

HMSO. 1928–9. Cmd 3211. xxiii. 763. Papers regarding the Limitation of Naval Armaments, 1928

HMSO. 1929. Cmd 3398. Misc. No. 6. Foreign Office: Protocol for the prohibition of the use in war of asphyxiating, poisonous or other gases, and of bacteriological methods of warfare, Geneva, 17 June 1925. pp. 7

HMSO. 1929–30. Cmd 3485. xxxii. 1071. Memorandum on the position of His Majesty's Government in the United Kingdom at the London Naval Conference, London, 4 February 1930. pp. 6

HMSO. 1929–30. Cmd 3547. xxxii. 1077. Memorandum on the results of the Naval Conference from 21 January to 15 April 1930. pp. 5

HMSO. 1929–30. Cmd 3556. xxxii. 1083. International Treaty for the Limitation and Reduction of Naval Armaments, April 1930. (Similar paper: 1930–1. Cmd 3758. xxxv. 159)

HMSO. 1929–30. Cmd 3597. xxxi. 1143. Exchange of Notes with the

United States Government on the interpretation of Article 19 of the London Naval Treaty, 1930, London, 15-30 June. pp. 3

HMSO. LONDON NAVAL CONFERENCE, 1930. Documents of the London Naval Conference, 1930, consisting of the Treaty signed on 22 April 1930, the minutes of plenary meetings, memoranda submitted by The United States, French, United Kingdom, Italian and Japanese delegations on their position at the conference, the reports of the first committee, and the letter addressed by the president of the conference to the Secretary-General of the League of Nations on 1 April 1930. pp. 4

HMSO. 1930-3. Cmd 3747. xxv. 207. Memorandum on Chemical Warfare presented to the Preparatory Commission for the Disarmament Conference by the Delegation of the United Kingdom

HMSO. 1930-1. Cmd 3757. xxxv. 209. Despatch from Viscount Cecil of Chelwood enclosing the Report of the Preparatory Commission for the Disarmament Conference and the draft Disarmament Convention, 10 December 1930. pp. 108

HMSO. 1930-1. Cmd 3812. xxxv. 199. Memorandum on the results of the negotiations with France and Italy (February—March 1931). pp. 7

HMSO. 1931-2. Cmd 4018. xxvii. 849. Speech by Sir John Simon at the opening of the Disarmament Conference, 8 February 1932

HMSO. 1931-2. Cmd 4122. xxvii. 857. Declaration of British Disarmament Policy

HMSO. 1931-2. Cmd 4189. xxvii. 865. Declaration of British Disarmament Policy in connexion with Germany's claim to Equality of Rights

HMSO. 1932-3. Cmd 4279. xxviii. 137. Draft Disarmament Convention submitted to the conference at Geneva on 16 March 1933 by Mr J. Ramsay MacDonald

HMSO. 1932-3. Cmd 4437. xxviii. 169. Proceedings of the Bureau of the Disarmament Conference, Geneva, 14 October 1933

HMSO. 1933-4. Cmd 4498. xxvii. 1103. Memorandum on Disarmament communicated by His Majesty's Government in the United Kingdom to the governments represented at the Disarmament Conference

HMSO. 1933-4. Cmd 4512. xxvii. 1115. Memoranda on Disarmament issued by the governments of the United Kingdom, France, Germany and Italy in January 1934

HMSO. 1933-4. Cmd 4559. xxvii. 1147. Further Memoranda on

Disarmament. 14 February to 17 April 1934

HMSO. 1934-5. Cmd 4930. xxiv. 141. Exchange of Notes between the United Kingdom and Germany regarding the Limitation of Naval Armaments (June 1935)

HMSO. 1934-5. Cmd 4953. xxiv. 145. Exchange of Notes between the United Kingdom and Germany regarding the Limitation of Naval Armaments (June 1935)

HMSO. 1935-6. Cmd 5136. xxvii. 377. Treaty between His Majesty in respect of the United Kingdom, Canada, Commonwealth of Australia, New Zealand and India, the President of the United States of America and the President of the French Republic for the Limitation of Naval Armaments. pp. 43. (Similar paper: 1936-7. Cmd 5561. xxviii. 475)

HMSO. 1935-6. Cmd 5317. xxvii. 421. Memorandum on the London Naval Conference, December 1935 to March 1936

HMSO. ROYAL COMMISSION ON THE PRIVATE MANUFACTURE OF AND TRADING IN ARMS (minutes of evidence). 1935-6. pp. 756

HMSO. 1936-7. xxviii. Treaty between His Majesty. . ., the President of the U.S.A. and the President of the French Republic for the Limitation of Naval Armaments. pp. 44

HMSO. 1936-7. xxix. Agreement between . . . the United Kingdom and the . . . Union of Soviet Socialist Republics providing for the Limitation of Naval Armaments and the Exchange of Information concerning Naval Construction. pp. 17

HMSO. 1936-7. Cmd 5519. xxix. 315. Agreement between the United Kingdom and Germany providing for the Limitation of Naval Armaments and the Exchange of Information concerning Naval Construction. pp. 43

HMSO. 1937-8. Cmd 5781. xxx. 385. Protocol modifying the Treaty of 25 March 1936 for the Limitation of Naval Armaments, London, 30 June 1938. pp. 2

HMSO. 1937-8. xxxi. Agreement between . . . the United Kingdom and the Polish Government providing for the Limitation of Naval Armaments, etc. pp. 31

HMSO. 1937-8. Cmd 5795. xxxi. 195. Protocol modifying the Anglo-German Agreement of 17 July 1937 for the Limitation of Naval Armament, London, 30 June 1938

HMSO. 1937-8. Cmd 5834. xxxi. 199. Protocol modifying the Anglo-German Agreement of 17 July 1937 for the Limitation of Naval

Armaments, London, 30 June 1938

HMSO. 1937-8. Cmd 5637. xxxi. 151. Agreement between His Majesty's Government in the United Kingdom and the German Government providing for the Limitation of Naval Armament and the Exchange of Information concerning Naval Construction (with Declaration Protocol of signature and exchange of Notes)

HMSO. 1937-8. xxxi. Agreement between . . . the United Kingdom and . . . the U.S.S.R. providing for the Limitation of Naval Armament . . . (with Protocol). 2 parts

HMSO. 1938-9. xxviii. Protocol modifying the Anglo-Soviet Agreement of . . . 1937 for the Limitation of Naval Armament. pp. 4

HMSO. 1938-9. xxviii. Agreement between . . . the United Kingdom and the Polish Government providing for the Limitation of Naval Armament . . . (with Protocol). 2 parts

HMSO. 1938-9. Cmd 5999. xxvii. 557. Agreement between the governments of the United Kingdom, Denmark, Finland, Norway and Sweden regarding the Limitation of Naval Armament and the Exchange of Information concerning Naval Construction (with Protocol of signature). pp. 16

PART TWO

30. A Note on Contemporary Government Publications

Her Majesty's Stationery Office publishes every year, for the Foreign and Commonwealth Office (up to October 1968, for the Foreign Office), a survey of the previous year's disarmament negotiations consisting in the main of the relevant documents of the UN and CCD. Examples of this series are

The Disarmament Negotiations 1967 (Cmnd 3767). London: HMSO, 1968. pp. 315. Price 25s.
The Disarmament Negotiations 1969 (Cmnd 4399). London: HMSO, 1970. pp. 209. Price 18s.

It has also published, in its 'Miscellaneous' category, certain disarmament documents on their presentation to Parliament by the Foreign (or Foreign and Commonwealth) Secretary. Notable among these documents are the various treaties concluded in the UN-CCD system: the *Convention on the Prohibition of the Development, Production and Stockpiling of Bacteriological (Biological) and Toxin Weapons and on their Destruction* was published as Cmnd 5053, for example, in 1972. Apart from actual treaties, a number of important texts have appeared under this imprint, such as (to take a trio relevant to disarmament in quite different ways)

Text of the Plan for Comprehensive Disarmament tabled by [the five Western delegations] at the Conference of the Ten Nation Committee on Disarmament in Geneva on 16 March 1960 together with an Extract from a Speech by the Foreign Secretary at the United Nations on 17 September 1959 (Cmnd 981). London: HMSO, 1960. pp. 8. Price 6d. (Miscellaneous No. 3 – 1960)
Draft Convention for the Prohibition of Biological Methods of Warfare and accompanying draft Security Council Resolution (Cmnd 4113). London: HMSO, 1969. pp. 7. Price 1s 3d. (Miscellaneous No. 27 – 1969)
Agreement between the United Kingdom of Great Britain and Northern Ireland, the Federal Republic of Germany and the Kingdom of the Netherlands *on Collaboration in the Development and Exploitation of the Gas Centrifuge Process for producing Enriched Uranium*, Almelo, 4 March 1970 (Cmnd 4315). London: HMSO, 1970. pp. 15. Price 2s. (Miscellaneous No. 5 – 1970)

84

Current lists may be found in the *Overseas Affairs* sectional catalogue of Government publications issued by HMSO.

Foreign Office pamphlets, e.g. *The Key to Disarmament* (1964), have been included in our main bibliography, as they constitute comment and analysis whereas the publications referred to in this Note are essentially documents or collections of documents. (There have in fact been no more pamphlets on disarmament since the creation of the FCO; this undoubtedly reflects the tighter budgetary situation of the Office since – though not because of – that amalgamation.)*

United Nations publications on disarmament do not fall within the scope of our bibliography, but any reader interested can obtain UN publications *for sale* through HMSO Government Bookshops; UN leaflets and pamphlets *for free distribution*, including treaty texts, from the UN Information Centre, 14–15 Stratford Place, London W1N ?AF; UN and CCD documents, at cost price (duplicated), from the Sales Section of the UN in Geneva or New York according to the location of the particular conference or committee generating the documents: e.g. the documents of each CCD session are distributed by the UN Sales Section in Geneva, a few weeks after the meeting to which they relate. UN publications for sale are listed in a special HMSO catalogue and many are on display at the Government Bookshop in High Holborn, London. (Full address: 49 High Holborn, London WC1V 6HB; HMSO's other Government Bookshops are situated in Edinburgh, Cardiff, Manchester, Bristol, Birmingham and Belfast.)

* In 1978, however, the FCO's Arms Control and Disarmament Department and its Research Unit issued several booklets in near-print form, using in-house reprographics because of the continuing budgetary restrictions: these booklets included *British Arms Control and Disarmament Policy: A Short Guide* (14 pp.), which was issued to participants in the non-governmental Assembly for Disarmament and Peace at Camden Town Hall, London, in January; the text of the Prime Minister's 2 June 1978 speech to the Special Session on Disarmament of the UN General Assembly; a leaflet (31 July), *The Special Session: A Brief Assessment*, prepared specially for non-governmental audiences; and *The Control of Arms Transfers*, ed. John Simpson, which consisted of papers presented at a seminar organised by the Department/Research Unit and the Arms Control Study Group of the British International Studies Association. Also in 1978 the Central Office of Information published *Arms Control and Disarmament* (38 pp.) as its Reference Pamphlet 155, produced for British Information Services overseas, but also available for home sale from HMSO (price 90p).

31. General: 1941-1945

Barlow, K. E. THE DISCIPLINE OF PEACE. London. 1942. pp. 214

Bedford, 12th Duke of (Hastings W. S. Russell). TOTAL DISARMA-
MENT OR AN INTERNATIONAL POLICE FORCE? Glasgow:
Strickland Press. 1944. Pamphlet. pp. 12

Bedford, 12th Duke of (Hastings W. S. Russell). WHY HAVE WAR?
Glasgow: Strickland Press. 1945. Pamphlet. pp. 24

Bennett, D. C. T. FREEDOM FROM WAR. London. 1945. pp. 90

Burns, C. D. AFTER WAR — PEACE? London. 1941. pp. 48

Capper-Johnson, Karlin. THE PROBLEM OF DISARMAMENT: In the
light of the atomic bomb and of the United Nations Charter.
London: Friends Peace Committee. [1945]

Cripps, Sir R. Stafford. SHALL THE SPELL BE BROKEN? London.
1943. pp. 16

Curtis, Lionel. WORLD WAR: ITS CAUSE AND CURE (1st edn).
London. 1945. pp. xx + 274

Curtis, Lionel. WORLD WAR: ITS CAUSE AND CURE: The problem
reconsidered in view of the release of atomic energy. (2nd edn).
London. 1945. pp. xxxii + 274

Davies, David (Davies) (1st Baron Davies of Llandinam). THE SEVEN
PILLARS OF PEACE. London. 1945. pp. ix + 149

Davies, Percival and Kathleen. FOUNDATIONS OF PEACE: A study
outline on the political implications of the letter from the Christian
Churches [in the Times of 21 December 1940]. Leeds: Northern
Friends Peace Board [1941] and London: [Society of Friends]
Industrial and Social Order Council. Pamphlet. pp. 38

Dell, Robert Edward. THE GENEVA RACKET, 1920-1939. London:
Robert Hale. 1941. (London, Geneva Conference on Disarmament,
1932-4)

Gollancz, Victor. SHALL OUR CHILDREN LIVE OR DIE? A reply to
Lord Vansittart on the German problem. London: Victor Gollancz.
1942. Hardback. pp. 170

Heymann, H. PLAN FOR PERMANENT PEACE. London. 1942.
pp. xx + 321

Martin, Kingsley. PROBLEM OF GERMANY: REPLY TO ARTICLE
BY F. A. VOIGT. New Statesman and Nation. Vol. 21. 22 March
1941. pp. 293. (Germany and Disarmament)

Martin, Kingsley. PROBLEM OF GERMANY; REVIEW OF CHATHAM HOUSE REPORT. New Statesman and Nation. Vol. 26. 24 July 1943. pp. 52-3. Reply by J. Lehmann. Vol. 26. 31 July 1943. p. 73. (Germany and Disarmament)

'Mercator'. GERMAN DISARMAMENT AND EUROPEAN RECONSTRUCTION. Political Quarterly. Vol. 13. October 1942. pp. 349-61

Morgan, J. P. ASSIZE OF ARMS. London: Methuen. 1945

Morgan, L. P. ARMAMENTS AND MEASURES OF ENFORCEMENT. Institute on World Organization. 1942. (World Organization). pp. 121-57

Morgan, L. P. DISARMAMENT. pp. 42-64 in H. I. E. Davies (ed.): PIONEERS OF WORLD ORDER. London. 1944

Oldham, J[ohn] H. THE ROOT OF OUR TROUBLES. London. 1941. pp. 24

Pollard, Francis E. − AND SO THE PEACE WAS LOST. London: Friends Peace Committee. 1942. Pamphlet. pp. 15

Quinn, E. FUNDAMENTALS OF PEACE. London. 1942. pp. 69

Thomson, D. *et al.* PATTERNS OF PEACEMAKING. London. 1945. pp. viii + 399

Winterton, Earl. THE GUNS TALK. Empire Review. May 1942. pp. 202-6

32. General: 1946-1950

Bedford, 12th Duke of (Hastings W. S. Russell). TOTAL DISARMAMENT OR AN INTERNATIONAL POLICE FORCE? (2nd edn). Glasgow: Strickland Press. 1948. Pamphlet. pp. 21

Capper-Johnson, Karlin. ENTER THE WORLD STATE: A CHRISTIAN PACIFIST COMMENT. London: Friends Peace Committee. 1946. Pamphlet. pp. 8

Capper-Johnson, Karlin. THE NEW INSTRUMENT OF GOVERNMENT: A COMMENTARY ON THE UNITED NATIONS CHARTER. London: Friends Peace Committee. 1946. Pamphlet. pp. 15

Curtis, Lionel. WAR OR PEACE. London. 1946. pp. vi + 66

Fuller, J. F. C. ARMAMENT AND HISTORY. London. 1946. pp. 246

Pollard, Robert S. W. THE STRUGGLE FOR DISARMAMENT. London: Friends Peace Committee. 1949. Pamphlet. pp. 36

Reves, E. THE ANATOMY OF PEACE. London. 1946. pp. 252

33. General: 1951–1955

Acland, Sir Richard, Brockway, Fenner (M.P.) and Hale, Leslie (M.P.).
WAGING PEACE: THE NEED FOR A CHANGE IN BRITISH
POLICY. London: Peace News, Peace News Pamphlets. 1954.
Pamphlet. pp. 24

Bernal, J[ohn] D. THE WAY TO PEACE. London: Labour Monthly,
Labour Monthly Pamphlets Series, No. 2. 1951. Pamphlet. pp. 23

Central Office of Information. THE DISARMAMENT QUESTION,
1945–54. London: Central Office of Information, Reference
Division Series (for overseas distribution only). 1954. Pamphlet.
pp. 53

Enock, Arthur Guy. THIS PLAYTHING PEACE. London: The Bodley
Head. 1952. Pamphlet

Fry, Anna Ruth. AN UNARMED WORLD. London: A. R. Fry. 1954.
Pamphlet. pp. 14

Kay, John A. CONSTRUCTIVE PEACEMAKING: THE QUAKER
CONTRIBUTION. London: Friends Peace Committee. 1951.
Pamphlet. pp. 7

Lonsdale, Kathleen. SECURITY AND RESPONSIBILITY. London:
Fellowship of Reconciliation. 1954. Pamphlet. pp. 32. (Alex Wood
Memorial Lecture, 1954)

Marwick, William H. THE ECONOMIC AND MORAL CONSEQUENCES
OF BRITISH REARMAMENT. London: Friends Peace Committee.
n.d. [1951]. Pamphlet. pp. 16

Metson, William. DEFENCE AND DISARMAMENT. London: UNA,
Peacefinder Series, No. 15. 1953. Pamphlet. pp. 16

Morrison, Sybil. SECURITY THROUGH DISARMAMENT. London:
Peace News, Peace News Pamphlets Series. 1954. Pamphlet. pp. 16

National Peace Council. WORLD DISARMAMENT: Report of the NPC
Disarmament Commission on the Political, Technical and Economic
Problems. London: National Peace Council, Peace Aims Pamphlet,
No. 58. [1953]. Pamphlet. pp. 78. (Contributors include: Ian
Mikardo (M.P.) (*q.v.*), Philip Noel-Baker, Harold Wilson (M.P.)
(*q.v.*), Leslie Hale (M.P.), Dr J. L. Michiels (*q.v.*) *et al.*)

Peace Pledge Union. THE MYTH OF BRITISH DISARMAMENT.
London: Peace Pledge Union. 1952. Pamphlet (illustrated by Mays).
pp. 8

Russell, Bertrand (3rd Earl Russell). DANGER TO MANKIND. Bulletin
of the Atomic Scientists. January 1954

Russell, Bertrand (3rd Earl Russell). HOW NEAR IS WAR? London: Ridgway, Fleet Street Forum Series. 1952. Pamphlet. pp. 39

Stewart, Michael (M.P.). POLICY AND WEAPONS IN THE NUCLEAR AGE. London: Fabian Society, Fabian Tract 296. 1955. Pamphlet. pp. 25

Thomas, Hugh. DISARMAMENT: THE WAY AHEAD. London: Fabian Society, Fabian Tract 307. 1957. Pamphlet. pp. 33. (Foreword by Kenneth Younger)

34. General: 1956-1960

Adam, General Sir Ronald and Judd, Charles. ASSAULT AT ARMS: A POLICY FOR DISARMAMENT. London: Weidenfeld & Nicolson, for UNA. 1960. Hardback. pp. 87

Angell, Sir Norman. DEFENCE AND THE ENGLISH-SPEAKING ROLE. London: Pall Mall Press. 1958. Hardback. pp. ix + 186

Bull, Hedley. DISARMAMENT AND THE INTERNATIONAL SYSTEM. Australian Journal of Politics and History. Vol. 5. May 1959. (Review of Noel-Baker (1958), *q.v.* Reprinted in Garnett (ed.), 1970, *q.v.*, pp. 136-148)

Buzzard, Rear-Admiral Sir Anthony. UNITY IN DEFENCE AND DIS-ARMAMENT. RUSI Journal. November 1959. pp. 390-404

Central Office of Information. THE DISARMAMENT QUESTION, 1945-56. London: HMSO, COI Reference Division Pamphlet, No. 18. 1957. Pamphlet. pp. iii + 54

Ennals, David. A UNITED NATIONS POLICE FORCE? London: Fabian Society, Fabian Research Series, No. 210. 1959. Pamphlet. pp. 24

Enock, Arthur Guy. THE CHOICE: CHRISTENDOM IN FETTERS OR EXERCISE PLOWSHARE. London: Marshall, Morgan & Scott. 1956. Hardback. pp. 160

Foreign Office. THE SEARCH FOR DISARMAMENT: A summary. London: HMSO. 1960. Pamphlet. pp. vi + 53

Goodwin, Geoffrey L. *THE ARMS RACE* BY PHILIP NOEL-BAKER: A review article. International Relations. Vol. 1. October 1958. pp. 483-93

Goold-Adams, Richard. THE ROAD TO DISARMAMENT. Brassey's Annual. 1960. pp. 4-13

Healey, Denis (M.P.). THE RACE AGAINST THE H-BOMB. London: Fabian Society, Fabian Tract 322: series Socialism in the Sixties.

1960. Pamphlet. pp. 20

King-Hall, Sir Stephen. COMMON SENSE IN DEFENCE. London: K-H Services. 1960

King-Hall, Sir Stephen. DEFENCE IN THE NUCLEAR AGE. London: Gollancz. 1958. Hardback. pp. 223

Labour Party and Trades Union Congress. DISARMAMENT AND NUCLEAR WAR: THE NEXT STEP. London: Labour Party. 1959. Pamphlet. pp. 8

Liddell Hart, B[asil] H. DETERRENT OR DEFENCE; A fresh look at the West's military position. London: Stevens. 1960. Hardback. pp. x + 257

Lonsdale, Dame Kathleen. IS PEACE POSSIBLE? Harmondsworth: Penguin (a Penguin Special). 1957. Paperback. pp. 127

Noel-Baker, Philip (M.P.). THE ARMS RACE: A PROGRAMME FOR WORLD DISARMAMENT. London: Stevens & Sons, Atlantic Books. 1958. Hardback. pp. xviii + 579. (See also the reviews by Bull (1959), and Goodwin (1958)) *or* (*q.v.*)

Noel-Baker, Philip (M.P.). THE ARMS RACE: A PROGRAMME FOR WORLD DISARMAMENT. London: John Calder, Calderbooks and New York: Oceana. 1960. pp. 579 or pp. xviii + 603

Noel-Baker, Philip (M.P.). PROSPECTS FOR WORLD DISARMA-MENT. Journal of the Royal Commonwealth Society. Vol. 3. 1960. pp. 91-3

Noel-Baker, Philip J. WELTABRÜSTUNG HEUTE MÖGLICH! (Fore-word by Jules Humbert-Droz, Afterword by Elisabeth Rotten). Zürich: Schweizerischer Friedensrat (Swiss Peace Council), Schriften-reihe des Schweizerischen Friedensrates Nr. 2. 1960. Pamphlet. pp. 31. (German translation of Nobel Peace Prize acceptance speech in Oslo, 11 December 1959)

Nutting, Anthony. DISARMAMENT, EUROPE AND SECURITY. International Affairs. Vol. 36. January 1960. pp. 1-6

Royal Institute of International Affairs. ON LIMITING ATOMIC WAR. London: RIIA (Chatham House). 1956. Pamphlet. pp. 46

Russell, Bertrand (3rd Earl Russell). COMMON SENSE AND NUCLEAR WARFARE. London: George Allen & Unwin. 1959. Hardback and Paperback. pp. 93

Russell, Bertrand (3rd Earl Russell). PHILIP NOEL-BAKER. Inter-national Relations. Vol. 1. April 1960. pp. 1-2

Standing Joint Pacifist Committee. UNARMED: SOME CON-SEQUENCES OF TOTAL DISARMAMENT. London: Peace News, for the Committee. 1957. Pamphlet. pp. 24

Thomas, Hugh. DISARMAMENT: DREAM OR REALITY? Political
Quarterly. Vol. 31. 1960. pp. 17-25

The Times. THE NUCLEAR DILEMMA (letters to the editor reprinted,
with a leading article). London: The Times Publishing Co. 1958.
Pamphlet. pp. 53

Toynbee, Philip (ed.). THE FEARFUL CHOICE: A DEBATE ON
NUCLEAR POLICY. London: Victor Gollancz. 1958. Hardback.
pp. 112

United Nations Association. DISARMAMENT AND DEFENCE.
London: UNA, Peacefinder Pamphlet, No. 32. 1960. Pamphlet.
pp. 12. (Contributors include Philip Noel-Baker and Sir Anthony
Buzzard)

Young, Wayland. STRATEGY FOR SURVIVAL: FIRST STEPS IN
NUCLEAR DISARMAMENT. Harmondsworth: Penguin (a Penguin
Special). 1959. Paperback. pp. 95

35. General: 1961-1965

Blackett, P[atrick] M. S. CRITIQUE OF SOME CONTEMPORARY
DEFENCE THINKING. Encounter. Vol. 16. April 1961. pp. 9-17.
(See also critique by Buchan (1961))

Blackett, P[atrick] M. S. THE FIRST REAL CHANCE FOR DIS-
ARMAMENT. Harper's Magazine. Vol. 226. January 1963.
pp. 25-32 and War and Peace. Vol. 1, No. 2. Summer 1963. pp. 2-12

Blackett, P[atrick] M. S. THE REAL ROAD TO DISARMAMENT:
THE MILITARY BACKGROUND TO THE GENEVA TALKS. New
Statesman. Vol. 63. 2 March 1962. pp. 295-300. (Reproduced in
French in LES TEMPS MODERNES 17 (June 1962) pp. 1895-
1913)

Blackett, P[atrick] M. S. STEPS TOWARD DISARMAMENT.
Scientific American. Vol. 206. April 1963. pp. 45-53

Boyd, Andrew. DISARMAMENT AND WORLD GOVERNMENT.
World Affairs (Washington, D.C.). Vol. 256. Summer 1962. pp. 41-5.
(Also in STUDIES IN DISARMAMENT AND ARMS CONTROL
(London: Institute for Strategic Studies, 1962). Adelphi Paper, No.
2)

Brown, Neville. AGREEMENTS FOR SELECTIVE ARMS REDUC-
TIONS in Luard (ed.): FIRST STEPS TO DISARMAMENT. 1965.
pp. 168-85

Buchan, (The Hon.) Alastair. ARMS AND SECURITY. Australian Outlook. Vol. 16. August 1962. pp. 113-59

Buchan, (The Hon.) Alastair. THE DETERRENT AND DISARMAMENT. Journal of the RUSI. Vol. 106. May 1961. pp. 186-94

Buchan, (The Hon.) Alastair. FOREIGN COMMENT in Donald G. Brennan (ed.): ARMS CONTROL, DISARMAMENT, AND NATIONAL SECURITY. New York: Braziller. 1961. pp. 443-45. (This book was published in Britain as ARMS CONTROL AND DISARMAMENT: AMERICAN VIEWS AND STUDIES (London: Jonathan Cape, 1961))

Buchan, (The Hon.) Alastair. P. M. S. BLACKETT AND WAR. Encounter. August 1961. (See also Blackett (1961))

Bull, Hedley. THE CONTROL OF THE ARMS RACE: DISARMAMENT AND ARMS CONTROL IN THE MISSILE AGE. London: Weidenfeld & Nicolson, for the Institute for Strategic Studies, Studies in International Security, No. 2. 1961. pp. xiv + 215. (Foreword by Richard Goold-Adams, Comment by the Rt. Hon. John Strachey (M.P.))

Bull, Hedley. THE CONTROL OF THE ARMS RACE: DISARMAMENT AND ARMS CONTROL IN THE MISSILE AGE. New York: Praeger. 1965. Paperback. pp. 235

Bull, Hedley. IS INTERNATIONAL INSPECTION NECESSARY? Spectator. 30 November 1962. pp. 853-54

Bull, Hedley. TWO KINDS OF ARMS CONTROL. Year Book of World Affairs. 1963. pp. 150-70. (Reprinted in the second (1965) edition of his book THE CONTROL OF THE ARMS RACE, *q.v.*)

Burton, John W. DISARMAMENT AND INTERNATIONAL ORGANIZATION [THE PROBLEM STATED]. Chapter 2 of his book PEACE THEORY: PRECONDITIONS OF DISARMAMENT. New York: Alfred A. Knopf 1962 (a Borzoi Book)

Carlton, David. ATTENTION, LORD CHALFONT! Socialist Commentary. January 1965. pp. 23-4. (See also reply by Noel-Baker (1965))

Cockcroft, Sir John. PROBLEMS OF DISARMAMENT. London: David Davies Memorial Institute of International Studies, David Davies Memorial Lecture. 1962. Pamphlet. pp. 14

Crane, Peggy. DISARMAMENT, 1963. London: UNA. 1963. Pamphlet. pp. 11

Crozier, Brian. THE DISARMING GAME. Spectator. 16 July 1965. pp. 74-5

Dunn, Ted (ed.). ALTERNATIVES TO WAR AND VIOLENCE.
London: James Clarke. 1963. Paperback. pp. 196
Foreign Office. THE KEY TO DISARMAMENT. London: HMSO.
1964. Pamphlet. pp. 72
Groom, A. J[ohn] R. LE CONTRÔLE DES ARMEMENTS: UN TOUR
D'HORIZON. Revue Militaire Suisse. January 1963
The Guardian. DISARMAMENT: PLANS AND ISSUES AT GENEVA.
Manchester. The Guardian. 1962. Pamphlet. pp. 19
Gutteridge, William. DEFENCE OR DISARMAMENT (review article).
International Affairs. Vol. 41, No. 4. October 1965. pp. 676-81
Hall, Stuart. END OF THE GRAND DESIGNS? War and Peace. Vol. 1,
No. 2. Summer 1963. pp. 14-18
Healey, Denis (M.P.). THE SEARCH FOR SECURITY. Views. Vol. 4.
Spring 1964. pp. 97-8
Howard, Michael. HOW CAN WE CONTROL THE ARMS RACE?
Listener. Vol. 65. 15 June 1961. pp. 1027-8
Howard, Michael. STRACHEY'S HOLY MOUNTAIN: *ON THE PRE-
VENTION OF WAR.* Encounter. Vol. 20. January 1963. pp. 65-72
Howard, Michael. STRATEGY OF SURVIVAL: PROSPECTS FOR
DISARMAMENT. Listener. Vol. 67. 29 March 1962. pp. 552-3
Institute for Strategic Studies. STUDIES IN DISARMAMENT AND
ARMS CONTROL. London: Institute for Strategic Studies, Adelphi
Paper, No. 2. 1962. Pamphlet. pp. 66. (Contributors include Luard,
q.v. (1964))
Johnstone, Kenneth (ed.). THE ROAD TO PEACE. London: SCM
Press, SCM Press Broadsheet, No. 6. Sponsored by the Conference
on Christian Approaches to Defence and Disarmament. 1965.
Pamphlet. pp. 54. (Contributors: Bennett, Johnstone (*q.v.*), von
Weizsäcker, Wright (*q.v.*))
Jones, Aubrey (M.P.). DISARMAMENT. Listener. Vol. 73. 18 February
1965. pp. 249-50
de Kadt, Emanuel J. BRITISH DEFENCE POLICY AND NUCLEAR
WAR. London: Frank Cass. 1964. Hardback. pp. 148
King-Hall, Sir Stephen. DEFENCE IN THE NUCLEAR AGE, 1961.
RUSI Journal. Vol. 106. May 1961. pp. 164-81
King-Hall, Sir Stephen. POWER POLITICS IN THE NUCLEAR AGE:
A POLICY FOR BRITAIN. London: Gollancz. 1962. Hardback.
pp. 224
Lister, Charles E. THE FOLKLORE OF GENERAL DISARMAMENT.
International Relations. Vol. 2. April 1963. pp. 427-42. (Essay

submitted for the Cecil Peace Prize, 1963)

Long, F. A. IMMEDIATE STEPS TOWARD GENERAL AND COM-
PLETE DISARMAMENT. Disarmament and Arms Control. Vol. 2.
Winter 1963-4. pp. 1-9

Luard, Evan. CONVENTIONAL DISARMAMENT. World Politics.
Vol. 16. January 1964. pp. 189-204

Luard, Evan. FIRST STEPS TO DISARMAMENT: A NEW APPROACH
TO THE PROBLEM OF ARMS REDUCTIONS. London: Thames &
Hudson. 1965. Hardback. pp. 277. (Chapters by Evan Luard:
(1) 'The Background of Negotiations to Date' (pp. 9-46); (2) 'Con-
clusions' (pp. 240-64). Other contributors: Brown (*q.v.*), Burns,
Halperin, Howard (*q.v.*), Levison, Mackintosh (*q.v.*), Schelling,
Slessor (*q.v.*), Thompson, Windsor (*q.v.*), Young (*q.v.*))

Luard, Evan. PEACE AND OPINION. London: Oxford University
Press. 1962. Hardback. pp. 170

Martin, Kingsley. ETHICS OF WAR. New Statesman. Vol. 66. 12
July 1963. pp. 40-1

Martin, Laurence W. POLITICAL SETTLEMENTS AND ARMS
CONTROL. Current History (Philadelphia). Vol. 42. May 1962.
pp. 296-301

Martin, Laurence W. *et al.* WEAPONS CONTROL TODAY. Current
History (Philadelphia). Vol. 47. July 1964. pp. 1-46

Moncrieff, Anthony (ed.). THE STRATEGY OF SURVIVAL. London:
BBC. 1962. Paperback. pp. 57. (Talks broadcast on the Third Programme in March 1962)

Neild, Robert. CHEATING IN A DISARMED WORLD. Disarmament
and Arms Control. Vol. 1. 1963. pp. 133-43

Noel-Baker, Philip. FOREIGN COMMENT in Donald G. Brennan
(ed.): ARMS CONTROL, DISARMAMENT AND NATIONAL
SECURITY. New York: Braziller. 1961. pp. 451-6. (This book was
published in Britain as ARMS CONTROL AND DISARMAMENT:
AMERICAN VIEWS AND STUDIES (London: Jonathan Cape,
1961))

Noel-Baker, Philip (M.P.). INTERNATIONAL DISARMAMENT: THE
ONLY DEFENCE POLICY. Disarmament (Paris). No. 7. September
1965. pp. 23

Noel-Baker, Philip. A POLICY FOR DISARMAMENT. London: UNA.
1965. Pamphlet. pp. 22

Noel-Baker, Philip (M.P.). THE SUPREME OBJECTIVE. Socialist
Commentary. March 1965. pp. 16-17. (Reply to Carlton (1965), *q.v.*)

Noel-Baker, Philip (M.P.). THE WAY TO WORLD DISARMAMENT –
NOW! London: Union of Democratic Control. n.d. [1963].
Pamphlet. pp. 48. (Foreword by the Rt. Hon. Harold Wilson, O.B.E.,
M.P.)

Ogley, R[oderick]. C. BELL, BULL AND CANON. International Relations. Vol. 2. April 1965. pp. 721-35. (The title refers to Dr Coral
Bell, Hedley Bull and the Rev. Canon L. John Collins, whose views
on unilateral nuclear disarmament are discussed in the article)

Raison, Timothy. STRATEGY FOR DISARMAMENT. London: Bow
Group, a Bow Group Memorandum. 1962. Pamphlet. pp. 17

Reece, Gordon. CURRENT LITERATURE AND RESEARCH. Disarmament and Arms Control. Vol. 2. Winter 1963-4. pp. 111-22

Roberts, John C. de V. DISARMAMENT IN FIFTEEN YEARS.
London: Federal Union. 1964. Pamphlet. pp. 12

Russell, Bertrand (3rd Earl Russell). HAS MAN A FUTURE? New
York: Simon & Schuster. 1962. Hardback. pp. 317. London:
Penguin (Special). 1961. Paperback. pp. 136

Seed, Philip. THE UNDEFENDED: Psychological aspects of the
problem of disarmament and possible solutions. London: Friends
Peace Committee. 1961. Pamphlet. pp. 15

Sington, Derrick. HOW THE PRESS COVERS THE GENEVA [ENDC]
NEGOTIATIONS. Disarmament and Arms Control. Vol. 2. Autumn
1964. pp. 141-8

Slessor, Sir John (Marshal of the Royal Air Force). WESTERN PRE-
CONDITIONS FOR DISARMAMENT AND ARMS CONTROL, in
Luard (ed.): FIRST STEPS TO DISARMAMENT. 1965. pp. 47-62

Strachey, John (M.P.). ON THE PREVENTION OF WAR. London:
Macmillan. 1962. Hardback and Paperback. pp. ix + 334

Tait, R. M. IN DEFENCE OF THE BIG CONFERENCE [ENDC].
Disarmament and Arms Control. Vol. 2. Summer 1964. pp. 331-41

United Nations Association. A CASE FOR HOPE: UNA's disarmament
policy 1964. London: UNA. 1964. Pamphlet. pp. 15. (Chairman of
the Disarmament Committee: Andrew Martin)

Verrier, Anthony. DISARMAMENT AND SECURITY. New Statesman.
Vol. 66. 30 August 1963. pp. 246-8

Verrier, Anthony. THE MEANING OF MULTILATERALISM. New
Statesman. Vol. 66. 11 October 1963. pp. 474-6

Verrier, Anthony. THE PRESENT STATE OF THE DISARMAMENT
DEBATE. The World Today. Vol. 18. June 1962. pp. 249-59

Watt, D[onald] C. THE POSSIBILITY OF A MULTILATERAL ARMS

RACE: A NOTE. International Relations. Vol. 2. October 1962

Watt, D[onald] C. DISARMAMENT AND PROBLEMS OF CIVIL-
MILITARY RELATIONS AMONG THE SMALLER POWERS.
International Relations. Vol. 2. October 1964. pp. 651-6

Wright, Sir Michael. THE CHOICE OF RISKS. Listener. Vol. 70. 12
December 1963. pp. 968-9

Wright, Sir Michael. DISARM AND VERIFY: An explanation of the
central difficulties and of national policies. London: Chatto &
Windus. 1964. Hardback. pp. xiv + 255

Wright, Sir Michael. DISARM AND VERIFY. New York: Praeger.
1964. pp. 275

Wright, Sir Michael. THE VIEW OF A BRITISH DIPLOMAT in
Johnstone (ed.): THE ROAD TO PEACE. 1965. pp. 42-54

Young, Wayland. BOMBS AND VOTES. London: Fabian Society,
Fabian Tract 354. 1964. Pamphlet. pp. 20

Young, Wayland. DISARMAMENT: PROPOSALS AND CONCES-
SIONS. Survival. Vol. 4. May–June 1962. pp. 127-9, 136

Young, Wayland. THE PROBLEM OF VERIFICATION in Luard (ed.):
FIRST STEPS TO DISARMAMENT. 1965. pp. 226-39

Young, Wayland. PUGWASH. Encounter. Vol. 20. February 1963.
pp. 54-7

Young, Wayland. VERIFICATION. Disarmament and Arms Control.
Vol. 2. Summer 1964. pp. 342-52

Young, Wayland and Young, Elizabeth. DISARMAMENT:
FINNEGAN'S CHOICE. London: Fabian Society, Fabian Tract
333. 1961. Pamphlet. pp. 20

Young, Wayland and Young, Elizabeth. DISARMAMENT *VERSUS*
ARMS CONTROL: A DISCUSSION OF CRITERIA. Commentary
(New York). Vol. 32. August 1961. pp. 124-34

36. General: 1966-1970

Bailey, Gerald. CRUSADE FOR DISARMAMENT? World Issues. No.
4. Summer 1967. pp. 1-2

Bailey, Sydney D. THE UNITED NATIONS AND WORLD ORDER
in George Cunningham (ed.): BRITAIN AND THE WORLD IN
THE SEVENTIES: A COLLECTION OF FABIAN ESSAYS. London:
Weidenfeld & Nicolson, on behalf of the Fabian Society. 1970.
pp. 83-106

Beaton, Leonard. DISARMAMENT. Chapter 12 of his book THE
   STRUGGLE FOR PEACE. London: George Allen & Unwin. 1966.
   Paperback, based on BBC series
Beaton, Leonard (ed.). THE STRUGGLE FOR PEACE. London:
   George Allen & Unwin. 1966. Hardback. pp. 118
Bull, Hedley. ARMS CONTROL: A STOCKTAKING AND PROSPEC-
   TUS in Buchan (ed.): 1970 (*q.v.*). pp. 9–20 of PROBLEMS OF
   MODERN STRATEGY, Part II
Burton, John W. *et al.* DISARMAMENT NOW! (three lectures given at
   a one-day conference on disarmament held jointly by UNA and
   FPAIRC at Friends House, November 1968). London: Friends
   Peace and International Relations Committee. 1969. Pamphlet.
   pp. 15
Burton, John [W.] UNILATERALISM AS A PROCESS in Carter (ed.):
   UNILATERAL DISARMAMENT. 1966. pp. 32–9
Calder, Ritchie (later Lord Ritchie-Calder of Balmashannar). PEACE
   AND DISARMAMENT. International Problems (Tel Aviv). Vol. 4.
   December 1966. pp. 20–5
Chalfont, Lord. THE POLITICS OF DISARMAMENT. Encounter.
   Vol. 27. October 1966. pp. 17–24
Chalfont, Lord. PROSPECTS OF DISARMAMENT in JOHNSTONE
   (ed.): PEACE IS STILL THE PRIZE. 1966. pp. 24–34
Crane, Peggy. DISARMAMENT STRATEGY FOR THE 1970s? Inter-
   State (Aberystwyth). No. 6. Summer 1969. pp. 22–5
Foreign Office.* DISARMAMENT: THE PATH TO PEACE. London:
   HMSO. 1968. Pamphlet. pp. 39. (*Pamphlet published in April 1968;
   the FO was superseded by the Foreign and Commonwealth Office in
   October 1968)
Garnett, John (ed.). THEORIES OF PEACE AND SECURITY. London:
   Macmillan. 1970. Paperback. pp. 272. (Includes the full text of Bull,
   1959 (*q.v.*))
Hanning, Hugh. THE PEACEFUL USES OF MILITARY FORCES.
   New York and London. Praeger (in co-operation with the World
   Veterans Federation), Praeger Special Studies in International
   Politics and Public Affairs. 1967. Hardback. pp. xxvii + 327
Howard, Michael. ARMS CONTROL AND DISARMAMENT. NATO's
   Fifteen Nations (Amsterdam). Vol. 15. December 1970–January
   1971. pp. 40–4
Howard, Michael. PROBLEMS OF A DISARMED WORLD in Herbert
   Butterfield and Martin Wight (eds.): DIPLOMATIC INVESTIGA-

TIONS: ESSAYS IN THE THEORY OF INTERNATIONAL POLI-
TICS. London: George Allen & Unwin. 1966. pp. 206–14. (Reprinted
in Howard's own book STUDIES IN WAR AND PEACE (London:
Maurice Temple Smith, 1970; New York: Viking, 1971), pp. 224–32)

Johnstone, Kenneth (ed.). PEACE IS STILL THE PRIZE. London:
SCM Press, SCM Press Broadsheet, No. 8. 1966. Sponsored by the
Conference on Christian Approaches to Defence and Disarmament.
Pamphlet. pp. 59. (Chapter by Kenneth Johnstone: 'What do we
want?' (pp. 7–17). Other contributors: Bailey, Booth, Buchan,
Chalfont (*q.v.*) Corbishley)

Luard, Evan. ARMS CONTROL. Chapter 7 of his book CONFLICT
AND PEACE IN THE MODERN INTERNATIONAL SYSTEM.
Boston: Little, Brown. 1968. Paperback. London: University of
London Press. 1970. Hardback. pp. 170–96

Luard, Evan. DISARMAMENT. Chapter 8 of his book CONFLICT
AND PEACE IN THE MODERN INTERNATIONAL SYSTEM.
Boston: Little, Brown. 1968. Paperback. London: University of
London Press. 1970. Hardback. pp. 197–226

Neild, R[obert] R. WHAT HAS HAPPENED TO DISARMAMENT?
London: David Davies Memorial Institute of International Studies,
David Davies Memorial Lecture. 1968. Pamphlet. pp. 20

Noel-Baker, Philip. THE ARMS RACE: ESCALATION OF TOTAL
MADNESS. UNESCO Courier (Paris). Vol. 23. November 1970.
pp. 4–12

Noel-Baker, Philip (M.P.). WE HAVE BEEN HERE BEFORE in Calder
(ed.): UNLESS PEACE COMES. 1968, 1970. (1968 edn) pp. 193–
205

Roberts, Adam. TRANSARMAMENT TO CIVILIAN DEFENCE in
Adam Roberts (ed.): THE STRATEGY OF CIVILIAN DEFENCE.
London: Faber & Faber. 1967. pp. 291–308. (This book was re-
issued in paperback as Adam Roberts (ed.): CIVILIAN RESIS-
TANCE AS A NATIONAL DEFENCE (Harmondsworth: Penguin,
1969))

Seed, Philip. THE PSYCHOLOGICAL PROBLEM OF DISARMA-
MENT. London: Housmans. 1966. Paperback. pp. 74

Sims, Nicholas A. DISARMAMENT: An analysis for Quakers. London:
Friends Peace and International Relations Committee. 1967.
Pamphlet. pp. 54

Sims, Nicholas. DISARMAMENT AND ARMS CONTROL: STRUC-
TURES FOR THE SEVENTIES. World Issues. No. 14. Spring 1970.

pp. 4-5

United Nations Association. DISARMAMENT: A POLICY AND A
PLAN. London: UNA. 1968. Pamphlet. pp. 16. (Chairman of the
Disarmament Committee: Sir Michael Wright)

Wilson, Andrew. PUBLIC OPINION AND DISARMAMENT. Disarmament (Paris). No. 11. September 1966. p. 8

Young, Wayland (ed.). EXISTING MECHANISMS OF ARMS CONTROL.
Oxford and London: Pergamon Press. Commonwealth and International Library. 1966. Paperback. pp. xiv + 150. (Reprinted from
articles in the Pergamon journal, DISARMAMENT AND ARMS
CONTROL, 1963-65)

37. General: 1971-1975

Bailey, Sydney D. DISARMAMENT, YES – BUT HOW? The Friend.
Vol. 131. 6 April 1973. pp. 404-7

Bailey, Sydney D. PROSPECTS FOR ARMS LIMITATION. Bulletin of
Peace Proposals (Oslo). Vol. 3, No. 4. 1972. pp. 356-61

Bailey, Sydney D. PROHIBITIONS AND RESTRAINTS IN WAR.
London: Oxford University Press, for the Royal Institute of International Affairs. 1972. Paperback and Hardback editions. pp. xiii +
194

Barnaby, Frank (SIPRI). DISARMAMENT OR DESTRUCTION?
Stockholm: SIPRI. 1975. Pamphlet. pp. 21

Barnaby, Frank (SIPRI). THE NUCLEAR AGE. Stockholm: Almqvist
& Wiksell International. 1974. pp. x + 148. (Published in collaboration with MIT Press, Cambridge (Mass.) and London)

Barnaby, Frank (SIPRI). NUCLEAR DISARMAMENT OR NUCLEAR
WAR? Stockholm: SIPRI. 1975. Pamphlet. pp. 27

Beaton, Leonard. THE REFORM OF POWER: A proposal for an international security system. London: Chatto & Windus. 1972
(published posthumously). (Foreword by Lester B. Pearson.)
pp. 240

Booth, Ken. DISARMAMENT AND ARMS CONTROL in John Baylis
et al.: CONTEMPORARY STRATEGY: THEORIES AND
POLICIES. London: Croom Helm. 1975. pp. 89-113

Burhop, E[ric] H. S. THE SOVIET PEACE POLICY: FOR DÉTENTE
AND DISARMAMENT. New World Review (New York). Vol. 40.
1972 (No. 4). pp. 33-4

Butler, Christopher (Bishop). DISARMAMENT – UNILATERAL OR MULTILATERAL? The Month. Vol. 6. March 1973. pp. 82-3

Carlton, David and Schaerf, Carlo (eds.). THE DYNAMICS OF THE ARMS RACE. London: Croom Helm. 1975. Hardback. pp. 244

Groom, A. J[ohn] R. BRITISH THINKING ABOUT NUCLEAR WEAPONS. London: Frances Pinter. 1974. pp. xliii + 614. (Extensive bibliography and index)

Gutteridge, William. ARMS CONTROL AND DEVELOPING COUNTRIES in Schaerf and Barnaby (eds.) (1972). *q.v.* pp. 121-39

Gutteridge, William. ARMS CONTROL AND DEVELOPING COUNTRIES in Carlton and Schaerf (eds.) (1975). *q.v.* pp. 212-14

Harding, (Rev.) David J. THE PEACE MOVEMENT IN ENGLAND. Reconciliation Quarterly. New Series. Vol. 3. September 1973. pp. 18-24

Kaldor, Mary. FACTORS GOVERNING THE SUPPLY AND DEMAND OF MAJOR WEAPONS in Schaerf and Barnaby (eds.) (1972). *q.v.* pp. 159-93

Kennet, Wayland (2nd Baron). STILL NO DISARMAMENT. London: Fabian Society. Fabian Tract 423. 1973. Pamphlet. pp. 24

Lee, Kenneth. DISARMAMENT, GCD, SMALL STEPS, AND THE FUTURE. World Issues. No. 26. Spring 1973. pp. 6-8

Lothian, 7th Marquess of (Peter F. W. Ker). ARMS CONTROL AND DISARMAMENT. RUSI Journal. Vol. 117. March 1972. pp. 12-19

Martin, Laurence W. DISARMAMENT AND ARMS CONTROL. Chapter 12 of his book ARMS AND STRATEGY. London: Weidenfeld & Nicolson. 1973. pp. 238-51. (Published simultaneously in New York by David MacKay)

Noel-Baker, Philip J. DISARMAMENT (originally published in 1926). New York: Garland. 1972. pp. 352

Noel-Baker, Philip. HUNGER WILL RAGE UNTIL THE ARMS RACE IS STOPPED. London: Friends Peace and International Relations Committee. 1972. Pamphlet. pp. 4. (Reprint from article in THE FRIEND)

Owen, David (M.P.). THE POLITICS OF DEFENCE. London: Jonathan Cape. 1972. Hardback. pp. 249

Purnell, Robert. ARMAMENTS, DISARMAMENT AND ARMS CONTROL in chapter 7 of his book THE SOCIETY OF STATES: AN INTRODUCTION TO INTERNATIONAL POLITICS. London: Weidenfeld & Nicolson. 1973. pp. 237-47

Roberts, Adam. IS GCD DEAD? War/Peace Report. Vol. 12. January-
February 1973

Schaerf, Carlo and Barnaby, Frank (eds.). DISARMAMENT AND ARMS
CONTROL. New York, London and Paris: Gordon Breach. 1972.
Hardback. pp. 414

Sims, Nicholas A. APPROACHES TO DISARMAMENT: An introduc-
tory analysis. London: Friends Peace and International Relations
Committee. 1974. Paperback. pp. vii + 81. (Foreword by Sir Michael
Wright, G.C.M.G.)

Sims, Nicholas A. THE RETURN OF GCD? Millennium/Journal of
International Studies. Vol. 1. Summer 1971. pp. 54-66

United Nations Association Disarmament Committee. ARMS AND
MAN: A pamphlet on disarmament. London: United Nations
Association. 1971. Pamphlet. pp. 23. (Chairman of the Disarmament
Committee: Sir Michael Wright, G.C.M.G.)

Windsor, Philip. GCD AGAIN? Millennium/Journal of International
Studies. Vol. 1. Summer 1971. pp. 66-70

Young, Elizabeth (Baroness Kennet). A FAREWELL TO ARMS
CONTROL? Harmondsworth: Penguin (a Pelican Original). 1972.
Paperback. pp. 256

38. General: 1976-

Bailey, Sydney D. PARTIAL DISARMAMENT — ESSENTIAL BUT
INADEQUATE. The Friend. Vol. 135. 25 November 1977. pp.
1389-90

Barnaby, Frank and Huisken, R. ARMS UNCONTROLLED. Cambridge, Massachusetts: Harvard University Press, for SIPRI. 1975

Barnaby, Frank. GLOBAL ARMAMENTS AND DISARMAMENT.
New Malden, Surrey: Fellowship of Reconciliation. 1978.
Pamphlet. pp. 19. (The Alex Wood Memorial Lecture 1978)

Barnaby, Frank. THE MOUNTING PROSPECTS OF NUCLEAR
WAR. Bulletin of the Atomic Scientists. Vol. 33. June 1977. pp. 10-
19

Barnaby, Frank. WORLD ARMAMENT AND DISARMAMENT.
Bulletin of the Atomic Scientists. Vol. 32. June 1976. (8-page
offprint, based on SIPRI YEARBOOK 1976)

Barnaby, Frank et al. SIPRI YEARBOOK OF WORLD ARMAMENTS
AND DISARMAMENT (annual). Stockholm: Almqvist & Wiksell.

Hardback. pp. 493 (in 1976), 421 (in 1977), etc. (Co-published in U.S.A. successively with the Humanities Press and the MIT Press; in London successively with Duckworth, Elek, the MIT Press and Taylor & Francis)

Booth, Arthur. TOWARDS A QUAKER VIEW OF DISARMAMENT. Reconciliation Quarterly. New Series. Vol. 6, No. 1. March 1976. pp. 25-33

Bull, Hedley. A DISARMED WORLD in his book THE ANARCHICAL SOCIETY: A STUDY OF ORDER IN WORLD POLITICS. London: Macmillan. 1977. pp. 234-8.

Cook, Robin (M.P.). THE THREAT TO PEACE AND THE NEED FOR DISARMAMENT in Judith Hart *et al.* DEFENCE CUTS AND LABOUR'S INDUSTRIAL STRATEGY. 1976. pp. 26-31

Cox, John. ON THE WARPATH. London: Oxford University Press. 1976. Paperback. pp. 65. 'Standpoints' series of illustrated paperbacks

Cox, John. OVERKILL: THE STORY OF MODERN WEAPONS. Harmondsworth: Penguin Books. 1977. A Peacock Book (hardback in Kestrel). Paperback. pp. 205. (Preface by Professor Joseph Rotblat)

Hembry, Basil. LET CIVILISATION BEGIN! The conflict of world armaments and world development. London: UNA. 1977. Pamphlet. pp. 10

Joyce, James Avery. ARMS RACE TO OBLIVION. Contemporary Review. Vol. 230. June 1977. pp. 311-15

Kaldor, Mary *et al.* GENERAL AND COMPLETE DISARMAMENT: A SYSTEMS-ANALYSIS APPROACH. Futures. October 1976. pp. 384-96. (Co-authored with J. P. Perry Robinson (*q.v.*) and R. Curnow, M. McLean and P. Shepherd, all with the Science Policy Research Unit, University of Sussex)

Kent, (Rev. Monsignor) Bruce. DISARMAMENT. Reconciliation Quarterly. New Series. Vol. 6, No. 1. March 1976. pp. 19-24

Mendl, Wolf. THE REALITIES BEHIND DISARMAMENT NEGOTIA-TIONS. The Friend. Vol. 136. 21 April 1978. pp. 477-8

Neild, Robert. APPROACHES TO DISARMAMENT in Richard Jolly (ed.): DISARMAMENT AND WORLD DEVELOPMENT [1978], *q.v.* pp. 113-17

Noel-Baker, Philip *et al.* DISARM OR DIE: A disarmament reader for the leaders and the peoples of the world. London: Taylor & Francis, on behalf of the Non-Partisan Fund for World Disarmament and Development. 1978. Paperback. pp. viii + 108. (Foreword (pp. vii–viii) by Noel-Baker. Contributors include Frank Barnaby (*q.v.*), Sean MacBride and Olof Palme, in addition to Noel-Baker (*q.v.*))

Pentz, Michael. THE NUCLEAR ARMS RACE: New dangers, new possibilities of disarmament. London: British Peace Committee. 1976. Pamphlet. pp. 24

Sims, Nicholas A. APPROACHES TO DISARMAMENT: An introductory analysis. London: Quaker Peace and Service. 1979. Paperback. pp. 170. (Revised and expanded edition, including the original (1974) Foreword by Sir Michael Wright)

Sims, Nicholas A. GENERAL AND COMPLETE DISARMAMENT: THE ITALIAN INITIATIVE OF 1969–70 AND THE SYNOPTIC APPROACH TO THE DISARMAMENT PROCESS. Reconciliation Quarterly. New Series. Vol. 6, No. 1. March 1976. pp. 40–6

Smith, Dan. THE DÉTENTE PUZZLE. Reconciliation Quarterly. New Series. Vol. 6, No. 1. March 1976. pp. 47–52

39. Science Aspects (see also under: **42. Military Aspects; 50. Chemical and Biological Warfare**)

Burhop, E[ric] H. S. ABC WEAPONS, DISARMAMENT AND THE RESPONSIBILITY OF THE SCIENTISTS. Scientific World. Vol. 16, No. 1. 1972. pp. 5–7

Calder, Nigel (ed.). UNLESS PEACE COMES: A SCIENTIFIC FORECAST OF NEW WEAPONS. London: Allen Lane, the Penguin Press. 1968. pp. 217. (Contributors include Cockcroft (*q.v.*), Noel-Baker (*q.v.*), Stratton (*q.v.*), Thring (*q.v.*), etc. Calder's chapter: 'Summary: The New Weapons', pp. 207–16)

Calder, Nigel (ed.). UNLESS PEACE COMES: A SCIENTIFIC FORECAST OF NEW WEAPONS. New York: Viking Press. 1968. pp. 243

Calder, Nigel (ed.). UNLESS PEACE COMES: A SCIENTIFIC FORECAST OF NEW WEAPONS. Harmondsworth: Penguin, Pelican edition. 1970. Paperback. pp. 253

Carlton, David and Schaerf, Carlo (eds.). ARMS CONTROL AND TECHNOLOGICAL INNOVATION. London: Croom Helm. 1977. Hardback. pp. 288

Clarke, Robin. THE SCIENCE OF WAR AND PEACE. London: Jonathan Cape. 1971. Hardback. pp. 349

Healey, Denis (M.P.). THE SPUTNIK AND WESTERN DEFENCE.

International Affairs. Vol. 34. April 1958. pp. 145–56

Jones, D. Carog. ADVANCE IN INVENTION: ITS RELATION TO WORLD PEACE. Nature. 16 May 1942. pp. 542–4

Kemp, Geoffrey (ed.). THE OTHER ARMS RACE. Lexington, Mass.: Lexington Books. 1975

Lindop, Patricia. EFFECTS OF ATOMIC RADIATION: EXTRACTS FROM THE REPORT OF THE UN SCIENTIFIC COMMITTEE. War and Peace. Vol. 1, No. 1. January–March 1963. pp. 32–41

Lonsdale, Kathleen *et al.* AN APPEAL TO SCIENTISTS: To consider their personal responsibility for the development of nuclear weapons and for other applications of science to warfare, issued by a group of members of the Society of Friends (Quakers) who are also professional scientists. Leigh-on-Sea, Essex: Quaker Scientists' Fellowship. 1957. Pamphlet. pp. 6

Noel-Baker, Philip (M.P.). SCIENCE AND DISARMAMENT. Impact of Science on Society (Paris). Vol. 15, No. 4. 1965. pp. 211–46

Rotblat, Joseph. PUGWASH: THE FIRST TEN YEARS: HISTORY OF THE CONFERENCES ON SCIENCE AND WORLD AFFAIRS. New York: Humanities Press. 1969. pp. 244

Rotblat, Joseph. SCIENCE AND WORLD AFFAIRS: HISTORY OF THE PUGWASH CONFERENCES. London: Dawson of Pall Mall. 1962. pp. 92

Rotblat, Joseph. SCIENTISTS IN THE QUEST FOR PEACE: A HISTORY OF THE PUGWASH CONFERENCES. Cambridge, Mass.: The MIT Press. 1972. pp. xix + 399

Russell, Bertrand. THE EARLY HISTORY OF THE PUGWASH MOVEMENT in Seymour Melman (ed.): DISARMAMENT: ITS POLITICS AND ECONOMICS. Boston: American Academy of Arts and Sciences. 1962. pp. 18–31

Stratton, Andrew. CONTESTS IN THE SKY in Calder (ed.): UNLESS PEACE COMES. 1968, 1970. (1968 edn) pp. 67–87

Thring, Meredith W. ROBOTS ON THE MARCH in Calder (ed.): UNLESS PEACE COMES. 1968, 1970. (1968 edn) pp. 207–16

Zuckerman, Sir Solly. JUDGMENT AND CONTROL IN MODERN WARFARE. Foreign Affairs (New York). January 1962

Zuckerman, Sir Solly. SCIENTISTS AND WAR. London: Hamish Hamilton. 1966. pp. xii + 177

40. Economic Aspects

Allaun, Frank (M.P.). THE WASTED £30,000,000,000 SPENT ON FALSE SECURITY. London: NATSOPA. n.d. [1974]. Pamphlet. pp. 39

Barnaby, Frank. THE SCALE OF WORLD MILITARY EXPENDITURES in Jolly (ed.): DISARMAMENT AND WORLD DEVELOPMENT [1978]. pp. 7-25

Blackaby, Frank. THE BURDEN OF DEFENCE SPENDING AND THE PROBLEMS OF TRANSITION in Judith Hart *et al.* DEFENCE CUTS AND LABOUR'S INDUSTRIAL STRATEGY. 1976. pp. 8-12

Brown, Professor A. J. THE ECONOMIC CONSEQUENCES OF DISARMAMENT. London: David Davies Memorial Institute of International Affairs. 1964. Pamphlet. pp. 20. (David Davies Annual Memorial Lecture for 1964)

CND. ARMS, JOBS AND THE CRISIS. London: CND. 1975. Pamphlet. pp. 20

Carter, Charles [Frederick]. SOME ECONOMIC PROBLEMS OF DISARMAMENT. London: Friends Peace Committee. n.d. [1959]. Pamphlet. pp. 13

Cooley, Mike. THE SEARCH FOR ALTERNATIVES: THE LUCAS AEROSPACE WORKERS' PLAN in Judith Hart *et al.* DEFENCE CUTS AND LABOUR'S INDUSTRIAL STRATEGY. 1976. pp. 13-18

Dale, Rowland. SWORDS INTO PLOUGHSHARES [Lucas Aerospace proposals]. The Friend. 30 June 1978. pp. 791-2

Dickinson, H. D. *et al.* THE ECONOMIC CONSEQUENCES OF DISARMAMENT IN BRISTOL: A GROUP STUDY. Bristol: Bristol Standing Conference on Disarmament. [1968]. Pamphlet. pp. 24

Economist Intelligence Unit. THE ECONOMIC EFFECTS OF DISARMAMENT. London: Economist Intelligence Unit, for the United World Trust for Education and Research. 1968. Hardback. pp. xiii + 224

Einzig, Paul. PLAN FOR GERMANY'S ECONOMIC DISARMAMENT. Economic Journal. Vol. 52. June 1942. pp. 176-85

Elliott, Dave, Kaldor, Mary, Smith, Dan and Smith, Ron. ALTERNATIVE WORK FOR MILITARY INDUSTRIES. London: Richardson Institute for Peace and Conflict Research. 1977. Large pamphlet format. pp. 68

Elliott, Dave. THE LUCAS AEROSPACE ALTERNATIVE CORPO-
RATE PLAN in Elliott *et al.* : ALTERNATIVE WORK FOR
MILITARY INDUSTRIES [1977] , *q.v.* pp. 62-8

Feinstein, Charles. THE ECONOMIC CASE FOR DISARMAMENT
(review article). War and Peace. Vol. 1, No. 2. Summer 1963. pp. 55-
64

Freedman, Lawrence. ARMS PRODUCTION IN THE UNITED
KINGDOM: PROBLEMS AND PROSPECTS. London: Royal
Institute of International Affairs, British Foreign Policy to 1985
Series. 1978. Large pamphlet format. pp. 50

Goodman, Geoffrey. THE ECONOMIC CONSEQUENCES OF STAY-
ING ALIVE. London: CND. n.d. [1964]. Pamphlet. pp. 29

Griffiths, David. INTRODUCTION in Judith Hart *et al.* DEFENCE
CUTS AND LABOUR'S INDUSTRIAL STRATEGY. 1976. pp. 2-7

Hart, Judith (M.P.) *et al.* DEFENCE CUTS AND LABOUR'S INDUS-
TRIAL STRATEGY. London: CND, a Labour CND Pamphlet.
1976. Pamphlet. pp. 36. (Contributors include Blackaby (*q.v.*),
Cooley (*q.v.*), Holland (*q.v.*), Cook (*q.v.*) and Griffiths (*q.v.*))

Holland, Stuart. LABOUR'S INDUSTRIAL STRATEGY AND
DEFENCE CONVERSION in Judith Hart *et al.* : DEFENCE CUTS
AND LABOUR'S INDUSTRIAL STRATEGY. 1976. pp. 20-5

Jolly, Richard (ed.). DISARMAMENT AND WORLD DEVELOP-
MENT. Oxford: Pergamon Press, Pergamon International Library.
1978. Hardback and Paperback. pp. xiii + 185. (Contributors
include Barnaby (*q.v.*), Neild (*q.v.*), Noel-Baker (*q.v.*), Robin
Luckham, Alva Myrdal, Inga Thorsson, Mary Kaldor, Brian Johnson
and Ruth Leger Sivard)

Jolly, Richard. OBJECTIVES AND MEANS FOR LINKING DIS-
ARMAMENT TO DEVELOPMENT in Jolly (ed.): DISARMA-
MENT AND WORLD DEVELOPMENT. [1978]. *q.v.* pp. 105-12

Kaldor, Mary. CASE-STUDY: THE ANTI-SUBMARINE WARFARE
(ASW) CRUISER (i) Background to the project; (ii) Alternative
employment for naval shipbuilding workers; in Labour Party:
SENSE ABOUT DEFENCE [1977]. *q.v.* pp. 139-54

Kaldor, Mary. DEFENCE CUTS AND THE DEFENCE INDUSTRY
(pp. 13-27) and THE ANTI-SUBMARINE WARFARE (ASW)
CRUISER: A CASE STUDY OF POTENTIAL FOR CONVERSION
IN THE SHIPBUILDING INDUSTRY (pp. 46-56) in Elliott *et al.* :
ALTERNATIVE WORK FOR MILITARY INDUSTRIES [1977],
q.v.

Kaldor, Mary. EUROPEAN DEFENCE INDUSTRIES: NATIONAL
AND INTERNATIONAL IMPLICATIONS. Brighton, Sussex:
Institute for the Study of International Organisations (University of
Sussex). ISIO Monograph No. 8. 1972. Large pamphlet format.
pp. 79

Kennedy, Gavin. DISARMAMENT. Chapter 9 of his book THE
ECONOMICS OF DEFENCE. London: Faber & Faber. 1975.
pp. 214–23

Mack, Andrew. THE UNDERCOVER ARMS RACE (the 'internalist'
theory of superpower arms procurement decisions). New Scientist.
Vol. 60, 29 November 1973. pp. 638–40

Mikardo, Ian (M.P.). THE ECONOMIC CONSEQUENCES OF RE-
ARMAMENT AND DISARMAMENT in National Peace Council:
WORLD DISARMAMENT, *q.v.* [1953]. pp. 60–9

Noel-Baker, Philip. DISARMAMENT AND DEVELOPMENT in Richard
Jolly (ed.): DISARMAMENT AND WORLD DEVELOPMENT
[1978], *q.v.* pp. 3–6

Rosenbaum, E. M. WAR ECONOMICS: A BIBLIOGRAPHICAL
APPROACH (to comprehensive bibliography). Economica.
February 1942. pp. 64–94

Shenfield, A. A. THE IMPACT OF REDUCTIONS OF DEFENCE
REQUIREMENTS ON BRITISH INDUSTRY. RUSI Journal.
February 1959. pp. 5–17

Smith, Dan. CASE-STUDY: TORNADO, THE MULTI-ROLE COMBAT
AIRCRAFT (MRCA) (i) Background to the project; (ii) Conversion
and diversification in the aerospace industry; in Labour Party: SENSE
ABOUT DEFENCE [1977], *q.v.* pp. 113–38

Smith, Dan. PRINCIPLES OF A CONVERSION PROGRAMME (pp.
28–35), MRCA TORNADO: A CASE STUDY OF POTENTIAL
FOR CONVERSION AND DIVERSIFICATION IN THE AERO-
SPACE INDUSTRY (pp. 36–45) and COMMUNITY PLANNING
AND BASE CONVERSION (pp. 57–61) in Elliott *et al.*: ALTERNA-
TIVE WORK FOR MILITARY INDUSTRIES [1977], *q.v.*

Smith, Ron. MILITARY EXPENDITURE AND THE ECONOMY in
Elliott *et al.*: ALTERNATIVE WORK FOR MILITARY INDUS-
TRIES [1977], *q.v.* pp 5–12

United Nations Association. DISARMAMENT AND JOBS: Report of
a working party. London: UNA. 1965. Pamphlet. pp. 30

United World Trust for Education and Research. DISARMAMENT:
WHAT IT WOULD MEAN TO BRITAIN'S ECONOMY. London:

United World Trust for Education and Research. 1963. Pamphlet. (Summary of the study by the Economist Intelligence Unit (*q.v.*) commissioned by the Trust)

Wilson, Harold (M.P.). THE PROBLEM OF WORLD POVERTY in National Peace Council: WORLD DISARMAMENT. 1953. pp. 70-8

41. Foreign Policy Aspects (see also under: **45. Nuclear Weapons: Other Countries; 42. Military Aspects; 56. Unilateral Nuclear Disarmament**)

Bailey, Gerald. THE EAST-WEST PROBLEM: A REASSESSMENT. London: Friends East-West Relations Committee. 1960. Pamphlet. pp. 71

Bailey, Gerald. PROBLEMS OF PEACE. London: Ginn, The World Today Series. 1970. Paperback. pp. 160

Blackett, P[atrick] M. S. (later Lord Blackett). ATOMIC WEAPONS AND EAST-WEST RELATIONS. London: Cambridge University Press. 1956. Hardback. pp. vi + 107. (Based on the Lees Knowles Lectures on Military Science delivered at Trinity College, Cambridge, 1956)

Buchan, (The Hon.) Alastair. THE MULTILATERAL FORCE: AN HISTORICAL PERSPECTIVE. London: Institute for Strategic Studies, Adelphi Paper No. 13. 1964. Pamphlet. pp. 18

Buchan, (The Hon.) Alastair. THE MULTILATERAL FORCE: A STUDY IN ALLIANCE POLITICS. International Affairs. Vol. 40. October 1964. pp. 619-37

Chalfont, Alun. THE DANGERS OF A NUCLEAR EUROPE. New Statesman. Vol. 81. 16 August 1971. pp. 520-1

Crossman, R[ichard] H. S. (M.P.). WESTERN DEFENCE IN THE SIXTIES. RUSI Journal. August 1961

Gittings, John and Gott, Richard. NATO's FINAL DECADE. London: London Region CND. 1964. Pamphlet. pp. 28

Gott, Richard and Gittings, John. NATO's FINAL DECADE. Views. Vol. 5. Summer 1964. pp. 140-51

Hall, Stuart. NATO AND THE ALLIANCES (CND's policy of positive neutralism). London: London Regional Council CND. n.d. [1960]. Pamphlet. pp. 8

Healey, Denis (M.P.). A LABOUR BRITAIN AND THE WORLD. London: Fabian Society, Fabian Tract 352. 1964

Healey, Denis (M.P.). NEUTRALISM. London: Ampersand, Bellman

Books No. 4. 1955. Paperback. pp. 64

Heelas, Terence. THE NATO SHEET-ANCHOR. London: CND. n.d. [1964]. Pamphlet. pp. 8. (A Labour CND Discussion Pamphlet)

Howard, Michael L. NOT EAST, NOT WEST (CND's policy of positive neutralism). London: London Regional Council CND. 1960. Pamphlet. pp. 8

Martin, Laurence W. DISARMAMENT: AN AGENCY IN SEARCH OF A POLICY. Reporter. Vol. 29. 4 July 1963. pp. 22-6

Mulley, F[rederick] W. (M.P.). NATO's NUCLEAR PROBLEMS: CONTROL OR CONSULTATION. Orbis. Vol. 8. Spring 1964. pp. 21-35

Mulley, F[rederick] W. (M.P.). THE POLITICS OF WESTERN DEFENCE. New York: Praeger. 1962. pp. 282. London: Thames & Hudson. 1962. Hardback. pp. xiv + 282

Newens, Stan. THE CASE AGAINST NATO: The danger of the nuclear alliances. London: CND and other organisations. 1972. Pamphlet. pp. 17

Russell, Bertrand (3rd Earl Russell). UNARMED VICTORY. London: George Allen & Unwin. 1963. Hardback. pp. 155. Harmondsworth: Penguin. 1963. Paperback. pp. 120

Sims, Nicholas A. DIPLOMACY OF DISARMAMENT: EUROPEAN CAPABILITIES IN THE SALT ERA. Clare Market Review. Vol. 66. Summer 1971. pp. 91-103

Sims, Nicholas A. NATIONALISM, INTERNATIONALISM, OR NON-ALIGNMENT (CND's policy of positive neutralism) in Carter (ed.) (q.v.). 1966. pp. 40-9

Slessor, Sir John (Marshal of the RAF). WHAT PRICE CO-EXISTENCE? A policy for the Western alliance. New York: Praeger. 1961. London: Cassell. 1962. pp. 153. (Cassell 1962 edn)

Verrier, Anthony. DEFENCE AND POLITICS AFTER NASSAU. Political Quarterly. Vol. 34. July-September 1963. pp. 269-78

Young, Wayland. THE INSOLUBLE ISSUE (MLF and NATO). Listener. Vol. 72. 30 July 1964. pp. 147-8, 169

Younger, Kenneth. DIPLOMACY IN THE AGE OF NUCLEAR STRATEGY. Nottingham: University of Nottingham. 1961. Pamphlet. pp. 16. (Series: Montague Burton Lectures in International Relations)

Zilliacus, Konni (M.P.). ANATOMY OF A SACRED COW: Ruthless realism about NATO, nuclear weapons and US bases. London: CND. 1962. Pamphlet. pp. 21

42. Military Aspects (see also under: 39. Science Aspects; 41. Foreign Policy Aspects; 44. Atomic Energy and Nuclear Weapons; 56. Unilateral Nuclear Disarmament)

Barnaby, Frank. THE BALANCE OF TERROR. Humanist. Vol. 85. May 1970. pp. 137-9

Barnaby, Frank and Boserup, Anders (eds.). IMPLICATIONS OF ANTI-BALLISTIC MISSILE SYSTEMS. London: Souvenir Press. 1969. Pugwash Monograph No. 2. pp. x + 246. (Chapters by Barnaby: 1 (pp. 3-25) 'The development and characteristics of Anti-Ballistic Missile systems' and 2 (pp. 26-35) 'Arguments for and against the deployment of Anti-Ballistic Missile systems'. Contributors include Carlton (*q.v.*), Feld, Leitenberg, etc.)

Barnaby, Frank. PRECISION WARFARE. New Scientist. Vol. 66. 8 May 1975. pp. 304-7

Barnaby, Frank. THE SCALE OF WORLD MILITARY EXPENDITURES and HIROSHIMA AND NAGASAKI: THE SURVIVORS in Richard Jolly (ed.): DISARMAMENT AND WORLD DEVELOPMENT [1978], *q.v.* pp. 7-33

Beaton, Leonard. THE WESTERN ALLIANCE AND THE McNAMARA DOCTRINE. London: Institute for Strategic Studies, Adelphi Paper, No. 11. 1964. Pamphlet. pp. 16

Bellany, Ian. THE CENTRAL BALANCE: ARMS RACE AND ARMS CONTROL in Carsten Holbraad (ed.): SUPER-POWERS AND WORLD ORDER. Canberra: Australian National University Press. 1971. pp. 41-63

Bellany, Ian. THE ESSENTIAL ARITHMETIC OF DETERRENCE. RUSI Journal. Vol. 118. March 1973. pp. 28-34

Bellini, James and Pattie, Geoffrey. BRITISH DEFENCE OPTIONS: A GAULLIST PERSPECTIVE. Survival. Vol. 19. September-October 1977 . 217-24. (Includes a critique of Robin Cook *et al.*: Defence Review: An Anti-White Paper (1975), *q.v.*)

Blackett, P[atrick] M. S. STUDIES OF WAR, NUCLEAR AND CONVENTIONAL. Edinburgh: Oliver & Boyd. 1962. Hardback. pp. viii + 242

Bow Group. STABILITY AND SURVIVAL: A Bow Group discussion about defence policy. London: Bow Group. 1961. Pamphlet. pp. 45

Brown, Neville. ARMS WITHOUT EMPIRE: British defence role in the modern world. Harmondsworth: Penguin (a Penguin Special). 1967. Paperback. pp. 159

Brown, Neville. BRITAIN IN NATO. London: Fabian Society, Fabian Tract 357. 1964. Pamphlet. pp. 16

Brown, Neville. BRITISH ARMS AND STRATEGY 1970-1980. London: RUSI. 1969. Pamphlet. pp. 73

Brown, Neville *et al.* DEFENCE IN A NEW SETTING. London: Fabian Society, Fabian Tract 386. 1968. Pamphlet. pp. 29

Brown, Neville. NUCLEAR WAR: THE IMPENDING STRATEGIC DEADLOCK. London: Pall Mall Press. 1964 (i.e. 1965). Hardback. pp. 238

Brown, Neville. TOWARDS A WORLD CRISIS in George Cunningham (ed.): BRITAIN AND THE WORLD IN THE SEVENTIES: A COLLECTION OF FABIAN ESSAYS. London: Weidenfeld & Nicolson, on behalf of the Fabian Society. 1970. pp. 30-57

Brown, Neville. AN UNSTABLE BALANCE OF TERROR? The World Today. Vol. 26. January 1970. pp. 38-46

Buchan, (The Hon.) Alastair. NATO IN THE 1960s: THE IMPLICA-TIONS OF INTERDEPENDENCE. London: Weidenfeld & Nicolson, for the Institute for Strategic Studies, Studies in International Society, No. 1. 1960. Hardback. pp. xii + 131. (Foreword by Marshal of the RAF Sir John Slessor)

Buchan, (The Hon.) Alastair. NATO IN THE 1960s: THE IMPLICA-TIONS OF INTERDEPENDENCE (revised edition). London: Chatto & Windus. 1963. Hardback. pp. 179

Buchan, (The Hon.) Alastair (ed.). PROBLEMS OF MODERN STRATEGY. London: Chatto & Windus, for the Institute for Strategic Studies, Studies in International Security. No. 14. 1970. Hardback. pp. 219. (Previously published by the Institute as Adelphi Papers 54 and 55, pp. 54 and 52 respectively, in pamphlet format, London. 1969. Contributors include Bull (*q.v.*))

Buchan, (The Hon.) Alastair. WAR IN MODERN SOCIETY: AN INTRODUCTION. London: Watts, New Thinker's Library, No. 4. 1966. Hardback. pp. xvi + 207

Buchan, (The Hon.) Alastair. WAR IN MODERN SOCIETY: AN INTRODUCTION. London: Fontana. 1968. Paperback. pp. xv + 208 (The 1966 (Watts) edition, corrected)

Buzzard, Rear-Admiral Sir Anthony. THE POSSIBILITIES OF CON-VENTIONAL DEFENCE. London: Institute for Strategic Studies, Adelphi Paper, No. 6. 1963. Pamphlet. pp. 19

Carlton, David. ANTI-BALLISTIC MISSILE DEPLOYMENT AND THE DOCTRINE OF LIMITED NUCLEAR WAR in Barnaby and Boserup (eds.): IMPLICATIONS OF ANTI-BALLISTIC MISSILE

SYSTEMS. 1969. pp. 126-38

Chalfont, Alun. SLOWING DOWN THE MISSILE RACE. New Statesman. 28 August 1970. pp. 231-2

Cook, Robin F. (M.P.), Holloway, David, Kaldor, Mary and Smith, Dan.
DEFENCE REVIEW: AN ANTI-WHITE PAPER. London: Fabian
Society, Fabian Research Series 323. 1975. Pamphlet. pp. 24

Cook, Robin F. (M.P.) and Smith, Dan. WHAT FUTURE IN NATO?
London: Fabian Society, Fabian Research Series No. 337. 1978.
Pamphlet. pp. 27

Freedman, Lawrence. THE BALANCE OF TERROR. New Society. 2
June 1977. pp. 441-2

Freedman, Lawrence. EUROPEAN SECURITY: THE PROSPECT OF
CHALLENGE. RUSI Journal. Vol. 123, No. 1. March 1978. pp. 20-
6

Garnett, John C. THE DEFENCE DEBATE. International Relations.
Vol. 2. October 1965. pp. 813-29

Greenwood, David. CONSTRAINTS AND CHOICES IN THE TRANS-
FORMATION OF BRITAIN'S DEFENCE EFFORT SINCE 1945.
British Journal of International Studies. Vol. 2, No. 1. April 1976.
pp. 5-27

Gwynne-Jones, Alun. MODERN STRATEGIC CONCEPTS. RUSI
Journal. Vol. 108. February 1963. pp. 4-13

Gwynne-Jones, Alun. THE ROLE OF BRITISH DEFENCE. Listener.
Vol. 69. 31 January 1963. pp. 193-5

Gwynne-Jones, Alun and McLachlan, Donald. THE STRATEGY OF
SURVIVAL: THE BRITISH RESPONSE. Listener. Vol. 67. 29
March 1962. pp. 548-51

Howard, Michael. THE CONTINENTAL COMMITMENT: THE
DILEMMA OF BRITISH DEFENCE POLICY IN THE ERA OF THE
TWO WORLD WARS. London: Temple Smith. 1972. (Ford Lectures
in the University of Oxford, 1971)

Howard, Michael. DISARMAMENT AND THE MILITARY BALANCE
(public lecture delivered at the University of Leeds, 1964), published
in his book STUDIES IN WAR AND PEACE. London: Maurice
Temple Smith. 1970. New York: Viking. 1971. pp. 213-23

Irwin, Christopher. NUCLEAR ASPECTS OF WEST EUROPEAN
DEFENCE INTEGRATION. International Affairs. Vol. 47. October
1971. pp. 412-15.

Labour Party. SENSE ABOUT DEFENCE: The Report of the Labour
Party Defence Study Group. London: Quartet Books. 1977. Paper-

112

back. pp. 166. (Introduction by Ian Mikardo, M.P. Includes case-studies by Mary Kaldor (*q.v.*) and Dan Smith (*q.v.*))

Mack, Andrew. STORMCLOUDS AHEAD FOR THE B-1 BOMBER. New Scientist. Vol. 64. 21 November 1974. pp. 562-4

Mackintosh, J. M[alcolm]. SOVIET THINKING ON WAR. Chapter 21 of his book STRATEGY AND TACTICS OF SOVIET FOREIGN POLICY. London: OUP. 1962. pp. 274-89. (Includes Soviet disarmament policy and ideas)

Mackintosh, Malcolm. DISARMAMENT AND SOVIET MILITARY POLICY in Louis Henkin (ed.): ARMS CONTROL: ISSUES FOR THE PUBLIC. Englewood Cliffs, New Jersey: Prentice-Hall, for the American Assembly and Columbia University. 1961. pp. 141-58

Martin, Laurence W. BALLISTIC MISSILE DEFENCE AND ARMS CONTROL. Arms Control and Disarmament (Washington). Vol. 1. 1968. pp. 61-7

Martin, Laurence W. BRITISH DEFENCE POLICY: THE LONG RECESSIONAL. London: Institute for Strategic Studies, Adelphi Paper, No. 61. 1969. Pamphlet. pp. 22

Mulley, F[rederick] W. (M.P.). EUROPE AND THE MEDITERRANEAN. RUSI Journal. Vol. 108. May 1963. pp. 121-30

Owen, David (M.P.). A NUCLEAR STRATEGY FOR EUROPE. New Scientist. Vol. 54. 1 June 1972. pp. 503-5

Raison, Timothy. THE MISSILE YEARS: THOUGHTS ON THE EVOLUTION OF BRITISH DEFENCE POLICY. London: Conservative Political Centre, CPC Publications, No. 203. 1959. Pamphlet. pp. 20

Richardson, James L. TWO THEORIES OF WESTERN EUROPEAN DEFENCE. Year Book of World Affairs. 1961

Slessor, Sir John (Marshal of the RAF). COMMAND AND CONTROL OF ALLIED NUCLEAR FORCES: A BRITISH VIEW. London: Institute for Strategic Studies, Adelphi Paper, No. 22. 1965. Pamphlet. pp. 16

Slessor, Sir John (Marshal of the RAF). NUCLEAR DETERRENCE IN A CHANGING STRATEGIC SETTING. RUSI Journal. Vol. 109. November 1964. pp. 309-14

Slessor, Sir John (Marshal of the RAF). STRATEGY FOR THE WEST. London: Cassell. 1954. pp. xv + 162

Smart, Ian. DISSUASION ET MAÎTRISE DES ARMES STRATÉGIQUES. Politique Etrangère (Paris). Vol. 35, No. 2. 1970. pp. 159-79

113

Smith, Dan and Cox, John. NATO RULES OK? London: CND. 1978.
  Pamphlet. pp. 22. (Foreword by Bruce Kent, Chairman of CND)
Strachey, John (M.P.). IS OUR DETERRENT VULNERABLE? A
  DISCUSSION OF WESTERN DEFENCE IN THE 1960s. Inter-
  national Affairs. Vol. 37. January 1961. pp. 1-8
Verrier, Anthony. AN ARMY FOR THE SIXTIES: A study in national
  policy, contract and obligation. London: Secker & Warburg. 1966.
  Hardback. pp. 288
Verrier, Anthony. THE END OF INDEPENDENCE. RUSI Journal. Vol.
  109. May 1964. pp. 136-40
Verrier, Anthony. STRATEGIC THINKING IN EUROPE. RUSI Journal.
  May 1962
Walker, Peter (M.P.). THE OPPOSITION's VIEW OF BRITISH DEFEN
  DEFENCE POLICY. RUSI Journal. Vol. 120. June 1975. pp. 3-8
Williams, Alan Lee. IS A EUROPEAN NUCLEAR FORCE DESIR-
  ABLE? Atlantic Community Quarterly (Washington). Vol. 10.
  Summer 1972. pp. 185-7
Young, Elizabeth (Baroness Kennet). WEAPONS FOR COLD WAR
  TWO. Listener. Vol. 78. 9 November 1967. pp. 591-3

43. Legal Aspects

Bailey, Sydney D. CAN THERE BE AN ETHICAL BASIS FOR THE
  REGULATION OF WEAPONS? Crucible. January 1974. pp.
  13-18
Bailey, Sydney D. PROHIBITIONS AND RESTRAINTS IN WAR.
  London: Oxford University Press, for the Royal Institute of Inter-
  national Affairs. 1972. Hardback and Paperback editions. pp. xiii +
  194
Bailey, Sydney D. PROTECTING CIVILIANS IN WAR. Survival. Vol.
  14. November-December 1972. pp. 262-7
Best, Geoffrey. THE GENEVA CONVENTIONS: PAST, PRESENT
  AND FUTURE. RUSI Journal. Vol. 119. June 1974. pp. 22-7
Bowett, D[erek] W. DISARMAMENT AND AN INTERNATIONAL
  FORCE. Chapter 16 of his book UNITED NATIONS FORCES: A
  LEGAL STUDY OF UNITED NATIONS PRACTICE. London:
  Stevens, for the David Davies Memorial Institute of International
  Studies. 1964

Bowett, Derek W. THE INTERNATIONAL DISARMAMENT ORGANISATION, THE UNITED NATIONS AND THE VETO in CAMBRIDGE ESSAYS IN INTERNATIONAL LAW: ESSAYS IN HONOUR OF LORD McNAIR. London: Stevens. New York: Oceana. 1965. pp. 1-23

Brownlie, Ian. INTERNATIONAL LAW AND THE USE OF FORCE BY STATES. Oxford: Clarendon Press. 1963. Hardback. pp. xxviii + 532

Brownlie, Ian. SOME LEGAL ASPECTS OF THE USE OF NUCLEAR WEAPONS. International and Comparative Law Quarterly. Vol. 14. April 1965. pp. 437-51

Draper, G[erald] I. A. D. THE EMERGING LAW OF WEAPONS RESTRAINT. Survival. Vol. 19. January-February 1977. pp. 9-15

Draper, G[erald] I. A. D. THE ORIGINS OF THE JUST WAR TRADI-TION. New Blackfriars. Vol. 46. November 1964. pp. 82-8

Draper, G[erald] I. A. D. THE RED CROSS CONVENTIONS. London: Stevens & Sons. 1958. Hardback. pp. ix + 228. (Includes the texts of the four Conventions (of 1949) and the Geneva Conventions Act 1957)

Johnson, D[avid] H. N. LEGALITY OF MODERN FORMS OF AERIAL WARFARE. Aeronautical Journal. August 1968

Martin, Andrew. LEGAL ASPECTS OF DISARMAMENT. London: Stevens, for the British Institute of International and Comparative Law. 1963. pp. v + 133. (INTERNATIONAL AND COMPARATIVE LAW QUARTERLY, Supplementary Publication, No. 7)

O'Connell, D[aniel] P. THE LEGALITY OF NAVAL CRUISE MISSILES. American Journal of International Law. Vol. 66. October 1972. pp. 785-94

Schwarzenberger, Georg. THE LEGALITY OF NUCLEAR WEAPONS. London: Stevens & Sons, for the London Institute of World Affairs, Library of World Affairs, No. 43. 1958. Pamphlet. pp. 61

Suter, Keith D. MODERNIZING THE LAWS OF WAR. Australian Outlook. Vol. 29. August 1975. pp. 211-19

Young, Elizabeth. NEW LAWS FOR OLD NAVIES: MILITARY IMPLICATIONS OF THE LAW OF THE SEA. Survival. Vol. 16. November-December 1974. pp. 262-7

44. Atomic Energy and Nuclear Weapons (see also under: **46. Nuclear Testing; 47. Nuclear Proliferation; 51. Strategic Arms Limitation Talks; 55. Christian Churches; 56. Unilateral Nuclear Disarmament**)

Barnaby, Frank. MAN AND THE ATOM: THE USES OF NUCLEAR ENERGY. New York: Funk & Wagnalls. 1971. pp. 216

Barnaby, Frank. THE NUCLEAR FUTURE. London: Fabian Society, Fabian Tract 394. 1969. Pamphlet. pp. 61. (Includes contributions by Alan Lee Williams, M.P. and Geoffrey Lee Williams)

Beaton, Leonard. DEFENCE IN THE NUCLEAR AGE. Listener. 30 April 1959. pp. 743-4

Blackett, P[atrick] M. S. THE ATOM AND THE CHARTER. London Fabian Society. 1949

Blackett, P[atrick] M. S. (later Lord Blackett). MILITARY AND POLITICAL CONSEQUENCES OF ATOMIC ENERGY. London: Turnstile Press. 1948

Blackett, P[atrick] M. S. NUCLEAR WEAPONS AND DEFENCE: COMMENTS ON KISSINGER, KENNAN AND KING-HALL. International Affairs. Vol. 34. October 1958. pp. 421-34

Buchan, (The Hon.) Alastair. BRITAIN AND THE NUCLEAR DETER-RENT. Political Quarterly. Vol. 31. January-March 1960. pp. 36-45

Buchan, (The Hon.) Alastair. THEIR BOMB AND OURS. Encounter. January 1959. pp. 11-18

Bull, Hedley. BOMBS AND BALANCES. Spectator. 25 October 1963. pp. 521-3

Bull, Hedley. EUROPE AND THE BOMB. Spectator. 29 June 1962. pp. 849-51

Bull, Hedley. LIMITATIONS IN STRATEGIC NUCLEAR WAR. Listener. Vol. 69. 24 January 1963. pp. 147-9

Bull, Hedley. LIMITED AND NUCLEAR WAR. Survival. March 1963

Burhop, E[ric] H. S. and Hasted, John. THE CHALLENGE OF ATOMIC ENERGY. London: Lawrence & Wishart. 1951. Paperback. pp. x + 137

Burhop, Eric. THE NEUTRON BOMB. London: CND. 1978 (2nd edn). Pamphlet. pp. 15. (A first, duplicated edition was published in 1977 by ASLEF)

Buzzard, Rear-Admiral Sir Anthony. MASSIVE RETALIATION AND GRADUATED DETERRENCE. World Politics. January 1956

Buzzard, Rear-Admiral Sir Anthony. THE H-BOMB: MASSIVE RETALIATION OR GRADUATED DETERRENCE? International

Affairs. April 1956

Carey, Roger. THE BRITISH NUCLEAR FORCE: DETERRENT OR
ECONOMY MEASURE? Military Affairs (Manhattan, Kansas). Vol.
36. December 1972. pp. 133-8

Carlton, David. GREAT BRITAIN AND NUCLEAR WEAPONS: THE
ACADEMIC INQUEST. British Journal of International Studies.
Vol. 2. July 1976. pp. 164-72

Chalfont, Lord. NUCLEAR WEAPONS AND FOREIGN POLICY.
Internationale Spectator (The Hague). Vol. 21. 8 October 1967.
pp. 1356-68

Chalfont, Lord. NUCLEAR WEAPONS AND WORLD POWER
(1. Dimensions of Violence; 2. Prospects of Peace). The Listener.
Vol. 75, Nos. 20 and 27. January 1966. pp. 83-5, 119-20, 139

Cochrane, (The Hon.) Sir Ralph. THE BRITISH NUCLEAR DETER-
RENT AFTER THE BAHAMAS AGREEMENT. RUSI Journal. Vol.
108. February 1963. pp. 31-5

Cook, Robin F. (M.P.). GERMANY'S DANGEROUS NUCLEAR DEAL.
New Statesman. 11 July 1975. pp. 48-9

Coulson, C[harles] A. SOME PROBLEMS OF THE ATOMIC AGE.
London: Epworth Press, Scott Lidgett Memorial Lectures, No. 2.
1957. Pamphlet. pp. 40

Crossman, R[ichard] H. S. (M.P.). THE NUCLEAR OBSESSION.
Encounter. July 1958

Edwards, Bob. WAR ON THE PEOPLE. Independent Labour Party.
1943. (The St. Helens speech presaging atomic destruction; see
Driver, 1964, *op. cit.*)

Glasgow, George. CHILD OF TERROR: THE PEACE BORN OF THE
THERMONUCLEAR MENACE. London: Pall Mall Press. 1958.
Hardback. pp. xi + 148. (Foreword by Dr. G. P. Gooch)

Gollancz, Victor. THE DEVIL'S REPERTOIRE: OR NUCLEAR
BOMBING AND THE LIFE OF MAN. London: Victor Gollancz.
1958. Hardback. pp. 192

Goold-Adams, Richard. THOSE AGAINST THE H-BOMB. Brassey's
Annual. 1958. pp. 90-7

Gott, Richard. THE EVOLUTION OF THE INDEPENDENT BRITISH
DETERRENT. International Affairs. Vol. 39. April 1963. pp.
238-52

Habgood, Rt. Rev. John S. (91st Bishop of Durham). THE PROLIFE-
RATION OF NUCLEAR TECHNOLOGY. London: Council on
Christian Approaches to Defence and Disarmament in association

117

with the British Council of Churches. 1977. Pamphlet. pp. 14

Hartley, Anthony. THE BRITISH BOMB: WHAT DETERS WHO, HOW AND WHY. Encounter. Vol. 22. May 1964. pp. 22–34

Heckstall-Smith, H. W. ATOMIC RADIATION DANGERS AND WHAT THEY MEAN TO YOU. London: Dent. 1958

Hodgson, Peter. NUCLEAR PHYSICS IN PEACE AND WAR. London: Burns & Oates, Faith and Fact Books, No. 128. 1961. Hardback. pp. 159

Howard, Michael. BOMBING AND THE BOMB. Encounter. Vol. 18. April 1962. pp. 20–6

Hudson, G. F. THAT TEN PER CENT: THE FOLLY OF 'OUR BOMB'. Encounter. Vol. 19. July 1962. pp. 54–5

Johnson, Paul. THE TORIES AND THE BOMB. New Statesman. Vol. 68. 9 October 1964. pp. 546–7

Johnson, Paul. WILL WILSON KEEP THE BOMB? New Statesman. Vol. 66. 13 December 1963. pp. 866–8

Jones, Roy E. NUCLEAR DETERRENCE: A SHORT POLITICAL ANALYSIS. London: Routledge & Kegan Paul, Library of Political Studies. 1968. Hardback. pp. viii + 113

Labour Research Department.* FACTS ON THE NUCLEAR ARMS RACE. London: Labour Research Department. 1958. Pamphlet. pp. 24. (*An independent socialist organisation, not to be confused with the Research Department of the Labour Party)

Lonsdale, Kathleen. ATOMIC ENERGY AND MORAL ISSUES, I in Rotblat (ed.): q.v. (1954). pp. 56–63

Lonsdale, Kathleen. CAN THE USE OF ATOMIC WEAPONS EVER BE JUSTIFIED? London: Friends Peace Committee. 1949. Pamphlet. pp. 4

Lonsdale, Kathleen. FACTS ABOUT ATOMIC ENERGY. London: Peace News, a Peace News Pamphlet. 1947 (two printings, May and November). Pamphlet. pp. 8

McAllister, Gilbert (ed.). THE BOMB: CHALLENGE AND ANSWER. London: Batsford. 1955. Hardback. pp. 160. (Contributors include Bertrand Russell and Lord Beveridge)

MacKinnon, D[onald] M. THE MORAL SIGNIFICANCE OF THE ATOMIC BOMB. Humanitas. Vol. 2. 1949. pp. 335–48

Maxwell, Stephen. RATIONALITY IN DETERRENCE. London: Institute for Strategic Studies, Adelphi Paper, No. 50. 1968. Pamphlet. pp. 19

Miller, Harold. THE NEUTRON BOMB. Reconciliation Quarterly. New

Series. Vol. 8, No. 2. June 1978. pp. 21-4

Moss, Norman. MEN WHO PLAY GOD: THE STORY OF THE HYDROGEN BOMB. London: Victor Gollancz. 1968. Hardback. pp. 352

Moss, Norman. MEN WHO PLAY GOD: THE STORY OF THE HYDROGEN BOMB. Harmondsworth: Penguin. 1970. Paperback. pp. 383

News Chronicle. IN THE SHADOW OF THE H-BOMB (a reprint of the articles of 1-11 March 1955 with some additional material). London: News Chronicle. 1955. Pamphlet. pp. 24. (Contributors include Bevan, Hailsham, Liddell Hart, Soper)

Peace News. THE BLACK PAPER: H-bomb war – what it would be like. London: Peace News. n.d. [1962]. Broadsheet format. pp. 16

Pirie, Antoinette (ed.). FALLOUT: RADIATION HAZARDS FROM NUCLEAR EXPLOSIONS. London: MacGibbon & Kee. 1957

Powell, C[ecil] F[rank]. THE HYDROGEN BOMB AND THE FUTURE OF MANKIND. London: London Co-operative Society Education Department. 1955. Pamphlet. pp. 16

Roberts, Professor John E. and Bell, George (97th Bishop of Chichester). NUCLEAR WAR AND PEACE: THE FACTS AND THE CHALLENGE. London: National Peace Council, Peace Aims Pamphlet, No. 60. 1954

Robinson, Kenneth. ATOMIC AND NUCLEAR WAR: YOUR CONCERN IN IT. London: James Clarke. 1958. Paperback. pp. 47

Rotblat, Joseph (ed.). ATOMIC ENERGY: A SURVEY. London: Taylor & Francis, for the Atomic Scientists' Association. 1954. (Contributors include Kathleen Lonsdale (q.v.) and Sir George Thomson (q.v.))

Russell, Bertrand (3rd Earl Russell). ATOMIC ENERGY AND THE PROBLEMS OF EUROPE. Nineteenth Century. January 1949. pp. 39-43

Russell, Bertrand (3rd Earl Russell). THE INTERNATIONAL BEARINGS OF ATOMIC WARFARE. United Empire. January-February 1948. pp. 18-23

Slessor, Sir John (Marshal of the R.A.F.). THE GREAT DETERRENT: THE DEVELOPMENT OF STRATEGIC POLICY IN THE NUCLEAR AGE. London: Cassell. 1957. Hardback. pp. xii + 322. (Foreword by General Alfred M. Gruenther, U.S.A.)

Slessor, Sir John (Marshal of the R.A.F.). THE H-BOMB: MASSIVE RETALIATION OR GRADUATED DETERRENCE? International

Affairs. April 1956

Thomson, Sir George. ATOMIC ENERGY AND MORAL ISSUES, II in Rotblat (ed.): *q.v.* (1954). pp. 64ff

Thomson, Sir George. HYDROGEN BOMBS: THE NEED FOR A POLICY. International Affairs. Vol. XXVI, No. 4. October 1950. pp. 463–9

United Nations Association. NUCLEAR ENERGY: ITS NATURE, CONTROL AND USE. London: UNA, Peacefinder Pamphlets, No. 29. 1959. Pamphlet. pp. 12. (Contributors include Cockcroft, Frisch, I. G. John)

Wharton, Nicholas. ALTERNATIVES TO THE WESTERN DETER-RENTS. Blackfriars. Vol. 44. March 1963. pp. 116–20

Wharton, Nicholas. NUCLEAR DETERRENCE BY BLUFF. Black-friars. Vol. 43. April 1962. pp. 169–74

Yool, W. M. THE CASE FOR THE DETERRENT. Brassey's Annual. 1960. pp. 62–70

Young, Elizabeth (Baroness Kennet). NATIONS AND NUCLEAR WEAPONS. London: Fabian Society, Fabian Tract. 1963. Pamphlet. pp. 19

45. Nuclear Weapons: Particular Countries (see also under: **47. Nuclear Proliferation; 48. Non-Proliferation Treaty**)

Barnaby, Frank. INDIA'S NUCLEAR VIEWS. New Scientist. Vol. 49. 4 February 1971. pp. 476–7

Beaton, Leonard. LA POSITION NUCLÉAIRE DE L'INDE ET D'ISRAEL. Politique Etrangère (Paris). Vol. 34, No. 1. 1969. pp 5–16

Bellany, Ian. AUSTRALIA'S NUCLEAR POLICY. India Quarterly (New Delhi). Vol. 25. October–December 1969. pp. 374–84

Bellany, Ian. AUSTRALIA IN THE NUCLEAR AGE: NATIONAL DEFENCE AND NATIONAL DEVELOPMENT. Sydney: Sydney University Press. 1972. Hardback. pp. 144

Desai, M[eghnad] J. INDIA AND NUCLEAR WEAPONS. Disarmament and Arms Control. Vol. 3. Autumn 1965. pp. 135–42

Edwardes, Michael. INDIA, PAKISTAN AND NUCLEAR WEAPONS. International Affairs. Vol. 43. October 1967. pp. 655–63

Hitchens, Christopher. THE NEUTRON BOMB AND THE CON-SCIENCE OF THE DUTCH. New Statesman. Vol. 95. 7 April 1978.

pp. 453-7

Kalicki, J[an] H. CHINA, AMERICA AND ARMS CONTROL. The World Today. Vol. 26. April 1970. pp. 147-54

Lindsay of Birker, Lord. DIALOGUE ON DISARMAMENT: THE CASE OF CHINA AND THE UNITED STATES. The World Today. Vol. 19. December 1963. pp. 523-32

Mackintosh, Malcolm. SOVIET PRECONDITIONS FOR DISARMA- MENT AND ARMS CONTROL in Luard (ed.): FIRST STEPS TO DISARMAMENT. 1965. pp. 63-84

Mendl, Wolf. THE BACKGROUND OF FRENCH NUCLEAR POLICY. International Affairs. Vol. 41. January 1965. pp. 22-36

Mendl, Wolf. DETERRENCE AND PERSUASION: FRENCH NUCLEAR ARMAMENT IN THE CONTEXT OF NATIONAL POLICY, 1945- 1969. London: Faber & Faber, Studies in International Politics. 1970. Hardback. pp. 256

Mendl, Wolf. FRENCH ATTITUDES ON DISARMAMENT. Disarma- ment (Paris). No. 14. June 1967. pp. 13

Slater, John and McCarthy, Tony*. THREATS TO PEACE: THE FRENCH NUCLEAR FORCE AND THE MULTILATERAL FORCE. London: International Confederation for Disarmament and Peace. n.d. [1965]. Pamphlet. pp. 58. (*Of the CND Information Office, London)

Smart, Ian. BEYOND POLARIS. International Affairs. Vol. 53. October 1977. pp. 557-71

Smart, Ian. FUTURE CONDITIONAL: THE PROSPECT FOR ANGLO- FRENCH NUCLEAR CO-OPERATION. London: International Institute for Strategic Studies, Adelphi Paper, No. 78. 1971. pp. 45

Smart, Ian. THE FUTURE OF THE BRITISH NUCLEAR DETER- RENT: Technical, economic and strategic issues. London: Royal Institute of International Affairs. 1977. (Abridged version reprinted in Survival, Vol. 20 (January-February 1978), pp. 21-4)

Smith, Dan. AFTER THE INDIAN BOMB . . . London: CND. n.d. [1974]. Pamphlet. pp. 12

United Nations Association Disarmament Committee. ANGLO- FRENCH NUCLEAR SHARING: A strategic conundrum. London: United Nations Association. 1972. Pamphlet. (Written by a study group under the chairmanship of Sir Michael Wright, G.C.M.G.)

Willetts, Harry T. DISARMAMENT AND SOVIET FOREIGN POLICY.
in Louis Henkin (ed.): ARMS CONTROL: ISSUES FOR THE
PUBLIC. Englewood Cliffs, New Jersey: Prentice-Hall, for the
American Assembly and Columbia University. 1961. pp. 158–73

46. Nuclear Testing

Bailey, Sydney D. UN REPORT ON RADIATION. The Christian
Century (Chicago). 13 August 1958. pp. 920–1
Barker, A. THE NUCLEAR TEST-BAN TREATY. Journal of the
RUSI. Vol. 107. August 1962. pp. 237–40
Bull, Hedley, THE ARMS RACE AND THE BANNING OF NUCLEAR
TESTS. Political Quarterly. October–December 1959. pp. 344–56
CND. IN IGNORANCE, REFRAIN! London: CND [1959]. Pamphlet.
pp. 4
Carter, April. NUCLEAR TESTING: DANGERS IN THE SEVENTIES.
London: CND and Friends Peace and International Relations Com-
mittee. n.d. [1971]. Pamphlet. pp. 8
Cockcroft, Sir John. EXTENDING THE NUCLEAR TEST BAN. Dis-
armament and Arms Control. Vol. 2. Winter 1963–64. pp. 16–22
Davies, David (SIPRI). SEISMIC METHODS FOR MONITORING
UNDERGROUND EXPLOSIONS: AN ASSESSMENT OF THE
STATUS OUTLOOK (report by a Study Group. Rapporteur: David
Davies). Stockholm: Almqvist & Wiksell, SIPRI, Stockholm Papers,
No. 2. 1969. pp. 99
Lindop, Patricia. EFFECTS OF ATOMIC RADIATION: EXTRACTS
FROM THE REPORT OF THE UN SCIENTIFIC COMMITTEE. War
and Peace. Vol. 1, No. 1. January–March 1963. pp. 32–41
Montagu, Ivor. A NEW CLIMATE? AN EVALUATION OF THE TEST
BAN TREATY AND ITS EFFECTS THROUGHOUT THE WORLD.
Labour Monthly. Vol. 14. November 1963. pp. 498–503
Pirie, Antoinette (ed.). FALL-OUT: RADIATION HAZARDS FROM
NUCLEAR EXPLOSIONS. London: MacGibbon & Kee. 1957
Pirie, Antoinette. THE STORY OF RONGELAP in Slater & McCarthy
(1965), q.v. pp. 49–58
Roberts, Adam. NUCLEAR TESTING AND THE ARMS RACE.
London: Peace News, Peace News Pamphlets series. 1962. Pamphlet.
pp. 11
Scott, Richard. A BAN ON NUCLEAR TESTS: THE COURSE OF

THE NEGOTIATIONS, 1958-1962. International Affairs. Vol. 38.
October 1962. pp. 501-10

Stubbs, Peter. DETECTION OF TESTS. War and Peace. Vol. 1, No. 1.
January-March 1963. pp. 42-6

UKAEA. THE DETECTION AND RECOGNITION OF UNDER-
GROUND EXPLOSIONS (a special report by the Atomic Weapons
Research Establishment [Aldermaston]). London: UKAEA. 1965.
pp. 50

Verrier, Anthony. TEST BAN TREATY: AFTERMATH IN NATO.
The World Today. Vol. 19. September 1963. pp. 369-71

Zilliacus, Konni (M.P.). BRITAIN AND THE TEST BAN TREATY.
New Times (Moscow). Vol. 33. 21 August 1963. pp. 14-15

47. Nuclear Proliferation (see also under: 48: Non-Proliferation Treaty)

Barnaby, Frank. IMPLICATIONS OF THE SPREAD OF NUCLEAR
TECHNOLOGY: With particular (*sic*) [reference] to the Gas
Centrifuge in Schaerf and Barnaby (eds): (1972), *q.v.* pp 69-76

Barnaby, Frank (ed.). PREVENTING THE SPREAD OF NUCLEAR
WEAPONS. London: Souvenir Press, Pugwash Monograph, No. 1.
1969. pp. xiv + 374. (Outcome of First Pugwash Symposium,
London, April 1968)

Barnaby, Frank. SALTING DOWN NON-PROLIFERATION. New
Scientist. Vol. 49. 4 March 1971. pp. 476-7

Beaton, Leonard. CAPABILITIES OF NON-NUCLEAR POWERS in
Buchan (ed): A WORLD OF NUCLEAR POWERS? (1966), *q.v.*
pp. 13-38

Beaton, Leonard. MUST THE BOMB SPREAD? Harmondsworth:
Penguin (a Pelican Original). 1966. Paperback. pp. 147. (Published
in association with the Institute for Strategic Studies)

Beaton, Leonard. NUCLEAR PROLIFERATION. Science Journal.
Vol. 3. December 1967. pp. 35-40

Beaton, Leonard. THE SPREAD OF NUCLEAR WEAPONS. Disarmament (Paris). No. 5. March 1965. p. 1

Beaton, Leonard and Maddox, John. THE SPREAD OF NUCLEAR
WEAPONS. London: Chatto & Windus, for the Institute for
Strategic Studies, Studies in International Security. 1962. New
York: Praeger. Hardback. pp. xi + 216

Brown, Neville. TOWARDS THE SUPER-POWER DEADLOCK. The World Today. Vol. 22. September 1966. pp. 366–74

Brownlie, Ian. NUCLEAR PROLIFERATION: SOME PROBLEMS OF CONTROL. International Affairs. Vol. 42. October 1966. pp. 600–8

Buchan, The Hon. Alastair (ed.). A WORLD OF NUCLEAR POWERS? Englewood Cliffs, New Jersey: Prentice-Hall, for The American Assembly. 1966. Paperback. pp. ix + 176. (Contributors: Buchan, Beaton (q.v.), Sommer, Gupta, Birnbaum, Wakaizumi, Hoffmann, Chalfont (q.v.), Schwarz)

Bull, Hedley. THE ROLE OF THE NUCLEAR POWERS IN THE MANAGEMENT OF NUCLEAR PROLIFERATION in James E. Dougherty and J. F. Lehman, jr. (eds): ARMS CONTROL FOR THE LATE SIXTIES. Princeton, New Jersey: Van Nostrand. 1967. pp. 143–150

Carlton, David. THE ANGLO-AMERICAN NUCLEAR RELATIONSHIP: PROLIFERATORY in Carlton and Schaerf (eds): ARMS CONTROL AND TECHNOLOGICAL CHANGE (1977), q.v.

Chalfont, Lord. ALTERNATIVES TO PROLIFERATION: INHIBITION BY AGREEMENT in Buchan (ed.): A WORLD OF NUCLEAR POWERS? 1966. pp. 123–42

Chalfont, Lord. ARMS CONTROL OR NUCLEAR ANARCHY? Review of International Affairs (Belgrade). Vol. 18. 5 May 1967. pp. 3–6

Chalfont, Lord. PEKING, MOSCOW AND THE SPREAD OF NUCLEAR ARMS. Internationale Spectator (The Hague). Vol. 20. 8 April 1966. pp. 437–52

Cockcroft, Sir John. THE PERILS OF NUCLEAR PROLIFERATION in Calder (ed.): UNLESS PEACE COMES. 1968, 1970. (1968 edn) pp. 37–47

Cook, Dan. THE ART OF NON-PROLIFERATION. Encounter. Vol. 27. July 1966. pp. 3–8

Griffiths, David and Smith, Dan. HOW MANY MORE? THE SPREAD OF NUCLEAR WEAPONS. London: CND. 1977. Pamphlet. pp. 32

Jacobs, Gary. NUCLEAR BRITAIN: THE 'POPULATION EXPLOSION'. International Relations. Vol. III, No. 1. April 1966. pp. 61–71

Maddox, John. PROSPECTS FOR NUCLEAR PROLIFERATION. London: International Institute for Strategic Studies, Adelphi Paper,

No. 113. 1975

Martin, Andrew and Young, Wayland. PROLIFERATION. Disarmament and Arms Control. Vol. 3. Autumn 1965. pp. 107-34

Patterson, Walter C. EXPORTING ARMAGEDDON. New Statesman. 27 August 1976. pp. 264-6

Windsor, Philip. THE MIDDLE EAST AND THE WORLD BALANCE. The World Today. Vol. 23. July 1967. pp. 279-85

Younger, Kenneth. THE SPECTRE OF NUCLEAR PROLIFERATION. International Affairs. Vol. 42. January 1966. pp. 14-23

Zuckerman, Sir Solly. TECHNOLOGICAL ASPECTS OF PROLIFERATION in THE CONTROL OF PROLIFERATION: THREE VIEWS, by Sir Solly Zuckerman, Alva Myrdal and the Rt. Hon. Lester B. Pearson. London: Institute for Strategic Studies. 1966. pp. 26. Adelphi Paper, No. 29. pp. 1-8

48. Non-Proliferation Treaty (see also under: 47. Nuclear Proliferation)

Barnaby, Frank (SIPRI). PREVENTING NUCLEAR-WEAPON PROLIFERATION: An approach to the Non-Proliferation Treaty Review Conference. Stockholm: SIPRI. 1975. Pamphlet. pp. 37

Beaton, Leonard. IMPLICATIONS OF THE NON-PROLIFERATION TREATY ON DETERRENCE AND THE PROSPECTS FOR DISARMAMENT. RUSI Journal. Vol. 114. June 1969. pp. 34-40

Beaton, Leonard. KERNWAFFEN-SPERRVERTRAG UND NATIONALE SICHERHEIT: DIE BEDEUTUNG DER SICHERHEITSZUSAGEN DER ATOMMÄCHTE. Europa-Archiv (Bonn). Vol. 24. 10 January 1969. pp. 5-12

Bellany, Ian. THE NON-PROLIFERATION TREATY: TWO YEARS ON. World Review. Vol. 10. March 1971. pp. 1-11

Bellany, Ian. NUCLEAR NON-PROLIFERATION AND THE INEQUALITY OF STATES. Political Studies. Vol. 25, No. 4. 1977

Bull, Hedley. IN SUPPORT OF THE NON-PROLIFERATION TREATY. Quadrant (Sydney). Vol. 12. May-June 1968. pp. 25-34

Bull, Hedley. THE NON-PROLIFERATION TREATY AND ITS IMPLICATIONS FOR AUSTRALIA. Australian Outlook. Vol. 22. August 1968. pp. 162-75

Bull, Hedley. RETHINKING NON-PROLIFERATION. International Affairs. Vol. 51. April 1975. pp. 175-89

Chalfont, Lord. PROSPECTS FOR NON-PROLIFERATION AGREE-

MENT. Disarmament. No. 9. March 1966. p. 1

'A Correspondent'. NON-PROLIFERATION: LAST CHANCE? The World Today. Vol. 21. August 1965. pp. 315-19

Keens-Soper, Maurice. NEGOTIATING NON-PROLIFERATION. The World Today. Vol. 24. May 1968. pp. 189-96

McKnight, Alan D. ATOMIC SAFEGUARDS: A study in international verification. New York: United Nations Institute for Training and Research. 1971. Hardback. pp. xxii + 301. (Foreword by Chief Simeon O. Adebo, Executive Director of UNITAR)

McKnight, Alan D. NUCLEAR NON-PROLIFERATION: IAEA AND EURATOM. New York: Carnegie Endowment, Occasional Paper, No. 7. 1970. pp. 103

Martin, Laurence W. NON-PROLIFERATION: WHO'LL KILL COCK ROBIN? Spectator. 18 August 1967. pp. 183-4

Ranger, Robert. DEATH OF A TREATY: A DIPLOMATIC OBITUARY? [NPT]. International Relations. Vol. 3. April 1969. pp. 482-97

Richardson, J[ames] L. AUSTRALIA AND THE NON-PROLIFERA-TION TREATY. Canberra: Australian National University Press, Canberra Papers on Strategy and Defence, No. 3. 1968. pp. 24

Smart, Ian. NON-PROLIFERATION TREATY: STATUS AND PROSPECTS in Anne W. Marks (ed.): NPT: PARADOXES AND PROBLEMS. Washington, D.C.: Arms Control Association and Carnegie Endowment. 1975. pp. 19-30

Smith, Dan. INSECURITY IN NUMBERS: THE THREAT OF NUCLEAR PROLIFERATION. London: CND. 1975. Pamphlet. pp. 35

Suter, Keith D. THE 1975 REVIEW CONFERENCE OF THE NUCLEAR NON-PROLIFERATION TREATY. Australian Outlook. Vol. 30. August 1976. pp. 322-40

Vital, David. DOUBLE-TALK OR DOUBLE-THINK? A COMMENT ON THE DRAFT NON-PROLIFERATION TREATY. International Affairs. Vol. 44. July 1968. pp. 419-33

Young, Elizabeth (Baroness Kennet). THE CONTROL OF PROLIFE-RATION: THE 1968 TREATY IN HINDSIGHT AND FORECAST. London: Institute for Strategic Studies, Adelphi Paper, No. 56. 1969. Pamphlet. pp. 22

49. Seabed Arms Control

Brown, Edward Duncan. ARMS CONTROL IN HYDROSPACE: LEGAL
ASPECTS. Washington, D.C.: Woodrow Wilson International Center
for Scholars, Oceans Series 301. 1971. pp. 131. (Foreword by
Gerard J. Mangone)

Brown, Edward Duncan. THE DEMILITARISATION AND
DENUCLEARISATION OF HYDROSPACE. Annals of International
Studies (Geneva). 1973. pp. 71-92

Luard, Evan. THE DISARMAMENT DEBATE. Chapter 6 of his book
THE CONTROL OF THE SEA-BED: A NEW INTERNATIONAL
ISSUE. London: Heinemann. 1974

O'Connell, D[aniel] P. THE SEA-BED. Chapter 11 of his book THE
INFLUENCE OF LAW ON SEA POWER. Manchester: Manchester
University Press. 1975

Sims, Nicholas A. ETAT ACTUEL DES NÉGOCIATIONS MULTI-
LATÉRALES POUR UNE RÉDUCTION DES ARMEMENTS.
Politique Etrangère (Paris). Vol. 36, No. 5. December 1972. pp.
672-705

Young, Elizabeth. OCEAN POLICY AND ARMS CONTROL. The
World Today. Vol. 26. September 1970. pp. 401-7

Young, Elizabeth (Baroness Kennet). TO GUARD THE SEA. Foreign
Affairs (New York). Vol. 50. October 1971. pp. 136-47

50. Chemical and Biological Warfare

Anti-CBW. CHEMICAL AND BIOLOGICAL WARFARE: A policy
statement. New Malden, Surrey: Anti-CBW. [1968]. Pamphlet.
pp. 6. (An information centre . . . to promote public debate on this
topic and to ensure that the facts, in so far as they are known, are as
widely distributed as possible)

Bailey, Sydney D. PROHIBITIONS AND RESTRAINTS IN WAR.
London: Oxford University Press, for the Royal Institute of International Affairs. 1972. Paperback and Hardback. pp. xiii + 194

Barnaby, Frank. CB WEAPONS AND ARMS CONTROL in Cornish
and Murray (eds.): THE SUPREME FOLLY. [1970]. pp. 22-6

Beaton, Leonard. A BAN ON GERMS. Survival. Vol. 12. January 1970.
pp. 17-18

Bull, Hedley. CHEMICAL AND BIOLOGICAL WEAPONS: THE

PROSPECTS FOR ARMS CONTROL. Australian Outlook. Vol. 24. August 1970. pp. 152–63

Carlton, David and Sims, Nicholas. THE CS GAS CONTROVERSY: GREAT BRITAIN AND THE GENEVA PROTOCOL OF 1925. Survival. Vol. 13. October 1971. pp. 333–40

Chalfont, Alun. THE CS GAS MUDDLE. New Statesman. 31 July 1970. pp. 108–9

Clarke, Robin. WE ALL FALL DOWN: THE PROSPECT OF BIO-LOGICAL AND CHEMICAL WARFARE. London: Allen Lane, The Penguin Press. 1968. Hardback. pp. xiii + 201

Clarke, Robin. WE ALL FALL DOWN: THE PROSPECT OF BIO-LOGICAL AND CHEMICAL WARFARE. Harmondsworth: Penguin, Pelican Book. 1969. Paperback. pp. xiii + 201

Cookson, John. C AND BW. London: Young Liberal Movement. 1970. Pamphlet. pp. 47

Cookson, John and Nottingham, Judith. A NEW PERSPECTIVE ON WAR: CHEMICAL AND BIOLOGICAL WARFARE: A study with special reference to Vietnam. Newcastle-upon-Tyne: Chemical and Biological Warfare Group (c/o University of Newcastle-upon-Tyne Students' Union). n.d. [1968]. Spiral-bound. pp. 129

Cookson, John and Nottingham, Judith. A SURVEY OF CHEMICAL AND BIOLOGICAL WARFARE. London and Sydney: Sheed & Ward. 1969. Hardback. pp. vii + 376. (This book has its origin in a document published by a group of students at Newcastle University and written by the two authors. In the present form it is the product of three years' work and research (Introduction))

Cornish, Mick D. and Murray, Robert (eds.). THE SUPREME FOLLY: CHEMICAL AND BIOLOGICAL WEAPONS. London: NCLC Publishing Society, c/o Fabian Society, format uniform with Fabian publications, for the Women's International League for Peace and Freedom, British section; papers from conference held 21–23 November 1969 in London. n.d. [1970]. Pamphlet. pp. 44. (Contributors: Barnaby (*q.v.*), Baroyan, Luard (*q.v.*), MacBride, MacCarthy, Meselson, Prawitz)

Harrigan, Anthony. THE CASE FOR GAS WARFARE. RUSI Journal. Vol. 108. November 1963. pp. 356–7

Jones, Robert. CHEMICAL WARFARE – THE PEACETIME LEGACY. New Scientist. Vol. 66. 24 April 1975. pp. 202–4

Liddell Hart, B[asil] H. IS GAS A BETTER DEFENCE THAN ATOMIC WEAPONS? Survival. September–October 1959

Luard, Evan (M.P.). CB WARFARE: THE BRITISH GOVERNMENT'S VIEW in Cornish and Murray (eds): THE SUPREME FOLLY. [1970]. pp. 31–4

Mulley, F[rederick] W. (M.P.). DIE BRITISCHE INITIATIVE ZUR TOTALEN ACHTUNG DER BIOLOGISCHEN METHODEN DER KRIEGFÜHRUNG. Europa-Archiv (Bonn). Vol. 24. 25 November 1969. pp. 787–94

Noel-Baker, Philip. PUTTING A STOP TO CBW. Science Journal. January 1970

Nottingham, Judith. THE DANGERS OF CHEMICAL AND BIO- LOGICAL WARFARE (CBW). The Ecologist. Vol. 2. February 1972. pp. 4–6

Perry Robinson, J[ulian]. BINARY NERVE-GAS WEAPONS in CHEMICAL DISARMAMENT: NEW WEAPONS FOR OLD. A SIPRI Monograph (Stockholm: SIPRI 1975). pp. 21–99

Perry Robinson, Julian (SIPRI). CB WEAPONS TODAY (Volume II of the SIPRI study, THE PROBLEM OF CBW). Stockholm: Almqvist & Wiksell. 1973. pp. 420. (Published in collaboration with Humanities Press, New York, and Paul Elek, London)

Perry Robinson, J[ulian] P. CHEMICAL WARFARE. Science Journal. April 1967

Perry Robinson, Julian (SIPRI) with Boserup, Anders, Neild, Robert *et al.* THE PREVENTION OF CBW (Volume V of the SIPRI study, THE PROBLEM OF CBW). Stockholm: Almqvist & Wiksell. 1971. pp. 287. (Published in collaboration with Humanities Press, New York)

Perry Robinson, Julian (SIPRI). THE RISE OF CB WEAPONS (Volume I of the SIPRI study, THE PROBLEM OF CBW). Stockholm: Almqvist & Wiksell. 1971. pp. 395. (Published in collaboration with Humanities Press, New York)

Perry Robinson, J[ulian] P. SHOULD NATO KEEP CHEMICAL WEAPONS? A framework for considering policy alternatives. Brighton, Sussex: University of Sussex Science Policy Research Unit (SPRU), SPRU Occasional Paper Series, No. 4. 1977. Pamphlet. pp. 93

Perry Robinson, J[ulian] P. THE SPECIAL CASE OF CHEMICAL AND BIOLOGICAL WEAPONS. Bulletin of the Atomic Scientists. Vol. 31. May 1975. pp. 17–23

Perry Robinson, J[ulian] P. THE UNITED STATES BINARY NERVE- GAS PROGRAMME (National and International Implications).

Brighton: University of Sussex Institute for the Study of International Organisation, ISIO Monograph, No. 10. 1975. Large pamphlet format

Ranger, Robin. THE CANADIAN CONTRIBUTION TO THE CONTROL OF CHEMICAL AND BIOLOGICAL WARFARE. Toronto: Canadian Institute of International Affairs, Wellesley Paper, No. 5. 1976. Pamphlet. pp. 65

Rose, Steven (ed.). CBW: CHEMICAL AND BIOLOGICAL WARFARE. London: Harrap (published simultaneously in USA by Beacon Press of Boston, Mass.). 1968. Hardback. pp. 209. (Based on papers presented to the Conference on CBW held in London, 22-23 February 1968)

Rose, Steven. THE REAL SIGNIFICANCE OF CBW. New Perspectives (Helsinki). Vol. 1. December 1971. pp. 53-7

Rose, Steven. THE REAL SIGNIFICANCE OF CBW. Instant Research on Peace and Violence (Tampere). Vol. 2, No. 1. 1972. pp. 9-16

Sims, Nicholas. BIOLOGICAL DISARMAMENT: BRITAIN'S NEW POSTURE. New Scientist. Vol. 52. 6 December 1971. pp. 18-20

Sims, Nicholas A. GERM WARFARE: THE SPECTRE RECEDES. The Friend. Vol. 133. 11 July 1975. pp. 793-4

Stares, John (SIPRI) (ed.). CHEMICAL DISARMAMENT: SOME PROBLEMS OF VERIFICATION. Stockholm: Almqvist & Wiksell, a SIPRI Monograph. 1973. Paperback. pp. 184. (Published in collaboration with Humanities Press, New York, and Paul Elek, London)

United Nations Association. FACTS ABOUT CBW (based on the UN report on the use of chemical and biological weapons). London: UNA. 1969. Pamphlet. pp. 14

Viney, D[eryck] E. CONSTRAINING CHEMICAL-BIOLOGICAL WARFARE. Disarmament (Paris). No. 15. September 1967. pp. 1-4, 20

Windsor, Philip. GAS: AN ISS VIEW (Institute for Strategic Studies). Survival. Vol. 7. May-June 1965. pp. 145-6

51. Strategic Arms Limitation Talks

Beaton, Leonard. SECONDARY AND 'ALMOST-NUCLEAR' POWERS: HOW DO THEY AFFECT STRATEGIC ARMS LIMITATIONS? in Morton A. Kaplan (ed.): SALT: PROBLEMS AND

130

PROSPECTS. Morristown, New Jersey: General Learning Press. 1973. pp. 169-81. (Papers presented to the University of Chicago Arms Control and Foreign Policy Seminar, Winter 1970-71)

Bull, Hedley. THE SCOPE FOR SUPER-POWER AGREEMENTS. Arms Control and National Security (Croton-on-Hudson, NY). Vol. 1. 1969. pp. 1-23

Bull, Hedley. STRATEGIC ARMS LIMITATION: THE PRECEDENT OF THE WASHINGTON AND LONDON NAVAL TREATIES in Morton A. Kaplan (ed.): SALT: PROBLEMS AND PROSPECTS. Morristown, New Jersey: General Learning Press. 1973. pp. 26-52. (Papers presented to the University of Chicago Arms Control and Foreign Policy Seminar, Winter 1970-71)

Burt, Richard. TECHNOLOGY AND EAST-WEST ARMS CONTROL. International Affairs. Vol. 53. January 1977. pp. 51-72

Chalfont, Lord. CONTROLLING THE WEAPONS OF MASS DES-TRUCTION: THE TASK OF THE SUPER-POWERS. The Round Table. Vol. 241. January 1971. pp. 33-41

Freedman, Lawrence. TOWARDS SALT II. The World Today. Vol. 33. November 1977. pp. 405-8

Freedman, Lawrence. US INTELLIGENCE AND THE SOVIET STRATEGIC THREAT. London: Macmillan. 1977. Hardback. pp. xv + 235

Institute for Strategic Studies. SOVIET-AMERICAN RELATIONS AND WORLD ORDER: Arms limitations and policy. London: Institute for Strategic Studies, Adelphi Paper, No. 65. 1970. Pamphlet. pp. 48

Kemp, Geoffrey and Smart, Ian. SALT AND EUROPEAN NUCLEAR FORCES in William R. Kintner and Robert L. Pfaltzgraff, jr. (eds.): SALT: IMPLICATIONS FOR ARMS CONTROL IN THE 1970s. Pittsburgh: University of Pittsburgh. 1973. pp. 199-235. (A Foreign Policy Research Institute Book. Based on the proceedings of the Fifth International Arms Control Symposium, Philadelphia, 1971)

Lapping, Brian. A PEBBLE IN THE DIPLOMATIC LAKE [SALT]. Venture. Vol. 22. December 1970. pp. 26-9

Martin, Laurence W. VLADIVOSTOK AND THE WILL FOR POWER. Listener. Vol. 93. 27 February 1975. pp. 260-1

Ranger, Robin. ARMS CONTROL NEGOTIATIONS: PROGRESS AND PROSPECTS. Canadian Defense Quarterly. Vol. 4. Winter 1974. pp. 16-25

Ranger, Robert. ARMS CONTROL WITHIN A CHANGING POLITI-

CAL CONTEXT. International Journal. Vol. 26. Autumn 1971. pp. 735-52

Ranger, Robert. THE POLITICS OF ARMS CONTROL AFTER VLADIVOSTOK. Millennium/Journal of International Studies. Vol. 4. Spring 1975. pp. 52-66

Roberts, Adam. THE MOSCOW SUMMIT AND ARMS CONTROL. The World Today. Vol. 30. August 1974. pp. 315-18

Smart, Ian. SALT: VERS UNE NOUVELLE STRATEGIÉ NUCLÉAIRE. Preuves (Paris). Vol. 7. 1971. pp. 105-18

Smart, Ian. STRATEGIC ARMS LIMITATION TALKS. Brassey's Annual. Vol. 81. 1970. pp. 39-52

Watt, Donald. HISTORICAL LIGHT ON SALT: PARALLELS WITH INTER-WAR NAVAL ARMS CONTROL. The Round Table. Vol. 245. January 1972. pp. 29-35

Werner, Roy A. VLADIVOSTOK AND SALT II: IS THE WORLD SAFER? RUSI Journal. Vol. 120. March 1975. pp. 56-8

Young, Elizabeth (Baroness Kennet). PROSPECTS FOR SALT AND THE ABM DEBATE. The World Today. Vol. 25. August 1969. pp. 323-8

52. Regional Negotiations and Proposals (see also under: 53. Arms Trade)

Bellany, Ian. BALANCING MUTUAL FORCE REDUCTIONS. Nature. Vol. 234. 10 December 1971. pp. 361-2

Bertram, Christoph. MUTUAL FORCE REDUCTIONS IN EUROPE: THE POLITICAL ASPECTS. London: International Institute for Strategic Studies, Adelphi Paper, No. 84. 1972

Bertram, Christoph. THE POLITICS OF MBFR. The World Today. Vol. 29. January 1973

Buchan, (The Hon.) Alastair and Windsor, Philip. ARMS AND STABILITY IN EUROPE: A BRITISH-FRENCH-GERMAN ENQUIRY: A REPORT. London: Chatto & Windus, for the Institute for Strategic Studies, Studies in International Security, No. 6. 1963. Hardback. pp. x + 236

Burton, John W. REGIONAL DISARMAMENT: SOUTH-EAST ASIA. Disarmament and Arms Control. Vol. 1. 1963. pp. 155-70

Chalfont, Lord. VALUE OF OBSERVATION POSTS IN NATO AND WARSAW PACT AREAS. European Review. Vol. 16, No. 4. 1966

Cook, Robin F. (M.P.). LOST IN THE VIENNESE WOODS (mutual force reduction negotiations). New Statesman. 14 January 1977. pp. 41-2

Fletcher, Raymond. EXISTING ARRANGEMENTS FOR INTER-NATIONAL CONTROL OF WARLIKE MATERIAL (the Agency for the Control of Armaments, of Western European Union). Disarmament and Arms Control. Autumn 1963

Gott, Richard. THE PURPOSE OF DISENGAGEMENT. Views. Vol. 4. Spring 1964. pp. 108-10

Healey, Denis (M.P.). A NEUTRAL BELT IN EUROPE? London: Fabian Society, Fabian Tract 311. 1958. Pamphlet. pp. 16

Howard, Michael. INSPECTED ZONES in Luard (ed.): FIRST STEPS TO DISARMAMENT. 1965. pp. 121-31

Howard, Michael. LIMITED ARMAMENT ZONES IN EUROPE. Bulletin of the Atomic Scientists. Vol. 17. February 1962. pp. 9-14

Institute for Strategic Studies. DISARMAMENT IN EUROPE. London: Institute for Strategic Studies, Adelphi Paper, No. 10. 1964. Pamphlet. pp. 22

Kirk, Peter (M.P.). SICHERHEITSKONFERENZ UND TRUPPEN-VERMINDERUNG. Wehrkunde (Munich). Vol. 21. March 1972. pp. 117-22

Palmer, Michael and Thomas, David. ARMS CONTROL AND THE MEDITERRANEAN. The World Today. Vol. 27. November 1971. pp. 495-502

Ranger, Robert. MBFR: POLITICAL OR TECHNICAL ARMS CONTROL? The World Today. Vol. 30. October 1974

Shuttleworth, Alan. DISENGAGEMENT: CHRONOLOGY AND ANALYSIS. War and Peace. Vol. 1, No. 2. Summer 1963. pp. 41-52

Windsor, Philip. ARMS CONTROL IN CENTRAL EUROPE. Disarmament (Paris). No. 3. September 1964. pp. 9-11

Windsor, Philip. OBSERVATION POSTS in Luard (ed.): FIRST STEPS TO DISARMAMENT. 1965. pp. 85-99

Young, Wayland. THE PROSPECTS FOR ARMS CONTROL IN EUROPE. Bulletin of the Atomic Scientists. Vol. 21. September 1965. pp. 22-4

53. Arms Trade

Bailey, Sydney D. CAN THE BOOMING ARMS TRADE BE HALTED?

The Christian Century (Chicago). 23 February 1972. pp. 220-2

Blackaby, Frank, Kaldor, Mary *et al.* (SIPRI). THE ARMS TRADE
WITH THE THIRD WORLD. Stockholm: Almqvist & Wiksell. 1971.
pp. 910. (Published in collaboration with Humanities Press, New
York, and Paul Elek, London. See also Stares (1975))

Camilleri, Joseph. BRITAIN AND THE DEATH TRADE. London:
Housmans, for Pax Christi. n.d. [probably 1971]. Pamphlet. pp. 16

Catholic Institute of International Relations. ARMS AND THE THIRD
WORLD. London: CIIR. 1974. Pamphlet

Christie, Michael J. THE SIMONSTOWN AGREEMENTS: BRITAIN'S
DEFENCE AND THE SALE OF ARMS TO SOUTH AFRICA.
London: Africa Bureau. 1970. Pamphlet. pp. 23

Commission for International Justice and Peace of the [Catholic]
Bishops' Conference [of England and Wales]. CHRISTIANS AND
THE ARMS TRADE. London: Commission for International Justice
and Peace. n.d. [1976]. Pamphlet. pp. 19

Committee on Poverty and the Arms Trade. BOMBS FOR BREAK-
FAST. London: COPAT. 1978. Pamphlet. pp. 42

Cook, Robin (M.P.). BRITAIN'S ARMS BAZAAR. New Statesman. 9
July 1976. pp. 37-8

Douglas-Home, Charles. THE ARMS SALES RACE. Yearbook of World
Affairs. Vol. 23. 1969. pp. 135-44

Fletcher, Raymond. WHERE ARE THE MERCHANTS OF DEATH?
Twentieth Century. Vol. 172. Spring 1963. pp. 89-96

Gutteridge, William. ARMS TO DEVELOPING COUNTRIES in
Schaerf and Barnaby (eds.) (1972), *q.v.* pp. 141-58

Hanning, Hugh. NIGERIA: A LESSON OF THE ARMS RACE. The
World Today. Vol. 23. November 1967. pp. 465-72

Harding, (Rev.) David J. BLOOD KEEPS THE WHEELS TURNING –
REFLECTIONS ON THE ARMS TRADE. Reconciliation Quarterly.
New Series. Vol. 5. September 1975. pp. 16-23

Hockaday, Arthur. THE TRANSFER OF ARMS. Crucible. January-
March 1977. pp. 20-7

Kaldor, Mary. ARMS AND DEPENDENCE in Jane M. O. Sharp (ed.):
OPPORTUNITIES FOR DISARMAMENT: A PREVIEW OF THE
1978 UNITED NATIONS SPECIAL SESSION ON DISARMA-
MENT. New York and Washington, D.C.: Carnegie Endowment for
International Peace. 1978. pp. 61-7

Kemp, Geoffrey. ARMS SALES AND ARMS CONTROL IN THE
DEVELOPING COUNTRIES. The World Today. Vol. 22. Septem-

ber 1966. pp. 386-95

Kemp, Geoffrey and Sutton, Colonel John L. (USAF). ARMS TO DEVELOPING COUNTRIES, 1945-1965. London: Institute for Strategic Studies, Adelphi Paper, No. 28. 1966. Pamphlet. pp. 45

Kemp, Geoffrey. ARMS TRAFFIC AND THIRD WORLD CONFLICTS. International Conciliation 577. March 1970. New York: Carnegie Endowment. 1970. Pamphlet. pp. 180

Kemp, Geoffrey. CONTROLLING ARMS IN THE MIDDLE EAST: Some preliminary observations. The World Today. Vol. 27. July 1967. pp. 285-92

Kemp, Geoffrey. DILEMMAS OF THE ARMS TRAFFIC. Foreign Affairs. Vol. 48. January 1970. pp. 274-84

Kemp, Geoffrey. THE INTERNATIONAL ARMS TRADE: SUPPLIER, RECIPIENT AND ARMS CONTROL PERSPECTIVES. Political Quarterly. Vol. 42. October-December 1971. pp. 376-89

Kemp, Geoffrey. REARMAMENT IN LATIN AMERICA. The World Today. Vol. 23. September 1967. pp. 375-84

Kemp, Geoffrey. REGULATING THE ARMS TRADE. Disarmament. No. 16. December 1967. p. 11

Kent, (Monseigneur) Bruce. POVERTY AND THE ARMS TRADE. London: Catholic Institute of International Relations, for the Committee on Poverty and the Arms Trade. 1975. Pamphlet

Lipton, Merle. BRITISH ARMS FOR SOUTH AFRICA. The World Today. Vol. 26. October 1970. pp. 427-34

Martin, Laurence W. THE ARMS TRADE. Listener. Vol. 84. 27 August 1970. pp. 274-5

National Peace Council. THE ARMS SALESMAN. London: National Peace Council. 1966. Pamphlet. pp. 6

'New Internationalist'. SWORDS AND PLOUGHSHARES IN THE GLOBAL VILLAGE. (special issue of) New Internationalist. No. 51. May 1977. pp. 34

Noel-Baker, Philip. THE PRIVATE MANUFACTURE OF ARMAMENTS (with a prefatory note by Viscount Cecil of Chelwood). New York: Dover. 1972. pp. xxiii + 574. (1936 edition reprinted with new introduction by the author)

Paskins, Barrie et al. THE SALE AND TRANSFER OF CONVENTIONAL ARMS, ARMS SYSTEMS AND RELATED TECHNOLOGY. Report of a Working Party of the Council on Christian Approaches to Defence and Disarmament (Convenor, Barrie Paskins; Chairman, Christoph Bertram) to the British Council of Churches.

135

London: British Council of Churches (BCC Publications). 1977.
Pamphlet. pp. 20

Sims, Nicholas A. THE AYACUCHO DECLARATION AND THE
ARMS TRADE WITH ANDEAN SOUTH AMERICA. The Pacifist:
Journal of the Peace Pledge Union. Vol. 14. November 1975. pp. 6-
10

Sampson, Anthony. THE CONTROLLERS. Chapter 17 (pp. 288-308)
of his book THE ARMS BAZAAR. London: Hodder & Stoughton.
1977

Stanley, John. THE INTERNATIONAL ARMS TRADE: CON-
TROLLED OR UNCONTROLLED? Political Quarterly. Vol. 43.
April-June 1972. pp. 155-68

Stanley, John and Pearton, Maurice. THE INTERNATIONAL TRADE
IN ARMS. London: Chatto & Windus, for the International Institute
for Strategic Studies. 1972. Paperback and Hardback editions.
pp. ix + 244

Stares, John (SIPRI) (ed.). THE ARMS TRADE WITH THE THIRD
WORLD. Harmondsworth: Penguin, Pelican Book. 1975. Paperback.
pp. 362. ('An abridged version of (the) major study' of the same
title, for which see under Blackaby and Kaldor *et al.* (1971))

Taylor, Trevor. THE CONTROL OF THE ARMS TRADE. International
Relations. Vol. 3. May 1971. pp. 903-12

54. History of Disarmament Negotiations (see also under specific
headings, e.g.: **46. Nuclear Testing; 48. Non-Proliferation Treaty;
49. Seabed Arms Control; 50. Chemical and Biological Warfare;
51. Strategic Arms Limitation Talks; 52. Regional Negotiations and
Proposals)**
[Approximate period covered is shown in square brackets]

Fitzgerald, Brigid. PROGRESS IN DISARMAMENT NEGOTIATIONS
[1972-75]. Reconciliation Quarterly. New Series. Vol. 6, No. 1.
March 1976. pp. 34-9

Ford, Boris. DISARMAMENT AND ATOMIC POWER. Chapter 6 of his
book DISCUSSING BRITAIN AND THE UNITED NATIONS [1945-
55]. London: UNA. 1958. pp. 67-76. (Study guide to Goodwin
(1957), *q.v.*)

Goodwin, Geoffrey L. DISARMAMENT [1945-1955]. Chapter 5 of
his book BRITAIN AND THE UNITED NATIONS. London: Oxford

University Press, for the Royal Institute of International Affairs; New York: Manhattan, for the Carnegie Endowment. 1957. (Part of the Carnegie-sponsored series National Studies on International Organization. See also Ford (1958))

Michiels, J. L. ATOMIC WEAPONS AND THE UN DISARMAMENT COMMISSION [1945-1952] in National Peace Council, WORLD DISARMAMENT, *q.v.* (1953). pp. 25-35

Noel-Baker, Philip (M.P.). THE ARMS RACE: A PROGRAMME FOR WORLD DISARMAMENT [1920-1958]. London: Stevens & Sons, Atlantic Books. 1958. Hardback. pp. xviii + 579. (See also the reviews by Bull (1959) and Goodwin (1958))

Noel-Baker, Philip. HISTORICAL DEVELOPMENTS ON DISARMA-MENT [1899-1978] in Noel-Baker *et al.*: DISARM OR DIE [1978]. pp. 19-33

Nutting, Anthony. DISARMAMENT: AN OUTLINE OF THE NEGO-TIATIONS [1945-58]. London: Oxford University Press, for the Royal Institute of International Affairs. 1959. pp. xi + 52

Pollard, Robert S. W. THE STRUGGLE FOR DISARMAMENT [1920-1949]. London: Friends Peace Committee. n.d. [1949]. Pamphlet. pp. 36

Ranger, Robert. ARMS CONTROL CONCEPTS AND PROPOSALS WITHIN A CHANGING POLITICAL CONTEXT, 1958-1972. University of London PhD thesis (LSE Department of International Relations). Typescript. 1973

Sims, Nicholas A. CONSULTATIVE COMMITTEES AS 'APPRO-PRIATE INTERNATIONAL PROCEDURES' IN DISARMAMENT-RELATED TREATIES [1969-78]. Transnational Perspectives (Geneva). Vol. IV, Nos. 1-2. 1978. pp. 15-19

Sims, Nicholas A. ETAT ACTUEL DES NÉGOCIATIONS MULTI-LATÉRALES POUR UNE RÉDUCTION DES ARMEMENTS [1968-1972]. Politique Etrangère (Paris). Vol. 36, No. 5. December 1972. pp. 672-705

Sims, Nicholas A. GENERAL AND COMPLETE DISARMAMENT: THE ITALIAN INITIATIVE OF 1969-70 AND THE SYNOPTIC APPROACH TO THE DISARMAMENT PROCESS [1969-1975]. Reconciliation Quarterly. New Series. Vol. 6, No. 1. March 1976. pp. 40-6

Sims, Nicholas A. UN DEADLOCKS AND DELAYING TACTICS: THE FIRST THREE YEARS OF THE SOVIET PROPOSAL FOR A WORLD DISARMAMENT CONFERENCE, 1971-1974.

Millennium/Journal of International Studies. Vol. 4. Autumn 1975. pp. 113-31

Thomas, Hugh. DEATH OF A CONFERENCE: An account of the negotiations for general disarmament, 1960. London: United Nations Association. 1960. Pamphlet. pp. 63

Wright, Sir Michael. DISARM AND VERIFY [1945-1963]: An explanation of the central difficulties and of national policies. London: Chatto & Windus. 1964. Hardback. pp. xiv + 255; New York: Praeger. 1964. pp. 275

Young, Elizabeth (Baroness Kennet). A FAREWELL TO ARMS CONTROL? [1961-1972]. Harmondsworth: Penguin (a Pelican Original). 1972. Paperback. pp. 256

World Today. DISARMAMENT PROPOSALS AND NEGOTIATIONS, 1946-1955. August 1955. pp. 336-7

55. Christian Churches (see also under: **44. Atomic Energy and Nuclear Weapons; 53. Arms Trade; 56. Unilateral Nuclear Disarmament; 57. CND – Histories and Memoirs**)

Alexander, Horace. RESISTING EVIL WITHOUT ARMS. York: Northern Friends Peace Board. n.d. (1956?). Pamphlet. pp. 12

Bailey, Sydney D. CAN THERE BE AN ETHICAL BASIS FOR THE REGULATION OF WEAPONS? Crucible. January 1974. pp. 13-18

Bailey, Sydney D. PROHIBITIONS AND RESTRAINTS IN WAR. London: Oxford University Press, for the Royal Institute of International Affairs. 1972. Paperback and Hardback editions. pp. xiii + 194

Bartlett, Percy W. DETERRENCE AND RETALIATION, OR CHRISTIANITY? London: Friends Peace Committee. n.d. [1958]. Pamphlet. pp. 31

Booth, (Rev.) Alan R. CHRISTIAN THEOLOGY AND MODERN WARFARE. Brassey's Annual. 1962

Booth, (Rev.) Alan R., Edwards, David L. and Jenkins, Daniel. CHRISTIANS AND NUCLEAR DISARMAMENT. Theology. Vol. 64. June 1961. pp. 222-7. (See also reply by Jude, 1961 (*q.v.*))

Booth, (Rev.) Alan R. CHRISTIANS AND POWER POLITICS. London: SCM Press, Living Church Books. 1961. Paperback. pp. 126

Booth, (Rev.) Alan R. CHURCH AND SOCIETY, A DISARMAMENT ASPECT. Disarmament (Paris). No. 13. March 1967. pp. 9

Booth, (Rev.) Alan R. A DISARMED WORLD in STUDIES IN DIS-
ARMAMENT AND ARMS CONTROL. London: Institute for
Strategic Studies, Adelphi Paper, No. 2. 1962
Booth, (Rev.) Alan R. NUCLEAR WEAPONS. Expository Times. Vol.
75. April 1964. pp. 220-3
British Council of Churches. THE BRITISH NUCLEAR DETERRENT:
Resolution of the British Council of Churches and Report of a
Working Group October 1963. London: SCM Press [SCM Press
Broadsheets, No. 1]. 1963. Pamphlet. pp. 48. (Report of a Working
Group (chairman, Kenneth R. Johnstone, C.B., C.M.G.) appointed
by the International Department of the British Council of Churches
and the Conference of British Missionary Societies. See also critique
by Vincent (1964))
British Council of Churches. CHRISTIANS AND ATOMIC WAR: A dis-
cussion of the moral aspects of defence and disarmament in the
nuclear age. London: British Council of Churches. 1959. Pamphlet.
pp. 40. (See also critique by Vincent (1962))
British Council of Churches. THE ERA OF ATOMIC POWER: Report
of a Commission (chairman: Dr. J. H. Oldham) to the British
Council of Churches. London: SCM Press. 1946. (See also critique
by Capper-Johnson (1946), and the report by the Church of
England (1948))
British Council of Churches, International Department. THE PATTERN
OF DISARMAMENT. London: British Council of Churches. 1962.
Leaflet.
British Council of Churches. THE SEARCH FOR SECURITY: A
CHRISTIAN APPRAISAL. London: SCM Press. 1973. Paperback.
pp. xii + 144. (Report of a Working Party on Defence and Disarma-
ment (chairman, the Rev. Edward Rogers; rapporteur, Nicholas A.
Sims) appointed by the Department of International Affairs of the
British Council of Churches and the Conference of British Mission-
ary Societies [1969-1972])
Butterfield, Herbert. HUMAN NATURE AND THE DOMINION OF
FEAR. London: CND. Christian CND Pamphlet, No. 3. n.d. [about
1962]
Buzzard, Rear-Admiral Sir Anthony. THE CHRISTIAN DILEMMA IN
THE NUCLEAR AGE. Journal of the RUSI. Vol. 107. May 1962.
pp. 145-8
Buzzard, Rear-Admiral Sir Anthony. THE CHRISTIAN DILEMMA
ON NUCLEAR WEAPONS. London: Mowbray. 1963. Pamphlet.
pp. 15
Buzzard, Rear-Admiral Sir Anthony. THE CRUX OF DEFENCE

POLICY. International Relations. April 1956

Buzzard, Rear-Admiral Sir Anthony. DEFENCE, DISARMAMENT AND CHRISTIAN DECISIONS. Survival. September 1961

CND. QUESTIONS AND ANSWERS FOR CHRISTIANS ON NUCLEAR DISARMAMENT. London: CND. Christian CND Pamphlet, No. 1. n.d. [1961]. Pamphlet. pp. 8

Capper-Johnson, Karlin. MAN VERSUS THE ATOM: A CHRISTIAN PACIFIST COMMENT. London: Friends Peace Committee. 1946. Pamphlet. pp. 22. (Critique of THE ERA OF ATOMIC POWER, *q.v.* under British Council of Churches (1946))

Catholic Institute of International Relations. ARMS AND THE THIRD WORLD. London: CIIR. 1974. Pamphlet

Chichester, The Rt. Rev. Dr. George Bell (97th Bishop of). THE BALANCE OF TERROR. Church Illustrated. May 1956. pp. 7–8

Church of England. THE CHURCH AND THE ATOM: A study of the moral and theological aspects of peace and war. London: Church Assembly. 1948. pp. 130. (Report of a Commission of the Church Assembly appointed to consider the Report of a Commission of the British Council of Churches (THE ERA OF ATOMIC POWER, *q.v.*))

Church of England. MODERN WAR: WHAT CAN CHRISTIANS DO TOGETHER? (a report by the Board for Social Responsibility of the Church Assembly (chairman, the Bishop of Leicester)). London: Church Information Office. 1962. Pamphlet. pp. 16. (Foreword by the Rt. Rev. R. R. Williams, 3rd Bishop of Leicester. See also the comment/response by Donald Groom (1963))

Collins, Diana. CAN CHRISTIANS ACCEPT THE NUCLEAR DETER-RENT? London: CND, a Christian CND Pamphlet. n.d. [1964]

Coulson, Charles A. NUCLEAR KNOWLEDGE AND CHRISTIAN RESPONSIBILITIES. London: Epworth Press, Foundery Pamphlets, No. 9. 1958. Pamphlet. pp. 16

Commission for International Justice and Peace of the [Catholic] Bishops' Conference [of England and Wales]. CHRISTIANS AND THE ARMS TRADE. London: Commission for International Justice and Peace. n.d. [1976]. Pamphlet. pp. 19

Crane, Paul. CATHOLICS AND NUCLEAR WAR. The Month. October 1959. pp. 223–9

Cullen, Peter J. CHRISTIANITY AND VIOLENCE: AN ALTERNA-TIVE TRADITION. New Blackfriars. Vol. 56. December 1975. pp. 532–42

Draper, G[erald] I. A. D. THE ORIGINS OF THE JUST WAR TRADI-

TION. New Blackfriars. Vol. 46. November 1964. pp. 82–8

Edwards, (Rev.) David L. WITHDRAWING FROM THE BRINK IN
1963: A plea for a Christian agreement in Britain concerning nuclear
weapons. London: SCM Press, Living Church Books. 1963. Pamphlet.
pp. 39

Evans, Canon Stanley. THE NUCLEAR DETERRENT AND
CHRISTIAN CONSCIENCE. London: CND, Christian CND Pamphlet,
No. 4. n.d. [about 1962]. Pamphlet. pp. 8. (Critique of Milford
(1961), q.v.)

Fawcett, G. Colin. THE UPHILL WAY: A Quaker comment on *The
Valley of Decision.* London: Friends Peace Committee. 1961.
Pamphlet. pp. 36. (Critique of Milford (1961), q.v.)

Feeny, Margaret Mary and Hodgson, Peter. JUST WAR? Papal
teaching on nuclear warfare with a scientific commentary. London:
Sword of the Spirit. 1958. Pamphlet. pp. 47

Frankau, Pamela. LETTER TO A PARISH PRIEST. London: CND,
Christian CND Pamphlet, No. 2. n.d. [1961]

Groom, Donald. THE [QUAKER] PEACE TESTIMONY TODAY: A
study outline. London: Friends Peace and International Relations
Committee. 1966. Pamphlet. pp. 32

Groom, Donald (compiler). THE VOICE OF THE CHURCH CON-
CERNING MODERN WAR: Extracts from official documents and
statements. London: Friends Peace Committee. 1963. Pamphlet.
pp. 20. (Response to Church of England (1962), q.v.)

Grubb, Sir Kenneth. COEXISTENCE AND THE CONDITIONS OF
PEACE. London: SCM Press, Burge Memorial Lectures. 1957.
Pamphlet. pp. 24

Hollis, Christopher. CATHOLICS AND THE NUCLEAR DILEMMA.
Spectator. 26 November 1965. pp. 684–5

Johnstone, Kenneth. CHRISTIAN APPROACHES TO DEFENCE AND
DISARMAMENT in Johnstone (ed.): THE ROAD TO PEACE.
1965. pp. 7–18

Jude, Francis. CHRISTIANS AND NUCLEAR DISARMAMENT.
Theology. Vol. 64. August 1961. pp. 330–3. (Reply to Booth,
Edwards and Jenkins, 1961 (q.v.))

Kenny, Anthony. CATHOLICS AGAINST THE BOMB. Blackfriars.
Vol. 42. December 1961. pp. 517–21

Kent, (Rev. Monseigneur) Bruce, Williams, Frank and Gray, Roger.
CHRISTIANS AND NUCLEAR DISARMAMENT. London: CND,
Christian CND Pamphlet. 1977. Pamphlet. pp. 18. (Foreword by

141

the Rt. Rev. Trevor Huddleston, [then] Bishop of Stepney)

Kent, (Rev. Monseigneur) Bruce. POVERTY AND THE ARMS TRADE.
London: Catholic Institute of International Relations, for the
Committee on Poverty and the Arms Trade. 1975. Pamphlet

Lee, A. D. AFTER *PACEM IN TERRIS* – WHAT? New Blackfriars.
Vol. 46. June 1965. pp. 505-10

Lonsdale, Kathleen. CHRISTIAN PACIFISM AND THE HYDROGEN
BOMB. London: Friends Peace Committee. [1954]. Pamphlet.
pp. 8

Lonsdale, Kathleen. EFFECTIVE CHRISTIANITY [AND ATOMIC
WEAPONS]. London: Fellowship of Reconciliation. n.d. [1948 or
1949]. Pamphlet. pp. 4

Lonsdale, Kathleen. PEACEFUL COEXISTENCE: THE CHRISTIAN
OBLIGATION. London: Friends East-West Relations Committee.
1955. Pamphlet. pp. 7

McCabe, (Father) Herbert. MORALS AND NUCLEAR WAR. Blackfriars.
Vol. 42. November 1961. pp. 446-58

Mason, David. A PACIFIST LOOK AT POLITICS. New Malden,
Surrey: Fellowship of Reconciliation. n.d. [1964]. Pamphlet. pp. 16

Methodist Church. DECLARATION OF THE METHODIST CHURCH
ON PEACE AND WAR: Statement of the 1957 Methodist Conference. London: Epworth Press. 1957

Midgley, Brian. NUCLEAR DETERRENTS: INTENTION AND
SCANDAL. Blackfriars. Vol. 44. September 1963. pp. 363-72

Milford, (Rev. [T]heodore) R. THE VALLEY OF DECISION: THE
CHRISTIAN DILEMMA IN THE NUCLEAR AGE. London: British
Council of Churches. n.d. [1961]. Pamphlet. pp. 47. (See also
critiques by Fawcett (1961), *q.v.*, and by Vincent (1962), *q.v.*)

Morton, (Rev.) Andrew. CHALLENGING THE JUST WAR DOCTRINE.
Reconciliation Quarterly. New Series. Vol. 5. June 1975. pp. 38-9

Mulleneux, Commander Hugh. CHRISTIAN APPROACHES TO
WORLD SECURITY AND PEACE. Wadhurst, Sussex: [the author].
1977. Pamphlet. pp. 25. (An unofficial history of CCADD (the
Conference, later Council, on Christian Approaches to Defence and
Disarmament) by its first (1963-73) Honorary Secretary)

Paskins, Barrie *et al.* THE SALE AND TRANSFER OF CONVEN-
TIONAL ARMS, ARMS SYSTEMS AND RELATED TECHNO-
LOGY. London: British Council of Churches (BCC Publications).
1977. Pamphlet. pp. 20. (Report of a Working Party of the Council
on Christian Approaches to Defence and Disarmament (convenor,

Barrie Paskins; chairman, Christoph Bertram) to the British Council
of Churches)

Rogers, (Rev.) Edward. THE CHRISTIAN APPROACH TO THE COM-
MUNIST. London: Edinburgh House Press, Christian Approach
Series, No. 4. 1959. Pamphlet. pp. 64

Spinks, (Rev.) G. Stephens. WORLD CONSCIENCE AND THE HYDRO-
GEN BOMB. Hibbert Journal. July 1950. pp. 334-8

Stein, Walter. CHRISTIAN ATTITUDES TO WAR. War and Peace. Vol.
1. January-March 1963. pp. 77-9

Stein, Walter. THE [VATICAN II] COUNCIL AND THE BOMB:
CASUISTRY OR WITNESS. New Blackfriars. Vol. 47. November
1965. pp. 68-83

Stein, Walter. DISCERNING THE REAL SITUATION. Blackfriars. Vol.
45. July-August 1964. pp. 302-7

Stein, Walter. MORALITY IN INTERNATIONAL POLITICS in Carter
(ed.): UNILATERAL DISARMAMENT. 1966. pp. 10-14

Stein, Walter (ed.). NUCLEAR WEAPONS AND CHRISTIAN CON-
SCIENCE. London: Merlin Press. 1961. Hardback. pp. 151. (Fore-
word by Mgr. T. D. Roberts. Re-published in 1963 under new title
NUCLEAR WEAPONS: A CATHOLIC RESPONSE)

Stein, Walter (ed.). NUCLEAR WEAPONS: A CATHOLIC RESPONSE.
London: Burns & Oates, Cardinal Books. 1963. Paperback. pp. 165.
(Foreword by Mgr. T. D. Roberts. Originally published in 1961 as
NUCLEAR WEAPONS AND CHRISTIAN CONSCIENCE)

Stein, Walter (ed.). PEACE ON EARTH: THE WAY AHEAD. London:
Sheed & Ward, Stagbooks series. 1966. Paperback. pp. x + 293

Taylor, Sir Thomas Murray and Bilheimer, Robert S. CHRISTIANS
AND THE PREVENTION OF WAR IN AN ATOMIC AGE: A theo-
locial discussion. London: SCM Press. 1961. Pamphlet. pp. 47

Thompson, Charles S. (ed.). MORALS AND MISSILES: CATHOLIC
ESSAYS ON THE PROBLEM OF WAR TODAY. London: James
Clarke. 1959. Paperback. pp. 76. (Introduction by Count Michael
de la Bedoyère)

Thrall, Margaret E. THE BISHOPS AND THE NUCLEAR DETER-
RENT. Theology. Vol. 75. August 1972. pp. 416-23

Vincent, John J. CHRIST IN A NUCLEAR WORLD. Rochdale: Crux
Press. 1962 (and second edition 1963). Paperback. pp. 160. (Foreword by the Rt. Rev. George F. MacLeod, M.C., D.D., later
elevated to the life peerage as Lord MacLeod of Fuinary. Critique of
Milford (1961) and British Council of Churches (1959) reports

$(q.v.)$)

Vincent, John J. CHRISTIAN NUCLEAR PERSPECTIVE. London: Epworth Press. 1964. Paperback. pp. 64. (Critique ('minority report') of British Council of Churches (1963), $q.v.$)

Walker, Derek (ed.). CHOOSE YOUR WEAPONS: CHRIST'S CHALLENGE TO EVERY CHRISTIAN. New Malden, Surrey: Fellowship of Reconciliation. n.d. [1964]. Pamphlet. pp. 40

Windass, G. S[tanley]. THE BIRD'S EYE VIEW: SOME THOUGHTS ABOUT THE JUST WAR TRADITION. Blackfriars. Vol. 45. May 1964. pp. 203-20

Windass, Stanley. DOUBLE THINK AND DOUBLE EFFECT. Blackfriars. Vol. 44. June 1963. pp. 257-66

Wood, J. Duncan. BUILDING THE INSTITUTIONS OF PEACE. London: George Allen & Unwin, Swarthmore Lecture (Quaker). 1962. Paperback. pp. 101

Zimmern, Sir Alfred. CHRISTIANITY IN THE ATOMIC AGE. Congregational Quarterly. October 1949. pp. 335-48

56. Unilateral Nuclear Disarmament (see also under: **40. Economic Aspects; 41. Foreign Policy Aspects; 42. Military Aspects; 44. Atomic Energy and Nuclear Weapons; 55. Christian Churches; 57. CND – Histories and Memoirs; 58. CND – Other Aspects; 59. Anti-CND Writings**)

Acland, Sir Richard. WAGING PEACE: The positive policy we could pursue if we gave up the hydrogen bomb. London: Muller. 1958. Hardback. pp. vi + 161

Allaun, Frank (M.P.). DISARMAMENT HOPES RISE: NEW MOVES IN THE STRUGGLE. Views. No. 3. Autumn-Winter 1963. pp. 13-18

Allaun, Frank (M.P.). NEW MOVES IN THE H-BOMB STRUGGLE. London: Union of Democratic Control. n.d. [1961]. Pamphlet. pp. 16. (Foreword by Bertrand Russell)

Allaun, Frank (M.P.). STOP THE H-BOMB RACE. London: Union of Democratic Control. 1959. Pamphlet.

Beswick, Frank (M.P.). THE HYDROGEN BOMB – WHAT SHALL WE DO? London: Co-operative Union. 1954. Pamphlet. pp. 24

Beswick, Frank (later Lord Beswick). WHEN WE RENOUNCE NUCLEAR WEAPONS. London: London Co-operative Society

Political Committee. 1960. Pamphlet.

Birkett, Stan. HUMANITY VERSUS THE HYDROGEN BOMB.
London: Independent Labour Party. n.d. [1955]. Pamphlet. pp. 31

Boulton, David. CND IN 1964. Views. No. 3. Autumn–Winter 1963.
pp. 136–7

Boulton, David (compiler). VOICES FROM THE CROWD: AGAINST
THE H-BOMB. London: Peter Owen. n.d. [1964]. pp. 185

Callow, Philip. LETTER TO A [ALDERMASTON] MARCHER. New
Statesman. Vol. 63. 20 April 1962. pp. 558–9

CND. THE BOMB AND YOU. London: CND. 1962. Pamphlet. pp. 16

CND. SANITY OR SUICIDE? London: CND. n.d. [1959]. Pamphlet.
pp. 12

CND. SIX REASONS WHY BRITAIN MUST GIVE UP THE BOMB.
London: CND. n.d. [1962]. Pamphlet. pp. 24

CND. TOMORROW'S CHILDREN. London: CND. n.d. [1959].
Pamphlet. pp. 7

Carter, April (ed.). UNILATERAL DISARMAMENT: Its theory and
policy from different international perspectives. London: Housmans.
1966. Reprinted from Carter (ed.): UNILATERALISM (*q.v.*) 1965,
with identical pagination. Pamphlet. pp. 68. (Chapter by April
Carter: 'Is there a theory of unilateralism?' Other contributors:
Becker, Burton (*q.v.*), Horowitz, Lapter, McReynolds, Roberts (*q.v.*),
Shuttleworth (*q.v.*), Sims (*q.v.*), Stein (*q.v.*))

Carter, April (ed.). UNILATERALISM. A special issue of Our Genera-
tion Against Nuclear War (Montreal and London). Vol. 3, No. 3.
April 1965. pp. 72. (Reprinted 1966 as Carter (ed.), UNILATERAL
DISARMAMENT (*q.v.*) with identical pagination)

Catlin, George E. G. ON UNILATERALISM. Contemporary Review.
Vol. 199. January 1961. pp. 1–6

Clark, George. FOR FREEDOM AND SURVIVAL (Campaign Caravan
Workshops). Views. No. 5. Summer 1964. pp. 128–34

Collins, (Rev. Canon) L. John. FORWARD FROM ALDERMASTON.
Labour Monthly. Vol. 44. April 1962. pp. 161–8

Fletcher, Raymond. £60 A SECOND ON DEFENCE. London: Mac-
Gibbon & Kee. 1963. pp. 141

Fletcher, Raymond. MILITARY THINKING AND UNILATERALISM.
London: Union for Democratic Control. 1961

Fletcher, Raymond. THE SUICIDE RACE. Twentieth Century. Vol.
170. Winter 1962. pp. 134–45

Griffiths, David. A TIME FOR DECISION: LABOUR AND DIS-

ARMAMENT. London: CND, Labour CND Pamphlet. 1977. Pamphlet. pp. 23

Hall, Stuart. BREAKTHROUGH. Oxford: Combined Universities CND. 1958. Pamphlet. pp. 33

Heelas, Terence. BALANCE OF RISKS. London: CND. n.d. [1964]. Pamphlet

Hughes, Emrys (M.P.). BOMB OVER BRITAIN. Glasgow: Civic Press. 1954. Pamphlet. pp. 32

Jones, Mervyn. FLOWING TIDE. London: CND. n.d. [1960]. Pamphlet. pp. 12

Jones, Mervyn. FREED FROM FEAR. London: CND. 1962. Pamphlet. pp. 20

Jones, Mervyn. LABOUR'S DEFENCE POLICIES (review article). War and Peace. Vol. 1, No. 1. January–March 1963. pp. 56–61

Levy, Benn W. BRITAIN AND THE BOMB: The fallacy of nuclear defence. London: CND. n.d. [1958]. Pamphlet. pp. 19

Lort-Phillips, Lt.-Col. Patrick. THE LOGIC OF DEFENCE: A short study of the 'nuclear' dilemma. Purley, Surrey: Radical Publications. 1959. Paperback. pp. 95

Lort-Phillips, Lt.-Col. Patrick. THE LOGIC OF DEFENCE: A short study of the 'nuclear' dilemma. Llandybie, Carmarthenshire: C. Davies. n.d. [1961]. New edition. Hardback. pp. 93

Lort-Phillips, Lt.-Col. Patrick. TOWARDS SANITY. Carmarthen: Radical Publications. 1960

McCarthy, Tony. NUCLEAR INFERNO. London: CND. n.d. [1967]. Pamphlet. pp. 12

Nettleton, Dick. THE CASE FOR NUCLEAR DISARMAMENT TODAY. London: CND. n.d. [1968]. Broadsheet format. pp. 10

Nettleton, Dick. IF YOU WANT PEACE . . .: The case for Nuclear Disarmament. London: CND. 1975. Pamphlet. pp. 30

Pirie, Antoinette (ed.). SURVIVORS. London: CND. n.d. [1962]. Pamphlet. pp. 24. (Foreword by James Cameron. Contributors include Marghanita Laski)

Priestley, J. B. BRITAIN AND THE NUCLEAR BOMBS. London: CND. n.d. [1958]. (Reprint of an article in New Statesman, 22 February 1957)

Rex, John. BRITAIN WITHOUT THE BOMB. London: New Left Review. 1960. Pamphlet

Roberts, Adam. UNILATERALISM – GESTURE OR POLICY? in Carter (ed.), *q.v.* 1966. pp. 4–9

Russell, Bertrand (3rd Earl Russell). THE CASE FOR BRITISH
NUCLEAR DISARMAMENT. Bulletin of the Atomic Scientists. Vol.
17. March 1962. pp. 6-10

Schaffer, Gordon. NUCLEAR 'DEFENCE' IS SUICIDE. London:
National Peace Council. 1970. Pamphlet. pp. 8

Shuttleworth, Alan. CUT OFF FROM THE SUN. New Left Review.
Vol. 18. January-February 1963. pp. 24-31

Shuttleworth, Alan. THE MEANINGS OF UNILATERALISM: A
PEACE MOVEMENT VIEW in Carter (ed.): UNILATERAL DIS-
ARMAMENT. 1966. pp. 27-31

Taylor, A[lan] J. P. THE GREAT DETERRENT MYTH. London: CND.
1958. Pamphlet.

Young, Wayland. AN ABOLITIONIST'S POSITION. Encounter.
November 1958. ('Conditional disarmament seems unobtainable.
Nations must disarm unconditionally')

Young, Wayland. THE NUCLEAR DISARMERS. Series of articles in
The Guardian. 12, 16 and 17 September 1959

Zilliacus, Konni (M.P.). ARMS AND LABOUR. London: CND, Labour
CND Pamphlet. n.d. [1965]. Pamphlet. pp. 58

Zilliacus, Konni (M.P.). MUTINY AGAINST MADNESS: H-bombs –
the case for political study. London: Housmans. n.d. [1957].
Pamphlet. pp. 24

Nature. NUCLEAR DISARMAMENT (leading article, on a House of
Lords debate). Vol. 183. 1959. pp. 1351-3

57. CND – Histories and Memoirs (see also under: 56. Unilateral Nuclear Disarmament; 58. CND – Other Aspects)

Brockway, Fenner (M.P.). THE DILEMMA OF THE LEFT (includes
CND). Chapter 13 of his continued autobiography OUTSIDE THE
RIGHT. London: George Allen & Unwin. 1963. pp. 170-81

Brockway, Fenner (Lord Brockway). TEN YEARS' REACTION.
Chapter 28 of his book TOWARDS TOMORROW: THE AUTOBIO-
GRAPHY OF FENNER BROCKWAY. London: Hart-Davis &
McGibbon. 1977. pp. 226-8. (CND and its precursors)

Cameron, James. [CND: PERSONAL MEMOIRS OF 1957-1963].
Chapter 16 of his autobiography POINT OF DEPARTURE. London:
Arthur Barker. 1967; Panther. 1969. pp. 284-95 of the Panther edi-
tion. (Routledge & Kegan Paul issued a new, 'definitive' edition

under their Oriel imprint in late 1978)

Clark, George. SECOND WIND: A HISTORY OF CND. London: Campaign Caravan Workshops. 1963. Pamphlet

Collins, (Rev. Canon) L. John. CND. Chapters 11 and 12 of his autobiography FAITH UNDER FIRE. London: Leslie Frewin. 1966. pp. 264-352

Driver, Christopher. THE DISARMERS: A STUDY IN PROTEST. London: Hodder & Stoughton. 1964. pp. ix + 256

Duff, Peggy. LEFT, LEFT, LEFT: A personal account of six protest campaigns, 1945-1965. London: Allison & Busby. 1971. Hardback (paperbacked in 1974). pp. 278

Jones, Mervyn. THE VOICE OF AN ERA (Collins's chairmanship of CND 1958-1964) in Ian Henderson (ed.): MAN OF CHRISTIAN ACTION. CANON JOHN COLLINS: THE MAN AND HIS WORK. London: Lutterworth. 1976. pp. 73-81

Purcell, William. THE ROAD TO ALDERMASTON. Chapter 6 of his book PORTRAIT OF SOPER: A BIOGRAPHY OF THE REVEREND THE LORD SOPER OF KINGSWAY. London & Oxford: Mowbrays. 1972. pp. 124-45

Ricks, Christopher. LAST THINGS: *THE DISARMERS* BY CHRISTOPHER DRIVER. New Statesman. Vol. 69. 1 January 1965. pp. 14-15

Rolph, C. H. KINGSLEY: THE LIFE, LETTERS AND DIARIES OF KINGSLEY MARTIN. London: Victor Gollancz. 1973. pp. 323-6. [Early CND]

Russell, Bertrand (3rd Earl Russell). TRAFALGAR SQUARE. Chapter 3 of his book THE AUTOBIOGRAPHY OF BERTRAND RUSSELL, VOLUME III: 1944-1967. London: George Allen & Unwin. 1969. pp. 101-53

58. CND – Aspects other than Unilateral Nuclear Disarmament –
political and sociological (see also under: 57. CND – Histories and
Memoirs)

CND. CIVIL DEFENCE AND NUCLEAR WAR. London: CND. n.d. [1963]. Broadsheet format. pp. 16

Carter, April. THE COMMON MARKET: A CHALLENGE TO UNILATERALISTS. London: Peace News. 1962. Pamphlet. pp. 35

Doncaster, L. Hugh. PERSONAL ACTION AND PUBLIC DEMON-

STRATION. London: Friends Peace Committee. 1964. Pamphlet.
pp. 12. (Swanwick Conference address, March 1963, reprinted from
The Friends' Quarterly, January 1964)

Fox, Alan. THE UNIONS AND DEFENCE. Socialist Commentary.
February 1961

Gittings, John. BRITAIN EAST OF SUEZ. London: CND. n.d. [1965].
Pamphlet. pp. 16

The Guardian. THE LABOUR PARTY CONFERENCE (Scarborough,
3–7 October 1960). Manchester: The Guardian. 1960. Pamphlet.
pp. 58

Haseler, Stephen. THE GAITSKELLITES: Revisionism in the British
Labour Party, 1951–1964. London: Macmillan. 1969. Hardback.
pp. xiv + 286

Hindell, Keith and Williams, Philip. SCARBOROUGH AND BLACK-
POOL: An analysis of some votes at the Labour Party conferences of
1960 and 1961. Political Quarterly. Vol. 33. July–September 1962.
pp. 306–20

Labour Party. ANNUAL CONFERENCE REPORT (Blackpool, 1959,
58th Annual Conference). London: Labour Party. 1960. pp. 216

Labour Party. ANNUAL CONFERENCE REPORT (Scarborough,
1960, 59th Annual Conference). London: Labour Party. n.d. [1960].
pp. 329

Labour Party. ANNUAL CONFERENCE REPORT (Blackpool, 1961,
60th Annual Conference). London: Labour Party. 1961. pp. 280

Martin, Kingsley. THE FUTURE OF CND. New Statesman. Vol. 66.
4 October 1963. pp. 436–8

Martin, Kingsley. WHERE TO FROM ALDERMASTON? New Statesman. Vol. 63. 27 April 1963. pp. 588–90

Martin, Kingsley and Howard, Anthony. WHERE HAVE ALL THE
FLOWERS GONE? (1. After Aldermaston [KM] ; 2. Leftist Legacy
[AH]). New Statesman. Vol. 67. 27 March 1964. pp. 482–4

Moncrieff, Anthony. THE RISE AND FALL OF CND. Listener. Vol.
77. 23 March 1967. pp. 385–7

Nuttall, Jeff. BOMB CULTURE. London: MacGibbon & Kee. 1968

Nuttall, Jeff. BOMB CULTURE. London: Paladin. 1970. Paperback.
pp. 252

Parkin, Frank. MIDDLE CLASS RADICALISM: The social bases of the
British Campaign for Nuclear Disarmament. Manchester: Manchester
University Press. 1968. pp. vii + 207. (Published in collaboration with
Praeger, New York)

Randle, Michael. THE COMMITTEE OF 100. Views. No. 1. Spring
1963. pp. 60-4
Rex, John. THE SOCIOLOGY OF CND. War and Peace. Vol. 1.
January-March 1963. pp. 47-55
Webbe, Harold. SCARBOROUGH AND AFTER. Quarterly Review.
Vol. 628. April 1961. pp. 123-34
Wolff, William. LIBERALS AT EASTBOURNE (1960 party confe-
rence). Contemporary Review. November 1960. pp. 624-9

59. Anti-CND Writings (see also under more general headings, e.g.:
44. Nuclear Weapons; 56. Unilateral Nuclear Disarmament;
42. Military Aspects)

British Atlantic Committee. NUCLEAR DISARMAMENT: Questions
and answers for those who want facts. London: British Atlantic
Committee. 1961. Pamphlet. pp. 8
Greer, Herb. MUD PIE: THE CND STORY. London: Max Parrish.
1964. pp. 108
Independent Labour Party and Solidarity. THE [COMMITTEE OF]
100 VERSUS THE STATE: Trafalgar Square . . . Wethersfield . . .
The Trial. . . . London: Independent Labour Party. n.d. [1962].
Pamphlet. pp. 19. (Attacks the CND Labour Advisory Committee
(predecessor of Labour CND) as the 'skeleton in the CND cupboard')
Marquand, David. BOMBS AND SCAPEGOATS: [LABOUR PARTY
OPINIONS]. Encounter. Vol. 16. January 1961. pp. 43-8
Marquand, David. ENGLAND, THE BOMB, THE MARCHERS. Com-
mentary. May 1960
Multilateral Disarmament Information Centre. THE BRITISH PEACE
MOVEMENT (articles reprinted from The New Daily). London:
British Newspaper Trust Society (The New Daily). 1963. Pamphlet.
pp. 8
Rees, David. THE MARCH TO NOWHERE [CND]. Encounter. Vol. 24
February 1965. pp. 70-4
Strachey, John (M.P.). THE PURSUIT OF PEACE: THE DEFENCE
DEBATE. London: Fabian Society, Fabian Tract 329 (series Social-
ism in the Sixties). 1960. Pamphlet. pp. 32
Strachey, John (M.P.). SCRAP ALL THE H-BOMBS. London: Labour
Party. n.d. [1958]. Pamphlet. pp. 20
Young Fabian Group. NATO OR NEUTRALITY? THE DEFENCE

DEBATE. London: Fabian Society. 1961. Pamphlet. pp. 30

60. United Nations General Assembly Special Session on Disarmament, 1978

Barnaby, Frank. LOCAL CONFLICTS AND NUCLEAR WORLD WAR
in Noel-Baker *et al.* DISARM OR DIE [1978]. pp. 91-105
Bennett, Ken and Wood, Jack. WHAT MIGHT FRIENDS SAY AT NEW
YORK? (UN Special Session). The Friend. Vol. 136. 31 March 1978.
pp. 387-8
Dean, Roy. BRITAIN AND THE UNITED NATIONS SPECIAL
SESSION ON DISARMAMENT. RUSI Journal. Vol. 123, No. 2.
June 1978. pp. 45-8
Dunn, Ted. HOPES AND FEARS FOR DISARMAMENT (UN Special
Session). Quaker Monthly. Vol. 57. July 1978. pp. 128-30
Evans, Cecil. WHAT ARE OUR HOPES OF THE UN SPECIAL
SESSION? The Friend. Vol. 136. 3 March 1978. pp. 247-8
Hewlett, Arthur. ADDING THE CRY OF THE MILLIONS TO THE
INSISTENT CALL. The Friend. Vol. 136. 23 June 1978. pp. 760-2.
(Text of Quaker Statement to the UN Special Session, 12 June 1978,
on pp. 757-9 of the same issue)
Hewlett, Arthur. SPECIAL SESSION'S FINAL STAGES. The Friend.
Vol. 136. 7 July 1978. pp. 825-6. (Previous reports on p. 727 (16
June) and pp. 760-2 (23 June))
Jolly, Richard (ed.). DISARMAMENT AND WORLD DEVELOP-
MENT. Oxford: Pergamon Press, Pergamon International Library.
1978. Hardback and Paperback. pp. xiii + 185. (Contributors include
Barnaby (*q.v.*), Neild (*q.v.*), Noel-Baker (*q.v.*), Brian Johnson, Mary
Kaldor, Robin Luckham, Alva Myrdal, Ruth Leger Sivard and Inga
Thorsson)
Mendl, Wolf. THE REALITIES BEHIND DISARMAMENT NEGOTIA-
TIONS. The Friend. Vol. 136. 21 April 1978. pp. 477-8
Noel-Baker, Philip *et al.* DISARM OR DIE: A disarmament reader for
the leaders and the peoples of the world. London: Taylor & Francis,
on behalf of the Non-Partisan Fund for World Disarmament and
Development. 1978. pp. viii + 108. (Foreword (pp. vii-viii) by Noel-
Baker. Contributors include Frank Barnaby (*q.v.*), Sean MacBride
and Olof Palme)
Sims, Nicholas A. APPROACHES TO DISARMAMENT: An introduc-

tory analysis. London: Quaker Peace and Service. 1979. Paperback.
pp. 170. (Revised and expanded edition, including the original
(1974) Foreword by Sir Michael Wright)

Terry, Carol. THE ROLE OF THE NGOs – 'CONSCIENCE OF MAN-
KIND'. The Friend. Vol. 136. 17 March 1978. pp. 321-2

Terry, Carol. WAS THERE AN 'AVALANCHE' AFTER ALL? The
Friend. Vol. 136. 22 September 1978. pp. 1183-4

TABLES

Table X: Members of Parliament

This table shows, for each of the authors in this bibliography who is known to have been at some time a Member of Parliament, her or his party, constituency or division, years as MP, and date of birth (and death, where applicable). An asterisk signifies a holder of Ministerial office, including Parliamentary Secretaries (but not parliamentary private secretaries to Ministers). Knighthoods and baronetcies conferred or assumed after leaving Parliament are not shown here; for these, and for peerages, see Table Y.

ACLAND Sir Richard (1906–) Ind, Barnstaple (Devon), 1935–45; Lab, Gravesend (Kent), 1947–55
ALLAUN Frank (1913–) Lab, Salford East, 1955–
ANGELL Sir Norman (1874–1967) Lab, Bradford North, 1929–31
BARCLAY Sir Thomas (1853–1941) Lib, Blackburn, 1910
*BARNES George (1859–1940) Lab, Glasgow Blackfriars (later Glasgow Gorbals), 1906–22
*BESWICK Frank (1912–) Lab, Uxbridge (Middlesex), 1945–59
*BRIDGEMAN William (1864–1935) Unionist, Oswestry (Salop), 1906–29
BROCKWAY Fenner (1888–) Lab, Leyton East (Essex), 1929–31; Lab, Eton & Slough (Bucks), 1950–64
BRYCE James (1838–1922) Lib, Tower Hamlets, 1880–85; Lib, Aberdeen South, 1885–96
*CECIL Robert (1864–1958) Con, Marylebone East, 1906–10; Ind Con, Hitchin (Herts), 1911–23
*CHURCHILL Sir Winston (1874–1965) Con, Oldham, 1900–04; Lib, Oldham, 1904–06; Lib, Manchester North West, 1906–08; Lib, Dundee, 1908–18; Coalition Lib, Epping, 1918–22; Con, Epping, 1924–31;[1] Con, Epping, 1931–45; Con, Woodford, 1945–64

[1] Although elected as a Constitutional candidate, he took the Conservative Whip.

153

COBB Sir Cyril (1861–1938) Unionist, Fulham West, 1918–29; Unionist, Fulham West, 1930–38

COOK Robin F. (1946–) Lab, Edinburgh Central, 1974 (Feb)–

*CRIPPS Sir Stafford (1889–1952) Lab, Bristol East, 1931–50 (Feb); Lab, Bristol South East, 1950 (Feb-Oct)

*CROSSMAN Richard (1907–1974) Lab, Coventry East, 1945–74

*DALTON Hugh (1887–1962) Lab, Camberwell Peckham, 1924–29; Lab, Bishop Auckland, 1929–31; Lab, Bishop Auckland, 1935–59

DAVIES David (1880–1944) Lib, Montgomeryshire, 1906–29

*DICKINSON Willoughby Hyett (1859–1943) Lib, St Pancras North, 1906–18

EDWARDS Bob (1906–) Lab, Bilston, 1955–74; Lab, Wolverhampton South East, 1974–

*ENNALS David (1922–) Lab, Dover (Kent), 1964–70; Lab, Norwich North, 1974 (Feb)–

FLETCHER Raymond (1921–) Lab, Ilkeston (Derbyshire), 1964–

GOOCH George Peabody (1873–1968) Lib, Bath, 1906–10

*GREY Sir Edward (1862–1933) Lib, Berwick-on-Tweed (Northumberland) 1885–1916

HALE Leslie (1902–) Lab, Oldham, 1945–50; Lab, Oldham West, 1950–68

HARRIS Henry Wilson (1883–1955) Ind, Cambridge University, 1945–50

*HART Judith (1924–) Lab, Lanark (Lanarkshire), 1959–

*HEALEY Denis (1917–) Lab, Leeds South-East, 1952–55; Lab, Leeds East, 1955–

*HENDERSON Arthur (1863–1935) Lab, Barnard Castle (Durham), 1903–18; Lab, Widnes, 1919–22; Lab, Newcastle upon Tyne East, 1923; Lab, Burnley, 1924–31; Lab, Clay Cross (Derbyshire), 1933–35

HUGHES Emrys (1894–1969) Lab, Ayrshire South, 1946–69[1]

*JONES Aubrey (1911–) Con, Birmingham Hall Green, 1950–65

KENWORTHY Joseph (1886–1953) Lib, Hull Central, 1919–26; Lab, Hull Central, 1926–31

KING-HALL Stephen (1893–1966) Ind National, Ormskirk (Lancs), 1939–44

*KIRK Sir Peter (1928–1977) Con, Gravesend (Kent), 1955–64; Con, Saffron Walden (Essex), 1965–77

LANSBURY George (1859–1940) Lab, Bow & Bromley, 1910–12 & 1922–40

*LEE Arthur Hamilton (1868–1947) Con, South Hants/Fareham, 1908–18

LEVY Benn (1900–1976) Lab, Eton & Slough (Bucks), 1945–50

*LLOYD George Ambrose (1879–1941) Unionist, Staffordshire West, 1910–18; Con, Eastbourne, 1924–25

---

[1] Deprived of the Labour Whip as a 'defence rebel' 1961-63.

*LLOYD GEORGE David (1863-1945) Lib, Caernarvon, 1890-1931;
   Ind Lib, Caernarvon, 1931-45
*LUARD Evan (1926-) Lab, Oxford, 1966-70 & 1974 (Oct)-
*MacDONALD James Ramsay (1866-1937) Lab, Aberavon (Glamorgan),
   1922-29; Lab, Seaham (Durham), 1929-31; National Lab, Seaham
   (Durham), 1931-35; National Lab, Scottish Universities, 1936-37
*McNEILL Ronald (1861-1934) Con, East Kent (St Augustine, later
   Canterbury, Division), 1911-27
 MANDER Geoffrey (1882-1962) Lib, Wolverhampton East, 1929-45
 MARQUAND David (1934-) Lab, Ashfield (Notts), 1966-77
 MIKARDO Ian (1908-) Lab, Reading, 1945-50; Lab, Reading South,
   1950-55; Lab, Reading, 1955-59; Lab, Poplar, 1964-74; Lab,
   Bethnal Green & Bow, 1974-
*MONEY Sir Leo Chiozza (1870-1944) Lib, Paddington North, 1906-
   10; Lib, Northamptonshire East, 1910-18 (joining the Labour Party
   in 1918)
*MORRISON Herbert (1888-1965) Lab, Hackney South, 1923-24; Lab,
   Hackney South, 1929-31; Lab, Hackney South, 1935-45; Lab,
   Lewisham East, 1945-51; Lab, Lewisham South, 1951-59
*MULLEY Frederick (1918-) Lab, Sheffield Park, 1950-
 NEWENS Stanley (1930-) Lab, Epping (Essex), 1964-70; Lab &
   Co-op, Harlow (Essex), 1974 (Feb)-
*NOEL-BAKER Philip (1889-) Lab, Coventry, 1929-31; Lab, Derby,
   1936-50; Lab, Derby South, 1950-70
*NUTTING Anthony (1920-) Con, Melton (Leics), 1945-56
*OWEN David (1938-) Lab, Plymouth Sutton, 1966-74; Lab, Plymouth
   Devonport, 1974-
 PATTIE Geoffrey (1936-) Con, Chertsey & Walton (Surrey), 1974
   (Feb)-
*PONSONBY Arthur (1871-1946) Lib, Stirling Burghs, 1908-18; Lab,
   Sheffield Brightside, 1922-30
*RAISON Timothy (1929-) Con, Aylesbury (Bucks), 1970-
*SALTER Sir Arthur (1881-1975) Ind, Oxford University, 1937-50;
   Con. Ormskirk (Lancs), 1951-53
*SINCLAIR Sir Archibald (1890-1970) Lib, Caithness & Sutherland,
   1922-45
 SMITH Rennie (1888-1962) Lab, Penistone (Yorks), 1924-31
*SNOWDEN Philip (1864-1937) Lab, Blackburn, 1906-18; Lab, Colne
   Valley (Yorks), 1922-31
 STANLEY John (1942-) Con, Tonbridge & Malling (Kent), 1974 (Feb)-
*STEWART Michael (1906-) Lab, Fulham East, 1945-55; Lab, Fulham,
   1955-
*STRACHEY John (1901-1963) Lab, Birmingham Aston, 1929-31;
   Ind, Birmingham Aston, 1931; Lab, Dundee, 1945-50; Lab, Dundee
   West, 1950-63
*SYKES Major-General Sir Frederick (1877-1954) Con, Sheffield
   Hallam, 1922-28; Con, Nottingham Central, 1940-45

*WALKER Peter (1932–) Con, Worcester, 1961–
WILLIAMS Alan Lee (1930–) Lab, Hornchurch (Essex), 1966–70; Lab, Hornchurch (Essex), 1974 (Feb)–
*WILSON Sir Harold (1916–) Lab, Ormskirk (Lancs), 1945–50; Lab, Huyton (Lancs), 1950–
*YOUNGER Kenneth (1908–1976) Lab, Grimsby, 1945–59
ZILLIACUS Konni (1894–1967) Lab, Gateshead, 1945–49; Ind, Gateshead, 1949–50; Lab, Manchester Gorton, 1955–67[1]

[1] Suspended from Labour Party membership, 1961–64.

Table Y: Peerages, Baronetcies and Knighthoods

Included in this table, alphabetically by *surname*, are the authors listed in this bibliography who became *peers* (cr = by creation of an hereditary peerage; s = by succession; Lp = by creation of a Life peerage), *baronets* (s = by succession) or *knights*, together with the relevant dates, titles (for peers) and orders of knighthood. Not included are courtesy titles (borne by heirs to peerages), Papal knighthoods and knighthoods of the Order of St John of Jerusalem. The main sources of information are *Debrett, Who's Who* and *Who Was Who*. An asterisk signifies a holder of Ministerial office, a category which is deemed to include Parliamentary Secretaries, but not parliamentary private secretaries to Ministers. For titles which differ significantly from surnames, see the concordance list attached to this table.

ACLAND Richard (1906-) 15th baronet, s 1939
ADAM Ronald (1885-) 2nd baronet, s 1926; KCB 1941; GCB 1946
ALLEN Clifford (1889-1939) 1st Baron Allen of Hurtwood, cr 1932
ANGELL Norman (1874-1967) Kt 1931
ASTON George (1861-1938) KCB 1913
BARCLAY Thomas (1853-1941) Kt 1904
*BESWICK Frank (1912-) Lp Baron Beswick, cr 1964
 BEVERIDGE William (1879-1963) KCB 1919; 1st Baron Beveridge,
    cr 1946
 BLACKETT Patrick (1897-1976) Lp Baron Blackett, cr 1969
 BRIDGEMAN William (1864-1935) 1st Viscount Bridgeman, cr 1929
 BROCKWAY Fenner (1888-) Lp Baron Brockway, cr 1964
 BRUCE Clarence Napier (1885-1957) 3rd Baron Aberdare, s 1929
*BRYCE James (1838-1922) 1st viscount Bryce, cr 1914; GCVO 1917
 BUTLER Harold (1883-1951) KCMG 1946
 BUTTERFIELD Herbert (1900-) Kt 1968
 BUZZARD Anthony (1902-1972) 2nd baronet, s 1945
 CALDER Ritchie (1906-) Lp Baron Ritchie-Calder of Balmashannar
    cr 1966
 CATLIN George (1896-) Kt 1970
 CARTER Charles (1919-) Kt 1978
*CECIL Robert (1864-1958) 1st Viscount Cecil of Chelwood, cr 1923
*CHURCHILL Winston (1874-1965) KG 1953
 CLARKE George Sydenham (1848-1933) KCMG 1893; GCMG 1905;
    GCIE 1907; GCSI 1911; GBE 1917; 1st Baron Sydenham of Combe,
    cr 1913
 COBB Cyril (1861-1938) KBE 1918
 COCHRANE Ralph (1895-1977) KBE 1945; KCB 1948; GBE 1950
 COCKCROFT John (1897-1967) Kt 1948; KCB 1953
*CRIPPS Stafford (1889-1952) Kt 1930
*DALTON Hugh (1887-1962) Lp Baron Dalton, cr 1960
 DAVIES David (1880-1944) 1st Baron Davies of Llandinam, cr 1932

DAVIES Percival (1915–) 2nd Baron Darwen, s 1950
*DICKINSON Willoughby Hyett (1859–1943) KBE 1918; 1st Baron
   Dickinson, cr 1930
FRY Edward (1827–1918) GCB 1907
GOLLANCZ Victor (1893–1967) Kt 1965
*GREY Edward (1862–1933) 3rd baronet, s 1882; KG 1912; 1st
   Viscount Grey of Fallodon, cr 1916
GRUBB Kenneth (1900–) Kt 1953; KCMG 1970
*GWYNNE JONES Alun (1919–) Lp Baron Chalfont, cr 1964
HALE Leslie (1902–) Lp Baron Hale, cr 1972
HEADLAM-MORLEY James (1863–1929) Kt 1929
HOCKADAY Arthur (1926–) KCB 1978
HURD Archibald (1869–1959) Kt 1928
KENWORTHY Joseph (1886–1953) 10th Baron Strabolgi, s 1934
*KERR Peter (1926–) 12th Marquess of Lothian, s 1940
*KERR Philip (1882–1940) 11th Marquess of Lothian, s 1930
KING-HALL Stephen (1893–1966) Kt 1954; Lp Baron King-Hall,
   cr 1966
*KIRK Peter (1928–1977) Kt 1976
LEE Arthur Hamilton (1868–1947) KCB 1916; GBE 1918; 1st Baron
   Lee of Fareham, cr 1918; 1st Viscount Lee of Fareham, cr 1922;
   GCSI 1925; GCB 1929
LIDDELL HART Basil (1895–1970) Kt 1966
LINDSAY Alexander Dunlop (1879–1952) 1st Baron Lindsay of
   Birker, cr 1945
LIVINGSTONE Adelaide Lord (d 1970) DBE 1918
*LLOYD George Ambrose (1879–1941) GCIE 1918; GCSI 1924; 1st
   Baron Lloyd of Dolobran, cr 1925
*LLOYD GEORGE David (1863–1945) 1st Earl Lloyd George of Dwyfor,
   cr 1945
LODGE Oliver Joseph (1851–1940) Kt 1902
LONSDALE Kathleen (1903–1971) DBE 1956
MacMUNN George (1869–1952) KCB 1917; KCSI 1919
*McNEILL Ronald (1861–1936) 1st Baron Cushendun, cr 1927
MALKIN Herbert (1883–1945) KCMG 1930; GCMG 1937
MANDER Geoffrey (1882–1962) Kt 1945
MAURICE Frederick (1871–1951) KCMG 1918
*MONEY Leo Chiozza (1870–1944) Kt 1915
*MORRISON Herbert (1888–1965) Lp Baron Morrison of Lambeth,
   cr 1959
*NOEL-BAKER Philip (1889–) Lp Baron Noel-Baker, cr 1977
*NUTTING Anthony (1920–) 3rd baronet, s 1972
*PONSONBY Arthur (1871–1946) 1st Baron Ponsonby of Shulbrede,
   cr 1930
RAGLAN Fitzroy Richard (1885–1964) 4th Baron Raglan, s 1921
RICHMOND Herbert (1871–1946) KCB 1926
RUSSELL Bertrand (1872–1970) 3rd Earl Russell, s 1931

158

RUSSELL Hastings (1888–1953) 12th Duke of Bedford, s 1940
*SALTER Arthur (1881–1975) KCB 1922; GBE 1944; 1st Baron
    Salter, cr 1953
*SINCLAIR Archibald (1890–1970) 4th baronet, s 1912; 1st Viscount
    Thurso, cr 1952
 SLESSOR John (1897–) KCB 1943; GCB 1948
*SNOWDEN Philip (1864–1937) 1st Viscount Snowden, cr 1931
*SYKES Frederick (1887–1954) KCB 1919; GBE 1919; GCIE 1928;
    GCSI 1934
 TAYLOR Thomas Murray (1897–1962) Kt 1954
*THOMSON Christopher Birdwood (1875–1930) 1st Baron Thomson,
    cr 1924
 THOMSON George Paget (1892–1975) Kt 1943
 WEBSTER Charles Kingsley (1886–1961) KCMG 1946
 WEMYSS Rosslyn Erskine (1864–1933) 1st Baron Wester Wemyss,
    cr 1919
 WHEELER-BENNETT John (1902–1975) KCVO 1959
 WILLIAMS John Fischer (1870–1947) Kt 1923
*WILSON Harold (1916–) KG 1976
 WRIGHT Michael (1901–1976) KCMG 1951; GCMG 1958
*YOUNG Wayland (1923–) 2nd Baron Kennet, s 1960
*YOUNGER Kenneth (1908–1976) Kt 1972
 ZIMMERN Alfred (1879–1957) Kt 1936
 ZUCKERMAN Solly (1904–) Kt 1956; KCB 1964; Lp Baron
    Zuckerman, cr 1971

Orders of knighthood
Garter (KG); Thistle (KT); Bath (GCB, KCB); Star of India (GCSI,
KCSI); St Michael and St George (GCMG, KCMG); Indian Empire
(GCIE, KCIE); Royal Victorian Order (GCVO, KCVO); British Empire
(GBE, DBE/KBE).

Concordance of titles and surnames
This list gives cross-references from title to surname where these differ
to any significant degree, or might be confused.

Title	*Surname*
Aberdare	Bruce (Clarence Napier)
Bedford	Russell (Hastings)
Chalfont	Gwynne Jones (Alun)
Cushendun	McNeill (Ronald)
Darwen	Davies (Percival)
Davies of Llandinam	Davies (David)
Grey of Fallodon	Grey (Sir Edward)
Kennet	Young (Wayland)
Lee of Fareham	Lee (Arthur Hamilton)
Lindsay of Birker	Lindsay (Alexander Dunlop)

Lloyd of Dolobran	Lloyd (George Ambrose)
Lloyd George of Dwyfor	Lloyd George (David)
Lothian (11th Marquess of)	Kerr (Philip)
Lothian (12th Marquess of)	Kerr (Peter)
Ponsonby of Shulbrede	Ponsonby (Arthur)
Ritchie-Calder of Balmashannar	Calder (Ritchie)
Strabolgi	Kenworthy (Joseph)
Sydenham of Combe	Clarke (George Sydenham)
Thurso	Sinclair (Sir Archibald)
Wester Wemyss	Wemyss (Rosslyn Erskine)

Table Z: Name Changes in Organisations

The following pairs of names relate to the same organisation at different times in its history (earlier name on the left):

Conference on Christian Approaches to Defence and Disarmament	Council on Christian Approaches to Defence and Disarmament
Institute for Strategic Studies	International Institute for Strategic Studies
National Peace Council (original *and present* name)	National Council for the Prevention of War (*but* it reverted to its earlier name in 1932 and has retained it)
Royal United Service Institution	Royal United Services Institute for Defence Studies
Sword of the Spirit	Catholic Institute of International Relations

The following organisations, although not identical, are related in that the one in the right-hand column is generally regarded as the lineal successor of the left-hand one, sometimes inheriting its assets:

No Conscription Fellowship (dissolved 1919)	1921	No More War Movement
No More War Movement	1937	Peace Pledge Union (founded 1936)
League of Nations Union	1946	United Nations Association
National Campaign for the Abolition of Nuclear Weapons Tests	1958	Campaign for Nuclear Disarmament
Friends East-West Relations Committee *and* Friends Peace Committee	1965	Friends Peace and International Relations Committee
National Assembly of the Church of England	1969	General Synod of the Church of England
Friends Peace and International Relations Committee	1978	Quaker Peace and Service

INDEX